Janner's Complete Speechmaker
Third Edition
including compendium of draft speeches
and retellable tales

'An invaluable addition to the library
of anyone who must speak in public . . .
I have read it and enjoyed it . . .
It's worth reading and worth having . . .'
The Rt Hon George Thomas MP,
then Speaker of the House of Commons,
now The Rt Hon Lord Tonypandy

JANNER'S COMPLETE SPEECHMAKER

Third Edition
including compendium of draft speeches
and retellable tales

Greville Janner

BUSINESS BOOKS

Copyright Greville Janner 1989

First published in Great Britain by
Business Books Limited
An imprint of Century Hutchinson Limited
62–65 Chandos Place, London, WC2N 4NW

Century Hutchinson Australia (Pty) Limited
89–91 Albion Street, Surry Hills,
New South Wales 2010, Australia

Century Hutchinson New Zealand Limited
P O Box 40-086, 32–34 View Road, Glenfield,
Auckland 10, New Zealand

Century Hutchinson South Africa (Pty) Limited
PO Box 337, Bergvlei 2012, South Africa

First published 1968 under the title
The Businessman's Guide to Speech-making
and to the Laws and Conduct of Meetings
First published under present title 1981
Second edition 1984
Reprinted 1986
Third Edition 1989

© Greville Janner 1981, 1984, 1989

British Library Cataloguing in Publication Data

Janner, Greville, 1928–
Janner's complete speechmaker. – 3rd ed
1. Public speaking – Manuals – for business
I. Title
808.5'1

ISBN 0–09–173973–X

Printed and bound in Great Britain by Mackays of Chatham, Kent

In-company training courses by Greville Janner include: effective
business presentation and speechmaking; speechwriting; radio and
TV skills; report and business writing skills; 'beauty contests'
training; effective telephone techniques; and 'rehearsals' and
'refreshers'.
For details of these and employment law training and consultancy
services by Greville Janner, contact Paul Secher, Effective
Presentational Skills Ltd, 8 Balfour Place, London, W1Y 5RS
Tel: 01-408 2063 Fax: 01-408 2079

In proud memory of my Father
Barnett Janner
Lord Janner of the City of Leicester
and with love to my mother
Elsie Janner
The Lady Janner CBE JP

Contents

Contents

Contents

Introduction

In business or in social life, competent speechmaking brings success. Disaster on your feet lands you on your back. This book is designed to keep you upright, articulate and succesful in speech by showing you how best to think on your feet – to provide the maximum of practical help with the minimum of misery. It is based on a lifetime of experience of hugely varied audiences and of oratorical and presentational occasions in many parts of the world.

The book divides conveniently into three sections. The first describes the basic arts of speechmaking: construction and delivery, audiences and occasions, technical aids – in short, the complete range of basic knowledge and guidance which is the essential equipment of the skilled speechmaker.

Whether you are addressing a meeting of colleagues or of employees at work, of shareholders in the UK or of stockholders in the USA, of family or of voters; whether you are making a presentation to commercial prospects or presenting a guest to an audience or prizes at a school, the techniques are essentially the same. Their application varies and is vital. Book 1 deals with them all.

You may have to chair a meeting, whether as major as a mass gathering or as minor as a company committee. In the same book we cover the rules on good chairing.

Book 2 contains models – a selection of draft speeches for varying occasions. Some revive great moments from the works of famed orators. They may be read and re-read, analysed and emulated, in the knowledge that they captivated audiences. Others are modern guides. Use both – as precedents. They should help you to make the best of your speechmaking opportunities and to minimise your prospects of tongue-tied collapse.

Finally, in Book 3, I offer a compendium of my own favourite Retellable Tales. Forced to listen to literally thousands of speeches, too many of them excruciatingly boring, I have carefully accumulated an array of over 500 gems. I have used them all – for laughter, effect or emotional impact. Here are my favourites: stories, jokes and epigrams which shine with wit or with vivid language; which delighted audiences; and above all, which made me or others laugh, rejoice or just contemplate.

Watch moonlight on the Taj Mahal, dawn breaking over the Palace of Westminster, or the play and change of light over any other great building: it never appears the same twice. Go back to your Bible and re-read your favourite tales and the words will achieve new form and meaning. Put my Retellable Tales before different people or varied audiences – or even the same people or audience in different mood – and they will change their reflection in the mirror or the mood of the moment.

So select and adapt those that suit you and your style as well as your victims and their reactions. With a modicum of that good fortune that every speaker always needs, but which is granted only on unpredictable and joyful occasions, these tales should provide you with a treasure house of spice for the seasoning of your speeches.

This third edition has emerged for a variety of reasons. Styles change. There were chapters and sentences to add, sections and phrases to chase away, and above all, I submitted the Retellable Tales to the critical eyes and ruthless pens of my daughters Marion and Laura. We argued our way through hundreds of stories. Out went those which they believed were irretrievably offensive. In came hundreds of others, selected and approved.

Revised, reviewed and renewed, resorted and reindexed, my expanded Retellable Tales are a tribute to the united efforts of father and daughers – and are all offered on the usual basis: responsibility for all errors is accepted by the older generation alone!

My thanks, then, to Marion and Laura and to all others who have contributed to the success of this new edition, including those who have (as will appear) given their consent to the republication of quotations. I thank those countless others whose speeches have provided me with examples – good and bad, worthy and laughable, splendid or sad – from which I have culled both advice and retellable tales.

I thank those delegates to whom I and my colleagues in Effective Presentation Skills have taught the allied arts of presentation and speechmaking for helping to develop so much of the material in this book – and in its sister Business Books' publications, *Janner on Presentation*, *Janner's Complete Letterwriter* and *Janner on Communication*.

Introduction

Finally, to you, my reader, I wish an overflow of those marvellous occasions when you return home from speechmaking knowing that the job was well done, the message duly delivered, the audience captivated and content.

London, 1989   *GREVILLE JANNER*

BOOK 1

Speechmaking

First I'll say I'm glad to be here, then I'll tell them the one about the Bishop, then I'll say I'm going to be brief, then I'll talk for half an hour and then sit down to thunderous applause...
......

PART 1

The speech – its structure and contents

Introduction: thinking on your feet

A renowned American trial lawyer called Louis Nizer once wrote a book entitled *Thinking on Your Feet*. It was the best in its field. Its title encapsulated the essential of every oratorical success – the ability to operate the mind and the tongue in tandem, with body upright.

An American president once remarked of his successor that he was so stupid that he was incapable of walking and chewing gum at the same time. (It has been suggested that the original quotation was even ruder – alleging that the unfortunate man was incapable of walking and passing wind simultaneously!) If your mind goes blank, you may still be able to read the words on the paper before you, but you will be unable to adapt them to match your audience or their reaction. They will react – you will not. You cannot win.

If you are attempting to plant your own ideas or thoughts in the minds of your audience, you have lost your chance. If your speech has been written for you, then you cannot now hope to make it appear your own.

Any interruption will throw you off your stride. You cannot draw ideas or allusions from your surroundings nor refer to speeches that have gone before or to speakers that are to come after. Your speech has lost its spontaneity, its charm and its effect.

Here, then, are the techniques of thinking while speaking – an art essential to the successful speechmaker.

1 The skeleton of a speech

The human spirit can live, flourish and be much admired even when the human body is frail, ugly or misshapen. Some brilliant minds can capture and hold an audience with a rambling, poorly formed oration. Meaning and sincerity shine through and all is forgiven.

But to the business executive who wishes to make a speech in a business-like way, to the average speaker who wishes to put on an above-average performance, or to the poor or timorous orator, forced into public speechmaking, the structure of the speech is of supreme importance.

Create the skeleton, clothe it with sensible thought, and all that remains is to deliver it. But without a healthy skeleton, the entire speech collapses. So here are the rules on forming a well-built talk.

Any speech may conveniently be divided into three parts – the opening, the body and the closing. Take them in turn.

The first and last sentences of a speech are crucial. The importance of a clear, resounding and striking first sentence and a well-rounded peroration cannot be over-emphasised. You must catch the interest of your audience from the start and send them away satisfied at the end. So, when building your skeleton, spend time on 'topping and tailing'. Many skilled speakers write out their opening and closing sentences, even if the rest is left entirely unfleshed.

Assume, now, that you have established a relationship with your audience. You have led in with your thanks for the invitation to speak, topical references, personal remarks, introductory witticisms and greetings to old friends. Now comes the substance of the speech – any speech. It must flow.

Like a first-class book, chapter or article, most fine speeches start their substance with a general introductory paragraph which sums up what is to come, catches the attention of the audience and indicates the run of the speaker's thought. Each idea should then be taken in sequence, and should lead on logically to the next.

Just as each bone of the human body is attached to its fellow, so the ideas in a speech should be jointed. The flow of ideas needs rhythm. Disjointed ideas, dislocated thoughts, fractured theories: these are the hallmarks of a poor speech.

5

So jot down the points you wish to make. Then set them out in logical order, so that one flows from the next. Connect them up, if you like, with a general theme. Start with that theme – and then elaborate, point by point.

Suppose, for instance, that you are explaining the virtues of a new product to your own sales staff. You begin in the usual way by asking for silence, smiling, looking round your audience and saying: 'Ladies and Gentlemen, sales staff of the X Company . . . It is a pleasure to see you here today, in spite of our reluctance to deprive the company's customers of your services . . .' Refer to Mr Y and Mr Z by name, congratulating them on their successes. Put your audience at ease. Tell them a joke or a story. Then launch into your theme.

'I have called you together today to introduce our new product.' (There it is, in a sentence.) 'Our research department has produced it. Now you must sell it. If you understand and exploit its full potential, you will not only benefit the company, but you should also add considerably to your own earnings.'

Personalise your message. Give your audience true incentive to listen. Whet their appetites for the substance to come.

Now for the speech proper. First, name and describe the product in broad terms. Next, preferably with the assistance of diagrams, transparencies or slides, describe the product in detail. Then take its selling features, one by one: 'The following features are entirely new . . .' Spell them out and explain them. 'But the following features are retained – they were too valuable to be lost . . .' (Once again, maintain logical sequence.)

'So there, Ladies and Gentlemen, we have our new product – and you are the first to see it. You will be supplied with full sales literature within the next week. It will be available for your customers by . . . The rest is up to you. I wish you the very best of good fortune.'

Precisely the sames rules of construction can be applied to any other discourse. Whether you are pronouncing a funeral oration over a deceased colleague or congratulating an employee on completing 25 years' service; whether you are making an after-dinner speech or haranguing your workers at the factory gates; whatever the circumstances, wherever the speech is made, if its skeleton is sound and solid, then even if the body is not as strong as it might be, the audience may not notice. Ignore the skeleton and the speech will prove a rambling disaster.

The skeleton of a speech

To summarise: introduce yourself and warm the audience . . .
'Good evening, Ladies and Gentlemen . . .'. Then say what you are
going to say; say it; then say what you have said.

2 In the beginning . . .

'In the beginning, God created the heavens and the earth.' What a marvellous first sentence, in the world's eternal best-selling book!

Now pick up any national newspaper. Read the first sentence in any news story and it should grab your attention, excite your interest and tell you to read on. It will also encapsulate the theme.

Any author or journalist will tell you that they may spend as long on preparing the first sentence as on the rest of the piece. A good opening is crucial to any presentation, written or oral.

Unlike the writer, the speechmaker has the starting benefit of a few formal words to get used to the acoustics and to settle into his audience. Do not rush them. 'Ladies . . . pause . . . 'and' . . . pause 'Gentlemen', – not 'Ladies-and-Gentlemen'. Look around and allow your audience to fix their attention on you, their minds on your words.

Next create a rapport. Latch onto some aspect of the introduction you have just received, or to a topical matter of particular interest to your listeners.

My late distinguished father (to whose memory this book is dedicated) was an MP for a total of some 30 years and then a life peer. I was (and often still am) introduced as his son – often by that well-intentioned cliché: 'The distinguished son of a distinguished father.' I have a standard opening which never fails: 'On behalf of my late father and myself – thank you for your kind introduction. When he was alive and active, we often got invited to meetings in mistake for each other. I treasure a letter, framed in the smallest room in my house, which was actually addressed to: "The Rt Hon. Lord Greville Janner QC MP, House of Commons, London." It begins: "Dear Sir or Madam!" The man was taking no chances!'

Listen to experienced speakers and you will find that they have opening gambits of their own – you will find a batch of some favourite standbys at the start of my Retellable Tales.

Once you have created contact with your audience and reassured them that they will be interested in your theme and will not be bored by your presentation, then – and only then – you launch into your subject. Your first sentence should be like those in the book or the newspaper – aimed precisely at the issue. Here are some random examples from one front page:

- 'The Prime Minister will return from her overseas visit tonight to find her Government in visible and increasing disarray over its controversial decision to . . .'
- 'The American space shuttle returned to earth yesterday from an eight-day mission . . .'
- 'British Coal yesterday closed a pit where the National Union of Mineworkers had withdrawn essential safety cover . . .'
- 'British American Tobacco announced yesterday that it is withdrawing from direct sales distribution in Britain, with the loss of over 1,800 jobs, mostly in Liverpool . . .'

You could start any of those sentences with the words: 'Did you know that . . .?', or 'We have come together because . . .', or 'It is essential for our industry/organisation that we should recognise that . . .', or 'As our local/trade newspaper announced on its front page only today . . .'

Sprinters who make a bad start can rarely win the race. Speechmakers who fail in the beginning are unlikely to succeed in the end.

3   In conclusion

Nothing so becomes a good speech as a fine ending. And nothing can be more ruinous than a weak termination trailing off into silence or into a lame 'Thank you'. So lavish as much care on the tail of a speech as you do on its top. Consider some common flops:

- Mr Brown rushes his last few sentences, gathers his notes and slides almost surreptitiously back into his seat.
- Mr Black ends his talk in what appears to be the middle of a sentence or at the height of an anti-climax.
- Ms Grey, who has been allotted 30 minutes to speak, runs out of material after 20, but is determined 'not to let the audience down', and says: 'In conclusion', 'finally', 'before I conclude', 'lastly', and 'to end up with', at least twice each – each time rekindling hope in the minds of her audience that she really means it.
- Ms Green thinks that she is narrating a serial story and leaves her audience in suspense by over-running her time, panicking and then forgetting to propose the resolution, which was the sole object of her speech.
- Mr Blue realises that he is not going to conclude his prepared talk within the time available if he keeps going at the same speed. So he runs out of script and breath at the same moment, leaving his audience miles behind.
- Mr White forgets that a peroration should be brief – and drags it out interminably, embellishing thoughts that were in the body of the speech, introducing new ideas in the guise of a summary of what he has said.

What, then, makes a really good ending or peroration? It should round off the speech and, in most cases, include the following:

- A summary, in a sentence or two, of the main purport of the speech;
- Any proposal or resolution arising out of the body of the speech; and
- A call for support or warm words of thanks.

If you were to attach the peroration to the opening, they should between them contain the core of the entire speech. The opening says what is coming; the closing says what has gone.

Here are some examples of good closing gambits:

- 'So this project does have great possibilities for our company. To succeed we must at once take the steps that I have suggested. I ask you all to support the resolution and to help put it into useful and urgent effect.'

- 'And so my argument is closed. I have tried to suggest the appropriate action which this company could now take. I believe that if my resolution is passed and put into urgent effect, it will transform the company's finances. I trust that no one will vote against it. I submit that it presents the best possible way out of our difficulties.'

- 'So this company stands in grave peril. The only way out is clear. The action I recommend could transform the situation. I am grateful to all of you for having listened so attentively to my arguments. Please do not reject them.'

- 'There is, then, no need for despair. The future presents great opportunities. But we must resolve not only to carry out the procedure proposed in my resolution, but also to ensure that the action which must follow will have the urgent and active support of us all. I therefore move that . . .'

- 'So those are the possibilities open to us. Only one of them really carries any hope of real success. It is the duty of this Board to protect and to advance the interests of our shareholders. That duty can only be performed if steps are taken in accordance with the resolution which stands in my name. I urge that it be accepted – fully, wholeheartedly and without amendment.'

*　*　*

There are many roads to Rome and countless ways to construct the end of the same speech. Purge the old clichés: 'My time is running short . . .', 'So without further ado . . .', 'I see that my time is nearly up and I must close . . .' Still worse: 'I see that you are beginning to get restless . . .', 'I have no wish to bore you any further . . .' Make your summary and your appeal – for support, for money, for understanding.

Other recommended endings:

- 'And so I thank you again for your kind hospitality.'
- 'Ladies and Gentlemen, it has been a delight to be with you. I hope that my words will have been of some help in promoting the cause for which you work and in which I – like you – believe so firmly. I wish you, your honorary officers, executives, members and workers, every possible success in your great venture.'
- So our Conference is over. It has been a delightful experience to meet you all. I trust that we shall see each other on many more such happy and useful occasions. Meanwhile, I know that I am expressing the warm

feelings of all of us when I wish you God-speed on your journeys home
and every success in all your ventures.'

- 'I know that the views I have put forward are not universally acceptable.
  But I know, too, that you would not have wished me to do otherwise
  than to speak my mind. That I have done, most earnestly. I do hope that
  the suggestions I have made will be adopted, or at least adapted. But
  whatever decision you take, I would like you to know how much I have
  appreciated the kind and courteous attention which you have given to
  me – and how much I care for the future of this organisation.'

Do not end by saying 'That you' or 'Good night'. Instead, build up
to a climax. A last powerful phrase, left hovering in the air – and
beckoning the applause.

Then do not rush back to your seat and flop quickly down into
your chair. Like any good trouper, wait for the applause. If it
comes, smile or bow slightly in acknowledgment. If it does not,
then look your audience straight in the eye. Pause. Then sit down.
The end of your speech should make as solid an impact as its start.

4 Wit and humour

Comedians labour hard for their living. If they are renowned for their wit, they may be able to make their audience laugh (if they are in the right mood) where no laughter is really deserved. Part of the art of all speakers is to let their hearers know what is coming . . . to lead them up to the climax . . . to prepare them to react as intended.

But speak to famous comedians and you will soon discover how carefully their impromptu laughs are prepared; how fickle and unpredictable an audience – any audience – can be; or even the best-woven tales may fall apart at the seams. You will then realise, if you do not already know it, that of all the skills of the public speaker, putting across humour is one of the most difficult. For the most experienced of humorists the path is tough. How much more difficult must it be for the beginner?

Still, the humourless speaker is weak. There are few occasions when a word of wit is not appreciated. The longer the speech, the more vital the touch of humour. The more sombre the subject, the more appropriate the tactful, tasteful touch of light relief. Humour is a weapon that every speaker should have readily available.

Humour must be tailored to the audience and to the occasion. This applies most obviously to the risqué, the rude or the plain vulgar. There is never any excuse for the obscene. But an element of dirt may sometimes add spice to the meal. When?

Obviously, the stag dinner is the place for the off-colour story. Conversely, those who introduce the risqué tale into solemn or sombre occasions invite contempt. In between come all the rest. You must judge each occasion as best you can. If in doubt – keep it clean.

Similar considerations apply to the dialect story. There is still a place for the saga of the Scotsman, the Irishman and the Jew. But to copy someone else's accent is usually a mistake. The only speakers who can do it without undue risk are those who belong to the group satirised.

Scotsmen, Jews, Irishmen, Blacks – they may delight in stories *about* themselves, but usually only when told *by* themselves.

If you enjoy the friendship of Jewish people, for instance, you will soon find that they poke merciless fun at their own foibles. Part

13

of their armour, acquired through centuries of persecution, is the ability to make laughter shine through the tears. No one can tell an anti-Semitic story with half the relish of the Jew. But then, masochism is reasonable. *Volenti non fit injuria* – the volunteer cannot complain of injuries brought about of his own free will. We cause no injury to ourselves when we make jokes at our own expense.

Sadism, on the other hand, is always unpleasant, and even a hint may be harmful. Minorities may consider themselves the subject for good humour. But the laughter is thin when the gibes come from tongues other than their own.

So be careful not to obtain cheap laughs at the expense of others. Many of the best jokes – and those most appreciated – are those about yourself.

'We Welsh' says the speaker with a smile, 'have, through our very name, given birth to an important word in the English language . . .'

'We foreigners find it very difficult to understand you English. I know that m-i-s-l-e-d spells misled. But when I pronounced t-i-t-l-e-d the same way, everyone laughed at me.'

Not great humour, and perhaps it has been heard before. But then, as one famous comic put it: 'There are basically only two jokes – the mother-in-law and the banana skin.' Make the joke fit the occasion and the audience.

The best way to suit the occasion is to extract the humour from the surroundings and from the people present. How do you put it across? Here are some hints.

First, you must appear confident. It is a mistake to say: 'I was going to tell you the story about . . .' and then to tell it, half apologetically. Believe in the comedy or you will never induce your audience to do so.

That confidence must be retained, even in the face of defeat. If a joke falls flat, never mind. Pretend it was not intended to be funny and carry on. Alternatively, face up the situation and say: 'Sorry . . . it wasn't a very good one, was it? Never mind – how about the tale of . . .?' Or: 'Sorry about that – I'll do better next time. But you must admit that after a meal such as we've just had, it really is the height of sadism to expect anyone to attempt to entertain you!'

Timing is all-important. This means that the joke, witticism or humorous thrust must be well placed in relation to the speech, the content of the talk or lecture, the mood of the audience. But it especially means that the joke must be told at the right pace . . . with the correct emphasis . . . with the appropriate pauses.

Listen to first-class comedians at work. Half their effect is achieved by timing. They know when to wait and when to rush forward. So listen and copy.

Some speakers keep a book of stories, notes of humorous tales that have gone down well and which they would like not to forget. Certainly the jotting down of the punch line on the back of a menu card or in the front of your dairy can provide useful ammunition. It may also have the opposite effect – it may help to save you from the gross error of telling an audience the same story that they heard the last time they met.

To avoid this fate, take some regular attender into your confidence. 'I'm thinking of telling the story of . . .' you say to the Chairman, 'Do you know it?' If not then the chances are that you will be safe. If he or she has heard it, then find out whether it was told at the same gathering. If in doubt, leave it out.

Jokes are for others to laugh at. Giggle at your own stories and you detract from their effect on your audience.

The best stories have a sting in their tails. The laughter should build up. The audience should expect the laughs. But if the first climax brings laughter and turns out to be a false one, giving rise to an unexpected twist, then the story has been a success.

The formal tale also has its place. But the bright phrase, the witty aside, the colourful remark – these are more important. If you cannot think of a suitable, funny story for the occasion, never mind. Some humorous thought may come to you as you speak. If it does not, at least make sure that your speech is shorter than if you had been able to lighten its darkness with a few shafts of light-hearted laughter.

Finally, mull over my Retellable Tales (Book 3). Use and adapt to suit yourself, your occasions and your audience.

5 Overstatement

Hyperbole – that is, exaggeration for effect – has its place, and is often used by humorists. There is nothing funny about a thin man; but a matchstick man, a creation of skin and bone, a fat head on a puny frame – that's different.

About the only time that deliberate exaggeration helps the presentation of a serious case is when that case is thin. 'If something is too silly to say, you can always sing it,' says the operatic librettist. 'If logic and argument are surplus,' says the skilled speaker, 'then it is just possible that if you shout loud enough, exaggerate sufficiently, thump with sufficient force, you may numb the minds of your audience.'

This type of behaviour is the last resort of the advocate and should only be used when *in extremis*. Otherwise, your exaggerations are likely to boomerang, to cause laughter, to ruin such case as you have. Two horrible examples:

- Reference to the speech immediately preceding: 'That magnificent and moving oration that we have just heard . . . that tugged at our heart strings and must now open our purses . . .'
- 'I only saw her passing by, but I shall love her till I die,' said Sir Robert Menzies, then Prime Minister of Australia, enthusing at a dinner in honour of the Queen. However well loved the Queen undoubtedly was and is, Sir Robert's hyperbole brought only ridicule.

Words, like drugs, may be highly beneficial in the correct quantity and dosage. Over-indulgence may cause death. Moderation pays.

6 Repetition

Repetition should be deliberate. Shakespeare did it best. 'Brutus is an honourable man . . .'

Repeating other people's points generally spells disaster: 'Mr Jones has put all the arguments which I had wished to put forward . . .' Try instead: 'Mr Jones has put forward his case with immense skill, and I commend it to the meeting. However, there are seveal aspects of his remarks which, I think, require further emphasis.'

'I will not bore you by reploughing the furrows so thoroughly covered by Mr Jones.' Watch out. Boredom is on its way. That sort of introduction, combining mixed metaphor with cliché, is a sure sign of impending audience distress. Leave the meeting if you can.

Then there are speakers who repeat their points in the same words. Most well-constructed speeches should begin with a summary of what is coming, followed by a full-blooded exposition of those points in the body of the speech and another brief summary at the end. 'To summarise, then: if we are to achieve success, we must take the following steps. First . . . second . . . third . . . and, above all . . .'

English is a rich language. If you cannot think of synonyms, consult the invaluable *Roget's Thesaurus* – which should be on the desk or at least in the library of every speaker. If you must repeat yourself, at least try not to do so in the current and boring clichés, which are merely a sign of speeches made without thought, and so reveal the thoughtlessness of the speaker.

Deliberate repetition of words or sentences is a great technique. See Martin Luther King's great speech, 'I have a dream . . .' (page 194).

Also, do repeat lists. Your listeners will not absorb them first time round. Or use visual aid (Chapter 33).

7 Jargon and clichés

My shorthand is your jargon. Your jargon is my cliché. Jargon is specialised speech, understood by insiders. Clichés are once-sparkling expressions or bright truths repeated to the brink of boredom. Avoid both.

Listening to the head of a financial institution, I jotted down the following jargon in his first few sentences: FIMBRA, LAUTRO, IMRO, TSA, AFBD . . . which reminded me of a visit to an African capital where the UK High Commissioner invited me to talk to his diplomats. First, though, would I mind if they discussed some urgent business? Of course not. I'd be interested. So, for some ten minutes, they discussed the QBP.

I was bemused. Talk swirled over well-known names, apparently to be included or excluded; delicacies to be served; British and local composers; diplomatic niceties . . .

Finally, I could contain myself no longer: 'I'm sorry to be dim', I said. 'But would you please tell me: What is the QBP?'

Every head turned at the vast ignorance of this politician. 'The Queen's Birthday Party, Mr Janner,' said His Excellency. When my turn came, I resisted the temptation to discuss the AGM of my GMC, or the preparations for the next meeting of the CLP, the DLP or the PLP. Meetings of the Labour Party are not tea parties, nor are they known for their diplomacy.

Anyway, there are two stages to avoiding this sort of embarrassment to others. Firstly, recognise your own jargon. None of us notices the familiar because habit dulls recognition. Secondly, once you have noticed it, use it only among your own colleagues or others afflicted by the same verbiage. Do not inflict it on those who are strange to it.

Final hint: here is an area in which your spouse is likely to be more useful than your secretary. In most families, spouses work and operate in different spheres and can recognise each other's jargon, point it out, chide, reprove and help to avoid. Ask yours to do so for you, or employ your older children in the hunt for the unacceptably obtuse. Unlike your secretary, they are likely to be jargon-free. You might even consider appropriate payment. We recommend £1 for every 'um' or 'er' (Chapter 19) or bit of jargon spotted by a spouse; or 50p for the same service performed by offspring.

Now apply similar rules to clichés, which are particularly prevalent in the business world. Take the 'track record' of your company or firm (what 'track' pray?); and who 'heads up' your department? (It's head down, when you are at the helm of your ship of state, as you steer it through the troubled economic waters . . .)

When Ernest Bevin was asked about someone's speech, he would often reply: 'Boring. Clitch after clitch after clitch!' Most clichés are universal. When you get bored with someone else's speech or presentation, spot the passing clichés and jot them down. Amongst my most despised are: 'We must stand up and be counted' (by whom? What, now?); 'At this moment in time', 'in this day and age' (why not 'now'? You are not being paid by the word); 'We must capture the hearts and minds of the people' (good idea – if you clitch long enough, their bodies will depart).

There is no limit, is there? Each is common, hackneyed, trite and commonplace (see *Roget's Thesaurus*, paragraph 496). Even though the sentiments expressed may be wise, sage, true, received, admitted, recognized (same paragraph), that flexibility of the language which can cloak even the most uninspiring and unoriginal thought with at least the appearance of charm or originality has not been brought into play.

It is no hyperbole to say that the oldest thought in the newest dress can have a rare and surprising appeal. 'There's nothing new to say about this subject,' is a cliché. 'Consider the problem from this new angle,' is a worthy start – and if the angle is sufficiently acute, its familiarity may well be forgotten.

You will not regard yourself as a bore. Your listeners should share your view. A good start to this hopeful process is to learn to recognize clichés in the speeches of others and ruthlessly to eliminate them from your own.

8   The vertical pronoun

Speakers of excellence treat the sound of their own voice as a drug to be taken in moderation. Restrain your use of the first-person singular.

There are two probable reasons why you have been asked to address a particular audience. Either the people *wanted* to hear you or they thought they *ought* to want to do so. These categories subdivide.

If you have been invited to speak in the hope that you will have something interesting to tell, then you are lucky. Do not push your luck too far by retelling what you are, rather than what you know.

Leave it to your introducer to sing your praises. To do so for yourself is to court ridicule. Oscar Wilde once remarked, 'Fall in love with yourself and you are in for a lifetime of romance!' Fine, but do not do your courting in public.

If you are asked to give advice, do you really need to praise your own success? To tell tales of the trade, you must draw on your own experience and a joke against yourself may be highly successful. But you do not need to alert your listeners to your excellence. Do so and they will not believe you. Fail to do so and they may think up the idea for themselves.

Naturally, if you have been the rounds of similar businesses, factories, offices or workshops to your own, at home or abroad, and are asked to give your impressions; if you wish to express views and to make it clear that they are yours and not those of your organisation or, perhaps, of your board, your partners or colleagues; if you wish to lighten the darkness of some drab subject with a personal anecdote – then go ahead. 'I once met . . . in Birmingham'; 'I was told the tale of . . .'; 'These are my views, I repeat, and if they turn out to be wrong, you will know where to place the responsibility.' All fair.

But: 'When I last saw the Prime Minister . . .'; or 'Now, I don't like to drop names, but when I was spending a weekend recently with Lord and Lady Blank in their country estate . . .' Terrible.

Remember the story of that famous General, Lord Montgomery of Alamein, whose first-person anecdote was accepted because of his undoubted greatness. He was telling an audience about his battle tactics. 'I could not decide what to do next,' he said. 'I thought to myself: "My God, what is to be done now?" "General," came the answer, "you decide. I have every confidence in you." So I did!'

Of course, people like to be given the inside information. Don the cloak of apparent modesty.

All this becomes even more important when you are Guest of Honour – which is not necessarily the same as the honoured guest. Maybe your hosts want your money . . . your support . . . your services . . . your backing. Maybe they are simply hoping to lubricate you sufficiently to obtain some useful information which, in a less cordial or obligated moment, you might never give. Whatever the reason, you are on show. So play up to it. Be grateful that you are to be honoured and not reviled. Help to keep it that way by making your speech extremely modest. Or try my father's favourite: 'After all those kind words, Mr Chairman, I can hardly wait to hear myself speak!'

'It is extremely good of you to honour me in this way,' you might continue. 'I fully appreciate that your intention is, through me, to honour my company / my organisation / my entire Board [or whatever the case may be]. We are deeply grateful to you.'

In the body of the speech, tell them about the work your organisation is doing. Give them as much inside information as you decently can. If you are honoured for long service, then reminisce – and mention as many individuals amongst your audience as you can.

Everyone honourably mentioned is flattered. You have achieved the all-important informal touch. Your audience are your friends. The ice is melted and you are revealed as one of the people instead of the complete egotist some had thought you to be.

Then continue: 'You are indeed lucky to have in your active ranks, tonight and always, Mr Reginald Property . . . Mr James Industry . . . and that lady, famous for her good deeds, Mrs Jewel.' The guest who gives honour will receive it.

'I now close . . .' (one hopes because of the time of the clock and not the time you have taken in your speech) 'but before doing so, I thank you again for the great kindness and generosity you have shown me. I have enjoyed being with you. I hope that we shall meet again often and always on happy occasions. And may this organisation/company/institute (etc.) flourish for many years to come, under your leadership.

Turn to the chairman, bow to your audience . . . You have produced a resounding ending to a good speech. Your hearers will tell you so – and mean it.

To sum up: substitute the most vital word in the English language – 'you' – for the vertical pronoun. In parliamentary language, 'The you's have it'!

9 Grammar – and the spoken word

Some of the more pedantic rules for writing have now been discarded. Freedom of expression and freedom of speech have followed in their wake. Sentences without verbs, split infinitives: they offend the ears of some but are generally forgiven. Still, here are some general rules which may prove helpful.

* * *

The most common grammatical error lies in the use of the first person. 'Between you and I' is wrong. So is 'Dr Brown and me were most impressed with our welcome', and 'You and me must give some careful thought to this problem'. If this sort of problem worries you, discuss it with a friend whose grammar is impeccable. If in doubt, change the sentences around and you will soon find whether your usage is or is not correct.

If you are inclined to say: 'You and me must go', try instead: 'Me must go' – and the error becomes obvious. Or: 'Thank you on behalf of Mr White and I for your kindness' cannot be correct when you leave out Mr White. 'On my own behalf ... on my behalf ... on behalf of Mr White' – but obviously, not on behalf of I!

Swear words and obscenities are best excluded, even from the stag-dinner oration. Some listeners will always be offended. But slang and modern idiom are expected. If in doubt, put the words 'in quotes'.

If in doubt about the precise meaning of a word, either avoid it or consult a dictionary. If given the choice between two words, one long and the other short, choose the shorter. Good old Anglo-Saxon monosyllables are usually the most effective.

Sentences, too, should be kept short. Apart from your audience losing the thread, you may yourself do so. 'Now, where was I?' is a sad admission of a speaker's failure.

Avoid statistics where you can: apart from the possibility of being found out, the effect of an understandable approximation is much greater than a detailed list of figures.

Clichés should be 'conspicuous by their absence' (see Chapter 7). You may use material full of sound and fury but signifying nothing. The higher you get in the government of a country or of an organisation, the more frequent those occasions become. But in general, direct speech is better than indirect, the active voice rather than the passive, and the straightforward far preferable to insinuation.

10   Brevity – the soul of success

Mort Mendels, long-time Secretary of the World Bank and top sufferer from the awful speeches of others, displayed a cartoon on his office wall. It showed a man being carried out of the Senate on a stretcher. 'Talked to Death!' was the caption. The corpse might as easily have been emerging from any one of thousands of meetings anywhere in Britain or the USA.

People who stand in front of the mirror admiring themselves for long periods are rightly regarded as freaks. But at least no one else is disturbed. Those who so rejoice in the sound of their own words that they impose them at great length upon their fellows should be granted the same privacy.

Have you ever heard an audience complain that the speaker did not go on long enough? Far more complain at the sluggishness of their watch hands. On the rare occasions when they do want more from the speaker – well, they can always be invited again.

The importance of this chapter is in inverse proportion to its length. Indeed, so vital is its theme that we shall return to it in Chapter 22.

PART 2

The art of delivery

11　Controlling your nerves

Human beings – which category includes most speechmakers – habitually have and suffer from nerves. I have seen great athletes coughing and moaning before races; experienced public speakers shaking and trembling before a major appearance; world leaders in agony before a crucial press conference. So join the club.

Nervous tension is a necessity for the performer in any sphere. It releases that amazing and invaluable secretion, adrenalin, which sharpens and tones up the functions of body and mind alike.

So if you do not feel nervous, your performance is unlikely to excel. Greet your anxiety with expectant understanding. It will be your ally.

Accepting, then, that pre-presentation nerves are an inevitable necessity, how can you control them?

First: recognise that once you start moving, they will disappear on their own. The runner may retch as he limbers up but *never* once he is in his starting blocks. The public speaker may shake before she begins but once her first words ring out and she actually hears her voice, she stops worrying whether her vocal cords will freeze.

Second: remember that your feelings are internal and your audience will not know of them unless you are inexperienced enough to tell them. Therefore:

- *Do not* say: 'I am a bag of nerves . . .' or any equivalent.
- *Do* look them straight in the eye.

The absence of eye contact is the greatest single give-away of the nervous presenter. An experienced audience may look for a tongue flickering over dry lips, but if speakers keep their eyes on floor, ceiling or notes, they are in trouble.

So look your audience in the face. Fix your eyes to theirs and they will concentrate on what you are saying and be far less likely to notice your mistakes.

Third: avoid whatever form of nervous twitch is your personal affliction. Do not:

- Put your hands in front of your mouth – you will muffle your words while leaving your nerve ends visible.

- Keep your hands in your pockets – a slovenly discourtesy made worse if you rattle coins or your keyring.
- Jiggle your handbag or bounce it up and down on the table.
- Twist your hair, excavate your ear, pick at your nose (however delicately), open and close buttons of your jacket, or engage in any other of those less entrancing pursuits of the nerve-ridden.

Above all, come to your presentation prepared with adequate notes, properly laid out (Chapter 34), knowing your case and (deep down, if not on the surface) confident that you can deal with your subject. Your nerves can then return to their quietude and you can make your presentation at your ease.

That said, here are a few hints to help you either to control your nerves or at least not to show how you are feeling:

- Take the position, sitting or standing, that suits you best (but see Chapter 37). Sometimes you have no choice; often you can say to the chairman: 'Do you mind if I sit?' Or, alternatively: 'If you have no objection, I shall talk to you standing.'
- Sit back, with your rear end tucked into the angle of the chair. If standing, try putting one foot ahead of the other – this is also better for your voice production. Sit or stand upright and keep your voice and eyes up.
- If you are superstitious, keep your favourite mascot or charm in your pocket or handbag – but do not rely on it so much that if one day you forget it, your confidence collapses. And please do not allow your nervousness to drive you into clicking your ball point, twiddling or tapping your pen or dashing doodles across a visible pad.
- Do not drink before you speak. Speaking, like driving, requires a sharp mind in a clear head.

A man I know was wrongly charged with arson. An honest, decent person, he arrived at his trial stuffed to his eyeballs with tranquillizers. He was not at all nervous. But he never answered the question he was asked; he was convicted and sentenced to three years' imprisonment; and it took the combined efforts of an investigative radio team and another MP and myself to get him released. Tranquillizers cost him an agonising year in jail.

Confidence comes with preparation, practice and training – not from drink or drugs.

12   Be yourself

Why is it that people who are charming, friendly and articulate in private conversation become wooden and charmless, remote and friendless, tongue-tied and wordless the moment they go public? Why, if the presentation is formal, does their backbone wobble and their knees knock, even if they stay seated?

The symptoms of this personality change are almost invariable.

- Speakers avoid eye contact. They look at floor or ceiling, or anywhere other than at their audience. They probably swivel their eyes, looking shifty and dishonest.
- They sit forward, elbows on table, hunched and hostile and as visibly screwed up physically as they are churned up mentally.
- If they stand, their fingers twist, their hands gyrate and their bodies jerk, with their heads sunk forward and their eyes downcast.
- Above all, instead of speaking ordinary, relaxed English, they adopt an unreal persona – not their own, but that which they believe others would expect them to be when making a formal presentation. They become pompous and formal.
- They speak fast, gabbling and rushing towards the end.

Colleagues and I teach and train all levels of business people, plus professionals at every level up to the very top. Our single most important, and often most difficult, task is to induce people to be themselves.

If you are talking to one person, eyeball to eyeball, your eyes should maintain contact. 'All the time he was talking to me, he was looking over my shoulder,' is a common complaint, however.

So do not lose eye contact with your audience just because the moment or the occasion is formal.

Do you sit back in the chair, relaxed and obviously at ease when at home? Then do not lean forward when you talk to your colleagues, your board, your customers or clients, actual or potential. You will not only show relaxed authority if you sit back but also retain the flexibility of occasional forward movement.

13   Style

For the speechmaker, style and success are synonymous. But the common idea that style will suffice without taught techniques is arrogant and ridiculous. So is the converse – the chip-on-the-shoulder, foot-in-the-mouth inferiority complex approach to public speaking in any form, especially endemic among business people at or near the top.

I invited a tycoon to address a private dinner. 'Sorry,' he replied, curtly. 'Nice of you to ask. You and your friends in Parliament do the speaking. I do the work!' What he really meant was: 'I'm afraid of opening my mouth while I'm on my feet in case I make a fool of myself.'

Another told me: 'I came up the hard way. I leave speeches to you fellows with the education.'

An education does no one any harm and many top people who missed it in their youth are unashamed to learn, when their money can buy them time and tuition. Presenting yourself to a public does take courage and is certainly an acquired skill. But if you have that intangible, inexplicable magic – that style of your own – you should not fear its public display. Printers and potters produce identical replicas, good or bad. Your style is unique and rules are made to be broken.

Take the orator's pause, for instance – a crucial weapon in the armoury of timing. (See also Chapter 18.) The space between words, sentences or thoughts should not be blurred by that most awful of sounds – 'er'. To 'err' (or to 'umm') is human – to pause, divine!

The art of successful speaking is to know the case you wish to present; to understand and to use the basic skills which will enable your audience to hear, to comprehend and to accept your words and their intent; and to stamp the process with your own particularity.

It follows that you should use the services of speechwriters with rare care. Unless you can find the writer who can step into your style as well as your mind, you are probably better off with a researcher. By all means use a ferret to produce your raw material, but knock it into your own shape.

If the speech or presentation is worth your while to make, is it not worth your own time to prepare? Then remember another of Churchill's dicta: 'If I have to make a two-hour speech,' he rumbled, 'I spend 10 minutes in preparation. If it is a 10-minute speech, then it can take me two hours . . .'

Stylists are as brief as their impact and their message permits. There is no reason why executives who are blunt, direct and lucid in conversation should allow their speeches to deteriorate into long-winded and indirect blather, the moment they climb to their feet.

Just as there is no one successful style in business – or, for that matter, in athletics or in football, in philosophy or in politics – so executives who seek success on their feet will project their personal individuality, their individual personality.

Every would-be excellent speaker needs education in the basic skills of speechmaking and presentation. They are universal. They range from voice production to microphone technique, from the skills of the construction of a speech or presentation to the art of the destruction of the arguments of others. But training in the use of their skills should be devoted to the creation and improvement of their own style.

True education and the best training teach students – however mighty – to make the best of their talents.

No presenter of ideas or maker of speeches has ever excelled the wondrous Shakespeare. 'This above all,' he admonished, 'to thine own self be true . . .'

If truth is the life of style, insincerity is its death.

14 Body talk

If self-presentation is an essential for self-preservation, then you must make your appearances and hence your appearance count. If your presentation is disembodied, you must take special care with your voice. You have no other way of showing your enthusiasm and your sincerity, your confidence and your command of the subject.

In person or on television, you are notable by your visibility. And while, for instance, dandruff may go unobserved at a meeting, on TV it stands out from a blue suit like chalk on a blackboard. So you *must* take note of detail.

Start, though, with the overall effect. How do you wish to appear? Authoritative, distinguished, sound and sensible? Then wear a dark suit or dress. Relaxed and informal? Then wear light-coloured, loose-fitting clothing. The choice is yours. The persuaders may try to influence your decision. But ultimately you make up your own mind.

Celebrated caricaturist Ranan Lurie, once said to me: 'Your father got his appearance right. A combination of pointed head, central bulk and above all of red carnation made him instantly recognisable. You, alas, are simply a pleasant and happy looking individual without even a treble chin.'

I convinced him that he should look more closely and he would see that I have at least six arms, most of them working at the same time. But I now usually wear a carnation.

Start at the top and work down. Do you cultivate polished head (David Nixon) or bushed hair (David Ben Gurion)? Do you groom your crowning glory (Margaret Thatcher) or allow it to dominate you (Michael Foot)? Do you permit your hair to turn grey or white (most men) or enjoy retaining or even enhancing its youthful blaze (most women)?

Do you wear your uniform (dark suit or working overalls)?

Safely married and at home or on holiday with your husband or wife, you may decide that appearances are skin deep and matter little. But when you appear in public, you woo the public – so present yourself with studied care, or take the consequences.

Study Desmond Morris's *The Naked Ape* – followed by his

Manwatching – and your speeches should gain an extra dimension
of excellence. In particular, you will learn how others give
themselves away through bodily indications, and how you can
avoid doing the same.

For instance, eye contact is crucial to successful speechmaking,
whether you are seated or on your feet. Lowering or swivelling your
eyes or failure to 'look people straight' in theirs is a classic symptom
of nervousness.

The more your stomach wobbles, the more you should hunt for a
friendly face in your audience and talk to it, eyeball to eyeball. (See
also Chapter 11.)

Keep your gestures to the minimum. They should emphasise your
words, not detract from their meaning. Keep your body still when
talking. Be upright to dominate your audience.

You may wish to move around, to involve your audience or for
effect. Or, like myself, you may have back trouble and be able to
run, jump or climb but not to stand still. Then get a high (or bar or
draughtsman's) stool, or perch on the edge of a table.

The effect of a gesture does not depend upon its vigour or
expanse. The more economic your movements the better. If you
make your presentation seated, keep your hands away from your
face and your mouth. To command your audience, do not slouch –
sit straight. Avoid minor, irritating gestures – from nail biting to
finger or pencil tapping to rattling coins in your pocket. Concentrate
on the body of your presentation and keep your own steady and
still.

Your facial expression should match your topic. President Jimmy
Carter used to speak with a fixed grin on his face. Eventually, a
professional speech teacher showed him on a video screen how
wicked it looked to preserve that smile when talking about, for
instance, those who had died in Vietnam. He stopped.

After chairing a memorial meeting. I was admonished for smiling
on the platform. My neighbour had told me a wistful and loving
story about the deceased. No matter. When on show, your face
must reflect the mood of the occasion.

Conversely if you are asking your audience to laugh, your face
should indicate that a joke is on its way.

Words matter; movements distract. We all recognise the speaker
who strides up and down while talking, like the American lawyer in
those television courtroom scenes. In Britain, lawyers stand still and
their speeches are the better for it.

Acrobats doing a tumbling act must gyrate and mime. Those who rely on words stand still and confine their movement to their faces.

The more motionless you stand, the greater the chance of your speech reaching the minds of your audience and making its impact. If you do move around, do so deliberately. Do not rock, or your speech will roll.

What do you do with your hands? Hold the lectern or rostrum before you. Grip the edge of the table. Put them behind your back, *à la* Duke of Edinburgh. Or simply hold the cards for your notes, firmly and calmly in front of you. Better still, rest them on the top of a chair back.

Keep your gestures sparing. The rarer and the more restrained the movement, the greater its effect. The days of the ranting, tub-thumping, rabble-rousing arm-waver are gone. The businessman who 'hams' is regarded (not always correctly) as an insincere show-off.

A contemptuous shrug, an occasional, accusing finger, a reference to the heavens and hand pointing to the sky: all have their place in the skilled speaker's repertoire.

You wear spectacles? Then use them as an occasional weapon. To emphasise a point, remove them gently from your nose, hold them still in your hand, bend forward and glare at your audience, brandish your glasses and then return them to your nose and your speech to its theme. Even the odd jab with the closed spectacles can be dramatic and useful.

Speakers with spectacles need not be shy. Many excellent performers who could do without their glasses, even for seeing their notes, deliberately wear them. Do not fear poor eyesight. Like other defects, it can be turned to good effect.

Generally, though, speakers should use their tongues, faces and minds, not their feet, arms or fingers. Otherwise, their audience may take to their heels. Gestures must add to words and to meaning. Otherwise, keep still.

15　Stand and deliver

'Give me a firm place to stand,' said Archimedes, 'and I will move the earth.' He might have said, 'Stand firmly and you are set to move your audience.'

As any toddler will tell you, there is an art to standing. Adult orators too soon forget.

'Here stand I. I can do no other,' said Martin Luther, refusing to budge. If more executives would stand with authority and determination, their audiences would listen to far greater effect.

As a start and at the start, rise before you shine. Say not one word until your feet are firmly in place, your clothing and your notes arranged to your satisfaction, your audience held with your eye.

To start before you stand erect has been described as *'oratus interruptus'*. To pause before you start takes confidence and skill, but is an absolute essential if you do not wish your beginning to fall limp.

Because you are upright, you automatically dominate. Given an audience of even moderate size and the choice between sitting and standing, stand.

To stand *with* ease, stand *at* ease, legs apart and one foot slightly in front of the other. Relax the body and you can then concentrate on balance in speech. With your chest upright and forward, you can produce sound with the least effort and to maximum effect.

Watch any accomplished opera singer. Forget the modern marvels, magnified, microphone to mouth. I mean those who have been taught to produce fine and varied sound by using the instruments with which God has endowed them. You do not need the training or the talent of a great singer if your words are to live. But you cannot project your voice without using your chest as a sound box. Like Woody Allen, you may want to achieve immortality not through your work, but by not dying. If you want to achieve success through your words and to avoid oratorical death, stand up for your case.

Once your presentation is moving, you may move with it. You are not a tree, rooted to one spot. You may stroll to your flip chart or your overhead, towards or away from your audience, as the spirit or the subject moves you.

Remember:

- Never turn your back on your audience, except for the occasional moment when you are actually writing on your flip charts.
- Never talk to your audience unless your eyes are on them.

If you are using amplification, then make sure that your mike is mobile. Plan in advance and, if possible, make your choice between:

- Neck mike – which hangs without effort. Advantage: you can forget it. Disadvantage: you probably will, thereby tripping over the cord and ripping the mike from your neck, which is most undignified. Also, you can neither adjust it nor use it as a weapon.
- Radio mike – expensive and liable to interference from (eg) radio cabs.
- Roving mike, clipped initially to a stand and then holdable by hand. This is my favourite. Keep your elbow tucked into your side and the mike will remain the same distance from your mouth, no matter what yours may be from your audience.

To create and to maintain intimacy with your audience, remove physical barriers. You may prefer to sit behind your desk while a recalcitrant employee stands trembling in front of it. But if you are trying to present a case to listeners whom you wish to carry with you, then shift the table, the lectern or the desk. Or (more likely) move yourself around it. Perch relaxed on the edge or speak from the side.

The longer your talk, the more appropriate it becomes to introduce action, movement, variety. The more complex the subject, the greater the need for well-prepared visual aids. Nor is there any law against at some stage taking a seat. The only vital rule when you move from standing to sitting or back again? Take your time; pause; and stay silent while you rise or fall.

At the start of your speech or presentation, then, rise to the occasion – with calm, relaxed authority. At its end, summarise your content, emphasise your message, work up to your climax. End in certainties. At your beginning should be an indication of your end, and you should finish as you began – on your feet until that last moment of vital control.

The Canadian humorist, Stephen Leacock, wrote of Lord Ronald: 'He said nothing; he flung himself from the room, flung himself up on his horse and rode madly off in all directions!' When you stand and think on your feet, you say your piece; fling yourself nowhere; and direct your words and your body in the required direction only.

16   Voice production

The human chest is a sound box. The voice should reverberate and carry. As a stringed instrument gains its volume through the resonance of its sound chamber, so the human voice should resonate through the chest.

Try saying the word 'war'. Through your nose and voice alone, it produces a puny sound. Now take a deep breath, put your hand on your chest and sigh out the word until you can feel the vibration. Deep and resonant sound reverberates an idea to immense effect.

The opposite also applies. To attract and hold the attention of an audience, you do not need to shout at them. The dramatic effect of a whisper may be intense.

Vary and change the volume and tone of your speech, but always within the hearing of your listeners. Address the woman in the back row. Imagine she is deaf – she may be!

Take special care not to drop your voice at the end of a sentence. Thoughts should rise to a climax, not fade with the final breath of a phrase. To avoid monotony, vary tone, speed and volume.

Words do not emerge from closed mouths. You may not consider this an especially brilliant observation, but if you saw the number of top people we train in presentation skills who speak like ventriloquists' dummies you would be amazed.

'Open your mouth, please,' we implore the executive, whose confidential whispers go unheard because he scarcely moves his lips. 'If ever you lose your job, sir, you should apply for another one as a ventriloquist's dummy!' He thinks we're joking. Not so.

We explain that if you want to eat, you have to open your mouth to put food in. If you want to get an unpleasant country to do what you want – including the release of hostages – you generally have to remain in communication with them. People do not come through closed doors, nor words through shut mouths.

If you do not open your mouth sufficiently wide, you cannot project your voice through it. For sound, you need breath. Full voice needs open mouth.

Take this book to a mirror. Read out a short sentence. Then repeat it several times, as naturally as you can. Watch. Is your mouth opening? Are your words coming out loud, crisp and clear?

When you talk, you should be able to put two fingers into your mouth, together and vertically. Try it. Then modulate your voice.

It has been said of one politician that he 'only opens his mouth when he has nothing to say'. When he wanted to say something, he would keep it closed and talk through gritted teeth. He needed a shoehorn to make a speech.

It may be true that the best way to get some people to agree with you is to keep your mouth shut. But if you are forced to speak, then please open it.

17   Speech reading

What is the main exception to the rule that you must not write your speech word for word? Where each word must count – and especially if time is strictly limited and your words are more 'for the record' than for the audience.

Consider the story told by that redoubtable dissident, Natan Sharansky, in his gripping story of his trial in Moscow and his trials in the Gulag, *Fear No Evil* (Weidenfeld and Nicolson). After the final speech for the prosecution, he had to consider his right of reply. He decided to prepare a list of 15 points. He sent for a clean sheet of paper and concentrated, trying to distil the essence of his case. He did not know how to begin.

Eventually, a sentence came into his head which he would use in the middle of his speech. Then, he tells us, 'something strange happened: I wrote without stopping or correcting a single word. I wrote quickly, but I could barely keep up with the words. I soon reached the end . . . Then I took a deep breath and returned to the beginning.

Now I knew how to begin . . . I practically didn't have to edit a word.'

If you know what you want to say and you have absorbed it, then it should pour out of your mind into good order.

When Sharansky came to court, he 'recited the text like a commander dictating a report to headquarters . . .' He knew that his words would have no impact on his immediate audience. The verdict and sentence had already been decided. He was talking for his brother, sitting in court; for his prosecutors and his persecutors; but above all, in the hope that his words would reach out to others and show that he would not relent.

If you decide that you must read, for whatever reason, and you value the reaction of your audience, then you must write and read well.

Remember that Churchill was probably the only man who ever wrote prose which sounded as great when read as when spoken. But one good trick is to speak words which you later intend to read.

Two methods:

- You may actually dictate your words, as I am dictating this chapter. Some writers sit behind typewriters or word processors; others scrawl in longhand or even in their own shorthand; but I find that talking into my dictating machines makes the words flow.

Sometimes the words cascade; other times, they dry up – which is the challenge of making a speech. How much greater is that challenge if the speech is to be written and then read.

- Conversely, you could write your words – or even get a speechwriter to do the job for you. Then you read them out.

Either way, you should rehearse and re-read and rewrite until you are satisfied with the rhythm, meaning and time.

Then get your secretary to type your final draft, widely spaced and with decent paragraphs. Sentences, phrases and paragraphs should be short. When an idea ends, start again on the next page.

Mark up your manuscript, using either strokes of the pen to mark emphasis or (if you prefer it, which I do not) pale coloured highlights.

Know your script well enough to be able to move from it in response to your audience's lack of response, or to deal with interruptions, or because of new ideas which leap into your mind during your delivery.

If you give advance copies to the press, warn them that you may move from your script.

Finally, if the occasion is sufficiently important and either you or your company or organisation are adequately rich, hire one of those machines that throws the words up onto plastic screens, which you can read but which are invisible to others. Whether called an 'autoprompt' or by some other name, these are the speechmaker's equivalent to the moving words which allow television newsreaders and announcers to keep their eyes apparently on their viewers while they are in fact reading.

If you use this or any other sort of equipment (see Chapter 33 on visual aids), practise in advance, rehearse with your operator, and recognise that even the most modern of wonders, like the human beings that use them, may suffer from a breakdown, nervous or otherwise.

All that said, the read speech should be the unavoidable exception to the oratorical rule.

18   The pause

The pause is the speechmaker's most useful weapon. Handled with confidence, it hides nerves and gives time for thought – and, above all, it is the basis of all dramatic timing.

Take your cue and your breath from the impresario: 'Ladies and Gentlemen' – pause – 'it is my honour to present' – pause – 'for the first time in this country' – pause – 'none other than' – pause – 'that most famous of all singers/comedians/boxers' – long pause – 'Mr' – pause – 'John' – pause – 'Smith!'

Refine that into the introduction: 'Ladies and Gentleman' – pause – 'Mr John Smith!'

The pause precedes the words and the sense mounts to a crescendo at the end of the sentence.

Churchill used the pause more and better than any other great orator. 'We . . . er . . . have no intention of allowing that . . . er . . . maniac to demolish our lives . . .' Each pause and each 'er' whetted the appetite for his next attack on the Nazis and their leader.

For those of us who are not Churchill, however, to 'er' is to err! If you cannot think what to say, keep silent. Your audience will believe that you are searching for the *mot juste*. Even if your mind is blank, look fierce, look around, stand firm. When you are ready with your next pearl, drop it.

At the start of your speech, talk or intervention, keep silent until you have the full attention of your audience. Pause.

If you are interrupted – whether by the drop of a window, the shrill of a passing jet, the intervention of a colleague, or by laughter or applause – wait again for silence before you proceed. A pause is not the sign of indecision or weakness, but the speaker's great weapon – and the one that the inexperienced speechmaker uses too little.

The pause before a crucial word is the orator's most superb trick. 'If we do not take the steps I have suggested, I foresee only one result' – pause – look around – wait: 'disaster'

'We all remember the terrible days of ' – pause. You are only using an extension of the suspense motivation, employed at the end of each properly constructed instalment of a radio play, or at the end of the chapter of a tightly written crime story. You are keeping your grip on your audience.

'After hearing all the views of this committee, I have come to my decision. I think that we have no alternative other than . . . to . . .' Wait for it . . . keep them waiting . . .'

Of course, the pause must not be too long. Just as brevity in a pause may show lack of confidence and cause it to lose its effect, so too long a pause may appear as 'ham'. To overdramatise is as bad as to underplay. Only experience can teach you how long to pause. Only practice can show the maximum period for the best effect. If in doubt, pause longer.

Prepare an important speech, and rehearse it more or less word for word and time yourself on a stop-watch. Then make the same speech on the important occasion and get someone to time you. It will take longer. So prepare less, and leave time for interruptions and questions.

The most common occasions for pauses:

- *The opening*: Make sure that your audience have settled down and are ready to hear you – whether you are making a major oration at a rally or a minor intervention at a board meeting.
- *In mid-sentence*: To emphasise a vital point.
- *After an interruption*: Once again, your audience must be settled in to hear what you have to say.
- *Before your last few words*: 'And now, Ladies and Gentlemen, I beg you once more to support your Board' – pause – 'so as to ensure' – pause '. . . that this modest organisation . . .' pause '. . . will continue to flourish.' Pause. Look around at those from whom you expect applause. And then sit down.

Which brings us to the final hint. Applause is a most helpful and invigorating leg-up for any speaker. If you did not want it, you would not speak. We all like to be liked. We all wish our words to be accepted. The 'hear, hear' or clapping is as gratifying to the speaker as the groan is a misery. It is essential to anticipate and to deal with the cheers – to fish *for* them and to pause *after* them.

Only rarely can a pause be used against the groaner. By all means look round and glare at the man who has the temerity to jeer at you. Then hit back at him 'You are not helping your cause by behaving in that manner.' Or, if kindness seems to be the best way to deal with the situation: 'I am sorry that you should see fit to jeer, sir. If you would be good enough to wait a little, you will hear my reasons. And you will find that they are correct.'

Then pause. Allow the effect of the jeer to die away. Do not pause so long that the interrupter is encouraged to have another go.

The borderline between the effective and the defective pause is narrow. Each case must be judged on its own, and immediately. Far more speakers rush forward in haste then regret the (apparently) confident wait for silence, attention . . . effect.

The pause is even more vital – and less of a risk – when fishing for cheers. If you are nervous, follow the sound theatrical first-night tradition of organising your own claque (see Chapter 31). 'We must give the impression of vast enthusiasm for the new project. So when I say how confident I am that it will be a success' – pause – 'clap!' (The pause gambit is even useful in ordinary speech.)

An audience generally likes to know when appalause is expected. 'We are all pleased to welcome our guest of honour from abroad, – pause – 'Monsieur' – pause – 'Jaune.' Turn to your guest – pause for the clap.

'Here, Ladies and Gentlemen, is the first sample of our new product. I present it to you ' – pause – 'with pride' – pause – 'I trust that you sell it, to your profit and that of the company' – pause. Look round. Someone will probably say 'hear, hear . . .' if only to please you.

One possible approach if no one applauds is to attack them for their silence. 'The success of each of you, as well as that of the company, depends upon the way you push this product. I invite you' – pause – 'to greet with pleasure' pause 'this new success from our research department.'

If that does not do the trick, if you cannot drag up the applause you want, then never mind. Move on. Change your tack. Alter your approach. Try again. But do not rush. Wait. Control your audience.

Do not be afraid of the pause. Silence is a weapon as valuable as speech itself.

19   To 'er' is human – but wrong

Once the skilled speaker has learned to punctuate by pausing, the next problem is how not to 'er'. The pause should be left empty, for the minds of both speaker and audience to expand, rotate, absorb. When you apply your oratorical brakes, you destroy their effect if you fill the air with an 'er', an 'um' or an 'ah'.

Timing – which means knowing how and when to pause and for how long – is the essence of the craft of the comedian, the actor and the orator alike. Thomas Hardy remarked, 'That man's silence is wonderful to listen to', and Sydney Smith commented on the boredom of a conversation with Macaulay, observing that it was his 'occasional flashes of silence that make his conversation perfectly delightful'! If you wish your talk to be appreciated, then your silences should be more than occasional, well-timed and free from sound.

20   Interruptions

Interruptions to the skilled speaker are like raids to the commando –
a challenge to draw on resources and to test the mettle. Handled
properly, the heckler can rouse the audience and put them on the
speaker's side. The unexpected break may bring variety to a dull
occasion.

From the platform or head table, the speaker has a total advantage.
Used properly, the interruption should bring or keep the audience
in sympathy.

To reap the benefit of useful interruption, speakers must be alert.
Tied to a script – written or memorised – they may be thrown off
balance. If they cannot think on their feet, they should have
remained seated.

Consider some common examples. Take the shareholder who
comes to a company meeting to criticise. He shouts interruptions.
How do you deal with him?

Maintain your dignity. Quiet but firm appeals for a fair hearing
usually earn applause. 'I appreciate that you have a point of view to
express and you will be given full opportunity to do so. Meanwhile,
please have the courtesy to listen.' Or: 'I ask you to give my
viewpoint the same fair hearing that I have given to yours.' Or: 'I
listened to you/your case without interrupting. I ask you to accord
the same courtesy to me/mine.'

You could try: 'If you would be good enough to listen to what
the Board/the company has achieved and is now proposing in the
present difficult circumstances, you will learn something to your
benefit'.

If the moment has come to attack, try: 'If you would listen to me,
sir, instead of to yourself, you would be doing both of us a favour.'

If you are coping, the Chair should not intervene. If the meeting
gets out of hand, then he or she must do so. At best, this will bring
calm; at worst, the interrupters will be asked to leave. Still, a wide-
awake speaker can usually keep the audience in reasonably good
humour and win a hearing without use of force.

Some interruptions are healthy and helpful – whether or not this
was the intent. Humorists' outcries can often be turned against
themselves. The scream of a jet engine overhead may drown you for

the moment, but gives you the opportunity to draw some moral about the point you are making. Even a friendly remark addressed to a member of your audience arriving late may save you both from embarrassment, as well as giving you the opportunity you may in any event need to sort yourself out: to vary the pace of your talk, or to give your audience the chance to relax for a moment, to shift about in their seats and to prepare for the rest of your speech.

The speaker must show self-confidence and self-command so as to achieve command of the situation and of the audience.

If you are needled by interrupters and are tempted to panic – pause, smile, retain control. The rowdier the meeting, the more disconcerting the interruption, the more aggravating the break in your train of thought, the more important it is for you to demonstrate to your audience that you are not to be thrown off your balance. Lose control of yourself and all is lost.

Go to first-class political meetings and watch accomplished politicians at work. Listen to them provoking then downing their hecklers. Watch them prompting their audience to turn on the interrupters. A few inefficient hecklers will do their work for them, rouse their supporters, bring the uncommitted to their side and enliven what might otherwise be a dreary occasion.

The more spontaneous the reply, the wittier the retort, the speedier the counter-attack, the more effective the speaker and the speech. A weak riposte now is better than that brilliant barb that you afterwards wish you had thought of at the time.

Do not let interrupters put you off your stroke. Make use of them.

21 Passion

Passions must be felt, recognised and controlled. Allow your mind to cloud with passion and your performance will collapse.

Studied calm is a powerful weapon. Let your audience share your feelings, but know that your mind guides your heart, or you will not influence their ideas, their votes or their pocket books.

You may wish your audience to feel sorrow *with* you, but they must not feel pity *for* you. You want them to laugh *with* you, but if they laugh *at* you, all will be lost.

So direct your words at your theme and not at your own feelings. Conclude with a thundering peroration or any icy blast, but retain your speech as a well-constructed, carefully presented offering.

Passionate eloquence has its place in the pulpit, but rarely works at a company meeting, an organisational gathering or a public conference. Open emotion seldom pays. If you must let off steam, do it at home.

22   Timing

Time is the enemy. Judge and use it well and your speech or presentation should prosper.

Experienced business people are expert in time management except when they are on their feet. Aloft in their private joy, they ignore both the minutes and the agony of their audience.

'Did I speak too long?' enquired the managing director.

'Not at all,' his host responded. 'You helped to shorten the winter!'

Whether you are making a speech or a presentation, your object is to capture, to captivate and to convince your audience. This means keeping it alive, not boring it to death.

'I could listen to him for hours'. How common is its converse: 'I thought he would never stop . . .'?

As a post-graduate student at Harvard, I debated at the famous Norfolk Penal Colony. My partner was Anthony Lloyd, now a High Court judge. Our opponents were Bill Flynn, forger, and Buzzy Mulligan, in for manslaughter. American debating is a tough art, with strict rules on timing, and judgment by both content and presentation.

We were briefed by Flynn. 'Remember, please,' he said, 'that in this place time is served, not enjoyed! Minutes, hours and days are notched up on the wall. Your audience is sensitive. Last year, we welcomed two debaters from your Cambridge Union. The opener did not start off very well. "It is a joy," he said, "to address a captive audience!" It is no fun being one!'

So respect your audience and its immobility. In Parliament, if you overrun a sensible time you will empty the chamber, keeping back only those who have to stay because they are waiting to speak. To antagonise any other audience – especially one that is either standing, or seated in discomfort – all you have to do is to speak too long. So work out your timing in advance; adapt it to your audience; and keep in touch with them while you speak.

A vicar found only one parishioner at his evensong service. With grim determination, he followed the prayer book to the letter and included a splendid half-hour sermon. When all was over, the vicar shook the sole listener's hand most warmly. 'Even if there is only one cow in the field,' he said, she must still be fed.'

'Indeed she must,' replied the parishioner. 'But you don't have to give her the whole load of hay!'

In general, the smaller your audience, the shorter you should keep your speech or your presentation. Why not use the time to communicate, to listen, to invite and to answer questions, to establish and to keep rapport? The object of your exercise is to win friends and to influence business? Then do your audience the courtesy of including them in your time calculations.

You recognise the importance of time in your business? You operate that inherently inhuman 'clocking' system for your workforce and perhaps even for your junior management? You regard such measures as part of the necessary discipline of commerce? Then at least apply *self*-discipline to your utterances, otherwise you will be talking to yourself, metaphorically if not literally.

So start by arriving on time. I once heard presidential candidate Adlai Stevenson apologising for turning up late at an election rally. 'I am deeply sorry. There is no greater thief than a man who steals the time of another. It is the only commodity that can never be recovered.'

Plan the timing of your speech. Recognise that while time creeps slowly for the prisoner, it races for the speaker. Concentrating on your subject and your audience, you will not notice the passing minutes.

So always overestimate the time you need and you will seldom be wrong. If you are preparing a half-hour presentation, then plan for 20 minutes. You can always use the balance for questions.

Speechmaking? Then ask the Chair – or even a colleague or confederate in the front row or your audience – to give you a signal when you have, say, five minutes left. Do not wait for the gavel to descend or the light to flash.

A well-known politician hideously overran his time at a dinner. The next speaker whispered to the Chair: 'Can't you stop him?' The Chair lifted his gavel but it slipped from his hand and hit his neighbour on the head. As the poor man slid under the table he was heard to exclaim: 'Hit me again! Hit me again! I can still hear him!'

Or why not prop up your watch well within view? Most skilled speakers have no compunction in doing so, so why should you?

I use a watch with an alarm. I set it for five minutes after my speech is due to end. I am happy that it has yet to sound off.

If you do not have a watch or clock within easy view, you must consult the time with due cunning. Your glance at your wristwatch will be noted by our audience – which is at least less disconcerting than your audience looking at theirs.

A vicar once said to an inattentive parishioner: 'Now, Mr Brown, I don't mind when you look at your watch during my sermon. But when you take it up to your ear and shake it . . .!'

Queen Elizabeth has elevated the art of surreptitious watch-watching to its ultimate. She wears hers on her right wrist, facing inwards. When she holds out her arm – whether to shake hands, to lift her cup or even in a simple gesture – time appears before her eyes.

PART 3

Handling your audience

My Lords, ladies & gentlemen—
Pray silence
for ...

23   Handling your audience

Experienced speakers may not talk to their audience. They look around for a kindly face. Even among the most hostile gathering, there is usually someone from whom they can extract a friendly or tolerant smile. They talk to that person.

Speakers who look over the top of their audience, out into space, indulging in soliloquy, are only a mite better than those who keep their head lowered and mumble into notes.

Audiences are people. They want to be entertained. They have presumably come to the gathering out of interest or curiosity – if not in what you are going to say, then in what the meeting is to undertake. Keep their interest by talking *to* them – and not over their heads, literally or metaphorically. Look at them. Speak to them.

If asked to address a gathering, try to find out the type and the size of the audience. Your preparation may depend on the number of listeners. Are they skilled or unskilled, simple or learned, well versed in your topic or new to it, likely to be friendly or hostile?

If you were working to put through a business deal in private you would tailor your talk to the nature, personality, interests and sensitivity of your hearer. Only common-sense? Well, if more public speakers would apply that same sense to their audiences, the market for public speaking would not be spoiled as it is. People would go to meetings, instead of preferring their television sets. And speakers would be a great deal more successful than most of them are.

Whatever and whomever your audience may be, watch them while you speak. See whether they are concentrating, or shifting around in their seats. If you have held them still for some time, then stop. Pause. Take a sip from your glass of water. Fiddle through your notes. Give your audience the chance to relax and then to resettle. No one can concentrate for any lengthy period of time without a break.

If your audience is restless when you do not intend it to be so, you must restore your hold on it. If you have been serious, then throw in a joke, a story, an anecdote. If you have been speaking at high volume, then switch to a confidential tone. If nothing works, then wind up – either permanently or for an extended question time.

There is no more important rule for public speakers than to keep a hawk-like watch on their listeners. It is different, of course, if you are talking to yourself – ignore this rule and you soon will be.

One of the speaker's problems is where to look. Facing your audience and fixing them with your eye is a problem. Why? Know the reason and the problem becomes easier to beat. Consider one paragraph in *The Naked Ape*, by Desmond Morris:

> A professional lecturer takes some time to train himself to look directly at the members of his audience, instead of over their heads, down at his rostrum, or out towards the side or back of the hall. Even though he is in such a dominant position, there are so many of them, all staring (from the safety of their seats), that he experiences a basic and initially uncontrollable fear of them. Only after a great deal of practice can he overcome this. The simple, aggressive, physical act of being stared at by a large group of people is also the cause of the fluttering 'butterflies' in the actor's stomach before he makes his entrance onto the stage. He has all his intellectual worries about the qualities of his performance and its reception, of course, but the massed threat-state is an additional and more fundamental hazard for him.

There it is. We fear those who stare at us. If you want to lift your head above the crowd, you must expect people to stare at it. Learn to stare right back.

24 Audience recognition

The best training sessions on the speechmaker's skills involve people at the same level (see Chapter 41 on training). No one is beholden to, jealous of or dependent for his or her living upon anyone else. The same principle applies to most presentations themselves.

When lecturing in-company, I try to induce my clients to bring together people at approximately the same level. If they want to include the boss, I warn them that the atmosphere may freeze, the jokes fall flat. The participants may be too apprehensive of their living to venture asking or answering questions when a foolish moment could lose them promotion or even their jobs.

I once addressed all the executives of a catering company, on Health and Safety. The first part of the morning took off in a gale of laughter and I was able to implant the required knowledge into a relaxed and receptive audience.

After coffee, everything froze. I only understood what had happened when I learned that the boss had, to everyone's knowledge other than mine, joined us after the break; and that earlier in the week he had sacked 20 executives.

So if you get the chance to choose your audience, aim not at uniformity of personality or approach, but at a similar level within the organisation. If you venture into the highly personalised and difficult task of teaching any of the arts of presentation, take extra care.

All these urgings are for the benefit of your victims themselves. They are also for you.

You may on occasion have to talk upwards, either to superiors on their own or to those embedded in a mixed audience. The basic rule is: never show up anyone in the presence of a superior. Tread on a person's dignity, said the sage, and they will hate you for life. Make them look small or stupid in the eyes of superiors or inferiors and you have acquired an enemy.

If those whom you have managed to lower in the eyes of others happen to be your superiors, then they are unlikely to raise you on their list of loyal disciples fit for promotion. If instead you have made an idiot out of a colleague, in the eyes of your shared boss, then you had better protect your back.

Banter and teasing – even harassing and tormenting – are invaluble weapons in the trainer's armoury. But they must be used with sensitivity or they will rebound off their target and strike you down.

If you are addressing an assembly of your elders, then indeed your mettle will be tried. How do you know and show more knowledge than they possess, without making them dislike or fear you, as present pain or future rival? How do you show respect without crawling, humility without being humble?

Tact, sensitivity, intelligence, common-sense and all those other virtues that you possess in such fine measure – you will now need them all. Plus good luck.

* * *

These rules apply especially to presentations to children, young people, or students. Have you ever been guest of honour at a school prize-giving? Or taken part in a university debate? Or given a talk about your business or your hobby to a youth club or group?

Those who talk down to the young are blighted. If you treat them as equals, with luck they will not only listen this time but ask you again. You fail to prepare your subject at your own risk. The young are swift to spot a fraud or a phoney. They have an instinct for the insincere.

Naturally, you will adapt your style and your material to your audience and to your intent. You would not talk in the same way to your sales force as you would to your shop stewards, nor use the same material when explaining why pay has to be held down as you would if launching a new product or scheme.

Sales people, for instance, are an extroverted race apart. Outgoing and thick-skinned by the nature of their craft, and crafty to the core of their nature, they (like all other good professionals) only respect knowledge and expertise that at least equals their own. You must talk their language if you wish them to listen.

A sales force needs to know what you are going to provide for the market and when and how. It needs detail on territories and prospects, on targets, plans and projections.

Shop stewards have a different job. They are elected to look after their members, and only if you can satisfy them that your proposals are indeed in their members' interests can you reasonably hope that they will co-operate with you.

Your sales force are as much employees as your workforce and their physical independence and initiative is far greater. But if the workforce is unionised, then it has a different type of independence, fed from the knowledge of its own unified strength.

If you are talking to union representatives, you should match their knowledge and determination with your own. Give them the maximum of information, accurate and honest. Recognise their loyalty to their union and to its members. If you can harness their members' interests to your own, you are in business.

When you speak to your managers, remember that they are probably more disgruntled than your workforce. Indeed, some of them are probably paid less than some of those they supervise. This unattractive result of employees receiving overtime, bonus rates and the like while management must work 'for such hours as may be necessary for the proper performance of their duties' and then at fixed rates causes vast ill will.

When you address your colleagues, recognise their problems, personal as well as managerial. Respect their jealousies and meet them head on.

Subordinate managers work *for* you? Fine – but *you* are also working *for* and *with* them. Get your approach into focus and your presentation should succeed.

* * *

Few executives or managers confine their conversations, speeches and ovations to their superiors. Most must at least spare an occasional word – and sometimes, a great string of them, dignified by the name of 'speech', 'lecture', 'talk', 'harangue' or 'presentation' – for their juniors.

So recognising that even a God-like Chair or a managing director must speak to those below them – and that there are very few who will talk only to Him or Her – here is your guide to addressing your staff or employees, workforce or salesforce or others upon whose success your own job and future may well depend.

● Do *not* talk down. Patronising, condescending bosses will never get the best from their team. Instead, chat them up; build them up; create in their minds the belief that they are part of a team which you are both happy and suited to lead.

- Regard these staff or employee talks as important – otherwise why should they? Follow the same procedures for them as you do for any other notable presentation – including careful preparation. There is no other than your immediate family who is more likely to spot or to be sensitive to your errors than your colleagues.
- Approach the subject matter and your effort to put it across from the viewpoint of a colleague or a team leader, and one whose income depends just as much upon their own successful effort as on yours. Together, you can make *their* business survive, blossom and flourish. But pull the business apart and it will fail – to the loss of all.

25   Sensitivity and tact

First-class presenters will react to their audience. They will watch them with care; coax them into concentration; convince them with their themes; enthuse them with their message.

From the moment you enter the room, sensitivity is the key to stylish success. It will, for instance:

- Guide you to the top people – so that you greet them, respect them, take care never to demean them, and, where possible, flatter them – if only by asking: 'Have I covered the points that you would wish?' Or: 'How would you deal with this matter in your organisation?'
- Help you to steer the conversation, discussion or presentation in the direction you wish – especially if it has veered on to an unexpected and unwanted course.
- Enable you to invite audience intervention or participation and make the best use of it. Just as any politician worth their salt will welcome a heckler, so presenters should be pleased with interventions which enliven their task and enlighten them on their listeners' interests and anxieties.
- Ensure that you avoid jargon, terminology and complications – especially in territory well known to you, but not to any or all of your listeners. You must never presume that others have too much knowledge. After all, Mr X may be new to his department or Ms Y, who should have prepared the ground before your talk, may have omitted to do so.
- Assist in recognising those people who would like to ask questions but are shy to do so for fear of revealing their ignorance to their colleagues. This applies to seniors, who must never be humbled before their subordinates; and to juniors, whose promotion depends upon their listening superiors.
- Help you to know when your audience is getting restless or inattentive, so that you can alter course, style or speed, introduce a story or a joke, invite your listeners to ask questions, or simply say: 'Are there any points that need clarification so far?'
- Sharpen your tact – so that, for instance, if someone asks a question which shows that he was either not listening or stupid, you say: 'I'm sorry. I am sure it was my fault. Let me try to explain again', or: 'It's a very complicated concept and I am so sorry that I did not succeed in explaining it clearly. Let me show you on a chart . . .', or: 'Thank you for that question. I'm pleased to expand on that important concept.'

If you do go wrong and cause unintentional offence, then apologise. An apology tells its recipient that they were right and you wrong, it raises them in their own estimation and does you no harm.

Make sure that you write down any names which you may have to quote – the Chair, the managing director, the company, the guest – and that you spell them correctly. People are very touchy about their names, which are themselves.

Train yourself to think ahead, so that you are not only watching your audience's reaction to what you are saying at the time, but thinking towards your next sentence, idea, theme . . . or change of rhythm or style.

If your listeners look at their watch, watch yours. You will know that their time is on their mind. And be prepared to move ahead on your notes, discard cards on which they are written, and either advance to your close or involve the timewatcher. 'I am sorry, Mr Brown,' you might say, 'that we are approaching our time limit. But are there any other points which *you* would like me to deal with?'

I once heard a computer salesman explaining to a major company in a depressed area why they should spend money on his equipment. 'We could help you to reduce your staff by 50 per cent if you buy one of our computers,' he announced. I could see each of his listeners saying to himself: 'I wonder whether I would be one of the staff that would go'. The contract was lost. Sensitivity matters.

These sensitivities apply to private as well as to public presentations – from person to person to a platform address. But when you are eyeball to eyeball, eye contact is both easier and more relaxed. The larger your audience, the greater your temptation to treat them as remote, but the greater your need to relate your sensitivities to those of individual listeners. Otherwise do not blame them if they take as little interest in you and your message as you do in them and their reactions.

If the intent of your presentation is to enthuse, then you must inject enthusiasm into your words and make them as infectious as possible. If the essence of a fine presentation lies in self-control leading into control of your audience, sensitivity is the presenter's top asset, and its absence an insurmountable obstacle to success.

26 Personal attacks

The word 'gentleman' has been defined as meaning 'one who is never unintentionally discourteous'. Mature speakers never unintentionally lose their temper. They also do their utmost to cause offence only by design.

Outside the realm of politics, most wounds are both regrettable and regretted. 'The moving finger writes and, having writ, moves on: Nor all thy piety nor wit shall lure it back to cancel half a line, nor all thy tears wash out a word of it.' In one off-guard moment, you may acquire an enemy for life, unnecessarily. The uttered word cannot be erased.

Humour and wit are vital to the speaker. But many a jest, however kindly meant, has been taken amiss. There is all the difference in the body of wit between pulling someone's leg in private and tweaking his or her sensitive tail in public. The same joke that went down splendidly at the dinner table may be a disaster when told from the platform.

No section of the public is more concerned with its own dignity than people of commerce. Lawyers may be pompous, but they recognise the bitter court battle as part of their trade – it bears no reference to their personal friendship outside court. The private jest is seldom resented, but the businessman whom you attack in public may not wish to speak to you in private.

It follows that apart from the laws of defamation, it is as well to keep the discussion on ideas, not personalities. If you do attack your opponent, be sure of your ground. Make certain that his or her discomfiture is intended and that it has a reasonable chance of leading to the results you seek. Whether you are speaking at a comparatively small meeting or a mighty gathering, be careful. You are not alone. If your attack is ill-chosen, you soon may be.

If you must attack a personality, then prepare your case with special regard to documentation: letters, quotations and firm facts. The more bitter your resentment, the quieter and the more apparently reasonable your tone should appear. Lose control of yourself and you will probably, and deservedly, also lose control of both situation and organisation.

Find out in advance whether your words are likely to be well received. There is no worse time to be shouted or voted down than during a personal attack. If the moment arrives for a personal vendetta, select your time and place with assiduous care. By launching an attack, you invite a counter-attack. By mentioning the names of your opponents you may give them the publicity that they seek plus – in the eyes of those who believe in fair play – the moral right to reply. Instead of being in sole occupation of the platform, you may have to surrender it to an opponent whom you would prefer to lurk unseen.

If your opponents descend to personal attack, it is rarely wise to lower yourself to their level. Your object, after all, is to win your case – to convince your audience of your rectitude, of the usefulness of your activities, of the excellence of the way in which you are running the business – or, conversely, of your opponents's error. The sharp intellect is a better weapon than the rough tongue. When the theme is laced with incivility, the audience may suspect a lack of factual backing or of self-control – or both.

For average speechmakers – company directors, trying to talk sense into the heads of their board in revolt, salaried directors or company secretaries dealing with the irascible chairman or managing director who is seeing fit to dress them down at a board meeting, or with an angry shareholder, making loud-mouthed, unwarranted and personal attacks against the company at a company meeting – the 'other cheek' policy is seldom out of place.

- 'I am extremely sorry that Mrs Jones has seen fit to deal with this serious matter in such a vituperative fashion . . .'
- 'If Mrs Jones would be good enough to listen to what the Board has achieved, I think he will regret the manner in which he has referred to it . . .'
- 'We are all here for a common purpose – to advance the business. The sort of remarks that have just been made are likely to send it into retreat. They can give comfort only to our competitors . . .'
- 'We will answer each criticism, in turn. We will ignore the personal and regrettably offensive manner in which some of these attacks have been made.'
- 'If Mr Black really is, as he says, concerned for the welfare of this organisation, I trust that when he has heard the case for the steps which he has so bitterly criticised, he will not only have the good grace to withdraw those criticisms, but also to apologise to those whom he has inevitably hurt by his unkind remarks. I hope that such was not his intention. He is, as we all know, a kindly man, and we all appreciate

what he has done for the company. We know how deeply involved he is, emotionally and otherwise, in its success . . . and no one will bear him the least ill-will because he has spoken his mind . . . But . . .'

- 'We all appreciate, I know, the customary frankness with which Mr White has dealt with this resolution. We do not appreciate, however, the personal insinuations he has made – which can only detract from the genuineness of his case and the real concern with which he and those who support him – and, indeed, many of us on your board – view the circumstances he discussed . . .'

Hostility breeds hostility, and an aggressive approach invites a like response. The converse also applies. Surprise your critics with your moderation, understanding, sensitivity and those views may mellow. It is, in any event, an approach far more likely to succeed than the frontal attack.

Once you have let rip with your hostility, not only has the reasonable possibility of future friendly relations been gravely affected, but you have even discounted the off-chance that the critic was really on your side all the time. Some apparently hostile questions are asked at meetings so as to obtain an answer for the benefit of those whom the questioner wishes to convince, and not for the questioner's benefit at all. 'All right, don't listen to me . . . We'll ask old White . . . He'll tell you a thing or two . . .' Blast the questioner for being an idiot and you have obliterated a friend and confirmed a foe in his enmity.

If you must lose your temper, then at least do so with deliberation. Choose your moment and your words with equal care. If you must tear at your opponent – do it properly.

A judge once said to a famous advocate: 'What you are saying to me is going in one ear and out the other.' To which the lawyer replied: 'That, my Lord, does not cause me any surprise, having regard to that which lies in between!'

Most of us think of the best repartee when the occasion is past. While swift retorts often produce acclaim far beyond merit, the rude, unkind, offensive or angry outburst, the facetious, sarcastic, ironic or spiteful suggestion, breeds contempt, derision, stony silence – and defeat for the speaker, not for the individual towards whom the words are directed.

27   Credits

Few speechmakers object to being thanked or resent receiving credit, even where it is not strictly due. But most get upset if their merit is not recognised or if thanks are withheld – especially if credit due to one goes to another. So good speakers are as liberal with their praise of others as they are parsimonious with their praise of themselves. The listener who feels that you recognise – and are prepared publicly to laud – his or her worth is more likely to be receptive to the excellence of your arguments.

Here, then, is a sample, generalised opening.

'First, I would like to express my appreciation to various people here. Were it not for Mr Brown, this gathering would never have been organised at all. Were it not for Ms Black, the company would be in grave difficulty. Were it not for Mr White, the scheme we are about to discuss would never have been born. In paying tribute to them, I express my gratitude to all of you for giving them the support and backing without which they could not have put forward this essentially constructive project.

'Now, let us look at the project.' Your audience is softened up. they are ready to listen to some constructive criticism from you.

Or: 'Under the guidance of Mr Green, this project has made great headway. With Mr Brown as treasurer and Ms Blue as honorary secretary, it is hardly surprising that it has gathered momentum. And now it is up to us to help them by applying constructive minds to the scheme they have created.

'I know they welcome criticism designed to forward their work. We all appreciate that their enthusiasm is only increased by suggestions, coming from people like ourselves who only want the scheme to succeed. They know that there is no element of destructive intent in the views that some of us hold. I am sure that you will give careful consideration to our submissions.'

Flattery? Certainly – but legitimate. Praise? Yes, indeed, and with every appearance of sincerity. Credit, thanks, tact – and all designed to prepare the ground for your forthcoming message. It is not only armies that do best when they advance from the side, and there is no shame in a swift strike from the rear.

To test the importance of these rules, listen to someone who ignores them. Beware the benefactor scorned, the doer of good deeds that go unrecognised, the creator whose idea, invention or brainchild is fathered onto another.

There exists, or course, the occasional *éminence grise* – the spectral backroom boy who takes as much pride in praise going to others whom he has built up as does the father who basks in the reflected glory of his child's exploits. But even he appreciates the oblique reference to the power that made the throne secure, to the modest mind that 'wishes to remain anonymous but must not go without being thanked . . . Those of us who are fortunate enough to realise just how and by whom the work has been done salute our silent and modest friends – we are grateful to them.'

As an editorial mention or the praise of a product in the general pages of a newspaper are public relations people's delight – and worth more to them than the advertisement that they have to pay for – so the 'plug' in the course of a speech and as part of it is often more valuable to the maker and more appreciated by the person referred to than the formal and expected vote of thanks. But even that is a weapon not to be despised in the campaign to get your own way – as we shall now see.

28   Persuading – the art of advocacy

Barristers, said Dean Swift, are 'bred up in the art of proving that white is black and black is white, according as they are paid'. He left out of account, of course, the ethics of the legal profession, which may often require its members to keep faith with the court by acting (and speaking) against the interests of their clients.

Advocacy is an art; deception an evil. Still, the Swift aphorism is too good to forget. Even business people may often be forced to propound or to defend in public policies or decisions with which, in private, they disagree.

It is not only the Cabinet that must stand by majority decisions. The same normally applies to the board of a company, to the partners of a firm, or to the committee of an organisation. Either you accept democracy – allowing your views to be overruled when the majority of your colleagues are against them – or you resign. If you remain in office, then you must stand by your colleagues. This may mean engaging in their public defence.

So advocates may have to propound not only views that are unpopular with their audience, but even some that they themselves have little sympathy with. Business people customarily attack lawyers and politicians as sophists and word-twisters. But just listen to that executive trying to make the creditors' meeting 'see sense' . . . the chairperson attempting to extract himself (and possibly the company secretary) from trouble . . . the sales director, drilling her sales force about an unpopular (and perahps not very satisfactory) product.

There is little art in persuading the convinced, preaching to the converted, or keeping your team behind you when they all agree with your views or policies. To argue a difficult case – or even one that seems impossible – is a far greater challenge. Business people may take many a leaf from the brief of the skillful lawyer-advocate.

Start with the quiet, sincere but firm approach. Call it 'the soft sell' if you like, but the studied lack of histrionics lies at the root of the modern persuader's art. Gone are the days of the ranter, the arm-waver, the loud shouter. The theatrical tugger at the strings of the heart may still have his place in a revivalist meeting or chapel, but he is a stranger to the court of law – and should be equally so to the company or organisational meeting.

The more your audience starts against you, the greater the importance of moderation – especially in your opening. Here are some well-tried gambits for when you are in a minority:

- 'I fully appreciate the difficulty of my task in convincing you that . . . But I hope and believe that if you will be good enough to give my case a fair and full hearing, you will be as convinced as I am that . . .'
- 'Mr Black, who has just addressed you, is an experienced advocate and has presented the case against with skill and eloquence. But there is another side to the picture. Before coming to a decision, I am certain that you would wish to hear both sides of the story, fully explained . . .'
- 'Many of us were saddened to hear the vehemence and even the venom with which the case for . . . has been put. While many of the attacks have apparent validity, when you go beneath the surface, all is not as some of our friends have suggested. I am sure that this committee/organisation/ meeting would not wish to take any decision on such a very important matter without having had both points of view put before it. I shall put mine, as briefly as possible; but I would be grateful for your indulgence if I take a little time to explain my case . . .'
- 'This is a small committee of busy people and we should expend no more time and energy in surplus pursuit of Mr X. He has made mistakes and is paying for them. Let us look to the future. Instead, let us look at some of the achievements of Mr X. He let us down? Yes – but he has also laid the foundations for our future success. First . . . Second . . . Third . . . Fourth . . . Fifty . . . Sixth . . .' By the time you are finished, Mr X appears to be quite a splendid character. If you had started with his virtues, you would have lost all hope of winning your case – and his.

Now for some traps to be avoided:

- 'Does anyone really think Mr Y has cheated the company?' Cries of 'Certainly . . .' Rhetorical questions are a menace. Thus:
- 'Could it conceivably be in the long-term interest of this organisation to follow the line proposed by Mr W?' Shouts of 'Yes!'
- 'Does anyone really think that I do not know my job after all these years?' Loud cries of 'Yes' – and laughter.
- 'I am . . . a man . . .' pause. Shouts of 'No, no . . .' The pause is a vital weapon – but watch where you place it.
- 'You may think that the statements you have just heard from Mr Z are about as untrue, misleading, ill-conceived and plain stupid as one could ever envisage.' This sort of attack – especially by someone in a minority

– can only lead to vituperation, and defeat. Softly, softly, catchee monkee. . .

- 'I am furious . . .' Then do not show it.
- 'I could weep when I hear such extravagant attacks.' They all know that tears are not in your line – so away with the crocodiles.

It is nearly always a mistake to walk out of a meeting. Still, there are occasions when there is no decent alternative. If decisions are taken that you regard as illegal, dishonest or so contrary to the welfare of the body concerned that you must dissociate yourself publicly from them, then you may have to leave. But otherwise, stay and fight.

You chances of winning from without are far less than of working your colleagues or audience round to your way of thinking from within. If you leave, you are not likely to be invited back. The dramatic exit may be required for the diplomat whose country is publicly attacked in his or her presence. It is seldom an answer for the orator spurned.

The threat of resignation is, of course, a powerful and a valid weapon. It must not be misused or over-employed. If your colleagues or the meeting would be happy to see you go, then you should not offer to provide satisfaction.

'If this decision is to be made, I hope it will not be taken amiss if I say that I shall have no alternative other than to reconsider my membership.' Fairly put.

'I have worked for this organisation for many years and am anxious to continue to do so in the future. I would not wish to sever my ties nor to be forced into a position where I would have no alternative but to do so. I do beg you to reconsider. Or at least, please do give me a fair hearing for the other point of view. I would put it like this . . .' You should get that fair hearing.

Avoid: 'If you do not change your minds, then I shall resign.' You invite the retort: 'Go ahead.'

29   In a tight corner

If in trouble, choose your words with special care. To borrow from the world of boxing – if you have been hit below the belt, are out for the count, or in a tight corner, you have three alternatives: you can throw in the sponge, trade blow for blow, or duck smartly under your opponent's fist and leap nimbly away.

You are proposing a toast to the bride and groom? The bride's father is dead. The groom's parents are divorced. What do you do? You can surrender by making no mention of the parents. This is abject cowardice, and generally regarded as such. You may neatly duck the situation with a few carefully chosen sentences: 'The bride's father . . . we wish he were not here only in spirit . . . but he would have been proud and happy today . . . How pleased we are that our groom's parents are both so well – and here together for the celebration . . .'

Finally, you can take the bull by the horns (to take a metaphor from another sport). You can start with the sort of comment given above – and then extend it into the appropriate elegy. 'Let us face the blunt truth, Ladies and Gentlemen – no occasion is completely perfect, no life without its problems. How sad we are that the bride's father is not here . . . but we admire her mother doubly for the fortitude with which she bore her loss and especially for the courageous and splendid way in which she brought up the bride . . . The extent of her triumph is revealed by the radiance of our bride. We rejoice too that the bridegroom's parents sit joyfully together with him, united in his happiness and good fortune . . .'

There are plenty of equivalent situations in business. A victory is achieved by an apology. The counter-attack is explained in Chapter 26. The method of ducking away from trouble will depend upon cirumstances. Here are some useful opening gambits:

- 'We fully appreciate the circumstances which have led to your anger and disappointment. But there is another side to the story and we do hope that you will give it your earnest consideration . . .
- 'You are, in theory, correct, fair and . . .'
- 'I do see your point of view – but am sure that you will give consideration to mine . . .'

- 'Yes, we made a mistake – but in good faith. The situation nevertheless remains that . . .'
- 'We see your viewpoint. Now do please consider ours . . .'
- 'You have set out your case admirably. It is only courteous, then, for me to set out as fully as possible the situation as we see it . . .'
- 'We believe that your complaint is based on a misunderstanding. We do see that . . . but we would urge you to consider . . .'
- 'No, we do not agree with you. But nevertheless . . .'

Have you noticed that people who use words as weapons employ similar tactics to those of the fencer or boxer? You give way a little, so as to attack a lot. You retreat gently, so as to counter-attack with firmness. You at least pretend to see the other person's viewpoint, so that he or she will be prepared to consider yours. Alternatively, you politely disagree – and then show your magnanimity, good sense or goodwill by offering a compromise or by giving in on some point, however small.

The French put it well: '*Il faut reculer pour mieux sauter*' – you must withdraw, the better to leap forward. You step back so as to throw your opponent off balance (boxing again).

Try these gambits when absolutely desperate:

- 'If you see fit to make these allegations to third parties, we shall have no hestitation in putting the matter in the hands of our solicitors . . .'
- 'In one last desperate attempt to remedy a situation which (we repeat) is not of our making, our Mr Jones will contact you and try to arrange some convenient time to visit your office . . .'
- 'Your threats are empty, their premise groundless. Nevertheless, if you wish to take the matter further, we must refer you to our lawyers . . .'
- 'We regard your allegations as both impertinent and groundless. If they are repeated, we shall take such steps as we are advised by our lawyers, to protect both our position and our good name . . .'
- 'If you are so ill-advised as to carry out your threats, then kindly direct all future correspondence to our lawyers . . .'
- 'Our lawyers will be in touch with yours . . .'

30   The reply

Debaters who content themselves with making their own speeches without referring to those which have gone before, deserve to fail. Many discussions – in public and private meetings of companies and organisations of all sorts – are in reality debates. The skilled speaker must study the art of reply, which requires alertness to what has gone before, and a keen eye and ear.

Proposers of motions or resolutions normally have 'right of reply'. They open the debate or discussion and, before the vote is taken, they have the privilege of closing it. Their second speech should not be a mere repetition of their first. They should deal – courteously, clearly and firmly – with the intervening debate.

Respondents should thank those who have spoken in favour of the resolution. Directly or by implication they should congratulate them on their perspicacity. 'I was not surprised to have the warm support of that respected businessman, Mr Brown – but I was grateful for it none the less . . . Mr Green is highly experienced in the trade and I do hope that everyone here will give his words due weight . . .'

'Ms White comes to us from a different side of the industry. So it is all the more significant that she approves of this resolution . . .'

'Mr Green, is, as you will all know, an extremely skilled and public-spirited lawyer. We must all be grateful to him for the careful analysis he gave to our problems – and for the legal light that he cast upon the dangers of action suggested by those who oppose this resolution.'

Skilled respondents demolish their enemies. 'I am sorry that Mr Diamond has not appreciated the warnings given by Ms Black . . .' 'If Mr Stone had really considered the argument that . . . I feel sure he would have come to a different conclusion . . .' 'Mr Ruby is wrong. The facts are not as he has suggested. The true position is . . .'

Then sum up your arguments once again, in a few brisk, crisp sentences. Commend your resolution to the meeting – and hope for the best.

Use notes when replying. No one will expect you to remember all that has been said. Once again, the card system is best. You may, if you wish, deal with the questioners or opponents in turn, but you would probably be better off to rearrange the comments and criticisms to suit your argument and its structure.

Remember, a reply is a speech like any other. It needs a good opening, a sound body, and a proper end. Some suggested openings:

- 'Thank you for permitting me to reply to some of the points raised . . .'
- 'I suggest that nothing that has been said against the resolution has in any way destroyed its essential validity . . .'
- 'We must all be grateful to those who have taken part in this debate. Even those who oppose the resolution do so in the interests of the company. But, as we have seen from the speeches of Mr Brown, Ms White and Mr Black, its opponents have not really grasped the advantage of the course of action suggested – and the risks of following any alternative . . .'
- 'The differences between us have been fully aired. Every possible alternative has been thrashed out. But, at the end of the day, are we not still left with only one real possibility? The resolution must be passed.'

Some of these rules also apply to many responses to toasts. Do *not* ignore the speeches that have gone before. *Do* deal with any points of criticism or suggestion raised by previous speakers. Do *not* fear to use notes to remind you of the words of others. And *do* make certain that your speech is properly constructed.

You have one great advantage over the person replying to a debate. His or her speech must not only appear extempore, but must actually be so. Yours may be carefully prepared, provided that you cover up that preparation by reference back.

31 Advance organisation

In Italy, opera singers employ claques. They pay the organisers who then ensure that the star receives the appropriate (or even inappropriate) applause, at the right time. If any star sees fit not to pay, then (as one a member of a claque recently remarked) 'We are quite capable of whistling and cat-calling instead.'

Those who speak in public may also have a claque – paid or unpaid. If the opportunity arises, no harm is done by ensuring that you get off to a good start, or that your words appear to be treated with such delight that (with luck) your opponents may prefer to stay silent.

People are like proverbial sheep, particularly in public. They want to follow the flock. Few have the courage to speak their minds openly in the face of a vociferous majority. 'What's the good of it?' they say – not realising that if they only did speak, they might well win. They might discover that the noise-makers were no more than a loud-mouthed minority.

The most inoffensive type of claque work is easily organized. 'Please show me some support,' you say to your friends. 'If you do not give me some loud "hear, hears", I shall stop trying. I refuse to be shot at on my own.'

Alternatively: 'This is going to be a difficult audience to warm up. If you would be kind enough to start the clapping when I am called upon to speak, I shall remember you in my will!' It only takes one or two people to clap the speaker for the rest to join in.

Again: 'I am going to tell them the story about the . . . So laugh!'

Of course, you may carry your claque along with you because they are under some obligation. Maybe you employ them, or are the kind benefactor on whom they rely.

In that case, no preparation should be needed. Wise lawyers soon learn to laugh at judges' jokes – and whenever possible to produce any of their own ideas in the guise of words of wisdom dropped by the Bench.

Of course, advance 'softening up' of an audience may often go far deeper than this. If you have a case to advance, do your best to sound out your audience. If you have a resolution to propose, make sure that someone will second it. Proposers without support are miserable fellows and, in most cases, would have been better off keeping silent. Good speakers prepare not only their case, but also their audience and supporters.

Of course, this preparation should not show. One reason why inexperienced speakers often take too little care in the preparation of their material is that they have seen how apparently easy the experienced speaker makes it all seem. Be not deceived. In general, the higher the polish, the greater the elbow grease; the more relaxed and effortless the style, the more careful the preparation.

Natural speakers may need to take less care than the rest. Follow them around and note how their performances vary. Those who stumble, repeat themselves, go on for too long, break the basic rules of good speaking and start to bore their audience have probably not prepared their speech.

The better the preparation of the material and of its reception, the less obvious that preparation will be. The more it shows, the less its effect. If audience preparation shows at all, the insincerity of the claque may rub off on your speech, and that could mean disaster.

So choose your supporters with as much care as your words, but do not be too proud to prepare both with equal attention.

If you are in the chair, make your preparations with special care. If there is to be a question time, prime someone to ask the first question – otherwise the silence may be embarrassing and ruin the evening.

If you have to appear neutral but need to espouse a particular viewpoint, make sure you get its best proponent ready with his or her speech – and someone else available to do a later mopping-up operation. If preparing a team, the basis used by most athletes for relays is helpful. The anchor – your best – goes last. The next best goes first. The third does the third leg. The worst goes second. Or you may want to put your anchor first – particularly if there is right of reply.

If you are not in the chair, but are especially interested in a particular topic or anxious to speak on it (or if you have to leave early or arrive late) do get the arrangements set up in advance with the Chair. Most will oblige. They will probably be glad to have advance notice of your intentions, so that they can plan operations accordingly. Planning is the partner of success.

PART 4

Visual aids, notes and venues

32 Microphones

Once upon a time, you had to speak to be heard. Nowadays, a whisper will do. The microphone has long since arrived. Know how to use it. Well employed, it is a trusty ally. Over-employed or misused it will blast away your audiences for ever.

A voice was a prerequisite for a singer – no more. With the aid of the 'mike', the men and women of music can make their fortunes without, in many cases, enough power in their lungs to fill a telephone booth or a breathalyser. They may belt out the tune, but the nuances and expressions that the opera singer spends years learning to create are absent. The effects that brighten so many otherwise even more miserable musical moments are created by the microphone – by the tricks of the audio trade.

Not everyone required to speak in public is blessed with a great voice. Some of us have voices that refuse to be produced. Never mind. We can learn much from the masters and mistresses of the mike.

First make sure that your mike is switched on. Speak into it, and you will soon find out. Adjust it to a convenient height at a rake of about 75 degrees. Whether it is a standing or a table model, you will probably find a turning ring near the centre. With luck and some reasonable wrist power, you should be able to fix the mike at about six inches below the level of your mouth.

If presented with a neck mike, test and adjust it so that your voice emerges at the correct volume. Then do not trip over the cord.

You may prefer, though – as I do – to use a wandering mike on a long lead. You retain your freedom of movement, and the mike becomes as much an asset for you as it is for stage and television performers who hold one by preference, when the wizards of the world of acoustics could well amplify without.

However long you have to keep your audience waiting, take your time to adjust and position your microphone. With the volume and position adjusted, you are ready to begin. If your voice emerges clear and undistorted, all is well. If there is a scream, a whistle or a shriek, you are too near or the volume is too loud. If your voice emerges as if from outer space, with Martian echo or eerie ululation, then adjust.

'Colleagues and friends . . .' Silence. Lift up your voice: 'Will someone kindly switch on this mechanical marvel?' Laughter. The engineer scurries around and flips the appropriate switch. 'Thank you.' Screams and whistles from the machine. More laughter. 'There's no need to overdo it.' The engineer tries again. 'Colleagues and friends . . .' Silence. 'Are you receiving me?' you say, smiling, tapping the dreaded instrument. 'Do you hear me at the back?' Loud cries of 'No, no' and more laughter. They are laughing *with* you and not *at* you. You have command of the situation. You are waiting until the conditions are as you require before you start speaking.

With luck and perseverance, the microphone will be put into proper order. If it is not – or if reception is intermittent or unpleasant – then you must make up your mind whether or not your voice will carry unaided. Is it better to risk being unheard than to submit your audience to squeals and screeches from the machine? Will you succeed in interesting your audience when the microphone is playing up? Have you, perhaps, a genius in the place who can adjust the amplifier, the loudspeaker, or some other unmentionable or unpronounceable part of this gadget? Think on your feet – fast.

'I shall do without the microphone,' you belt out. 'I hope that you will all hear me.' Applause.

Alternatively: 'I apologise for the inefficiency of this miserable apparatus. I think I had better submit you to the occasional grunt and growl, so that at least I may grant you the pleasure of hearing a part of my presentation!' Hear, hear!

You are off – to a late and unhappy start. But your audience have noted your confidence.

More good speeches are ruined because the speaker is not prepared to take time and make preparations with the microphone than for any other reason.

Make the mike your ally. Never panic when it goes wrong. Be prepared to fall back on your own voice power, if you must. Remember that great orators of the past had to manage unamplified – and they did not do too badly – presumably because they knew the rules of voice production (see Chapter 15).

33　Visual aids

There is an art to all excellence – not least in the use of visual aids. So why is this use so seldom taught? Consider:

- Which aids are best for the particular occasion? Slides (35 mm) are splendid – but generally only for projecting pictures or for large audiences. Overhead projection transparencies can be switched or even amended or added to during the presentation. They should be treated with respect, their contents carefully thought out and the transparencies themselves professionally produced. (These sheets of clear plastic, usually mounted in card frames, are known by a variety of names.)
- Do not use your visual aids to replace your verbal message. Your charts, etc., should either:
  Provide the skeleton for your presentation, so as to attract the eye and direct the mind, later to revive the memory, and/or
  Illustrate and explain through graphs, etc., concepts and/or detail which cannot be explained simply and/or adequately and/or swiftly in other ways.
- Keep the wording on all visual aids to a sensible minimum. This does not mean putting one simple sentence onto a separate transparency, but dividing a mass of hard-to-assimilate material between two or more projections.
- Transparencies, etc., should be concise, compact and uncluttered. Use abbreviations and symbols to summarise and to emphasise. Use artwork sparingly and for results, not effects.
- Remind your graphics department or other aid makers to make the transparencies with backgrounds clear and light – not obscure and dark. The darker the background, the poorer the view. Green or blue as well as black come out well on a white background, as black does on yellow. Red on green or green on red are even worse than white on red, orange on black, or red on yellow. Clarity of overhead vision should never be sacrificed for artificial and artistic impression.
- Beware of 'funnies'. Humour is much better presented orally, if only because you can quickly move on and away from a failed joke. If you must use cartoons, caricatures or illustrative, graphic humour, then make sure that it is thoroughly professional.
- Choose your overhead projectors or machinery with care. I deeply dislike projectors with fans that change the atmosphere when they come on, often do not go off along with the light, and disturb speaker and audience. Watch out especially for those that blow air out sideways,

depositing papers all over the show. Better – in any event with a smaller audience – to use a modern, mirror-type, fanless projectors.

- Ensure that your visual aids are properly set up before your audience arrive, i.e. properly focused and with the first slide, transparency, etc., in position.
- The first transparency should generally provide an overall summary – to which you can return, filling in the detail with your further projections.
- To point at a slide, you must use (and have ready) a stick or other pointer. For a transparency, you have four possibilities, which can be used in combination, for variety and as required:

  Point with a pencil, pen or even a finger on the slide itself, casting the shadow of the pointer onto the screen.

  Put your pencil or pen down on the transparency. Do not hold it or the slightest jiggle or movement will create a major flicker on the screen. Make sure it will not roll.

  Use pointer or finger on the screen itself – but beware of casting the shadow of your body onto the screen at the same time; and/or use a sheet to cover up that part of the transparency that you do not require the audience to see – and then move it. Use the masking technique sparingly: it irritates audience who find themselves wondering what is hidden, rather than thinking about what is revealed.

- Change of transparency should be slick. Hold the replacement in your right hand; remove the existing transparency with your left and put the new one into its place, all in one movement; and practise until you can put the replacement into a firm, central position without fiddling. To recognise a transparency, put its title at the top of its frame; then lay out all of them on your table, with the title of each sticking out above the next.
- Ensure that all the audience can see – if anyone cannot do so, then move the viewer or the screen.
- Be deliberate – do not jog, jolt or jiggle an item on the screen.
- Talk to your audience, not to the machine – and even if you are reading out what is on the screen, do not turn your back on your audience or put your face down to the machine. Try not to turn your back on your listeners.
- Minimise your own movement and that of the visual aids; do not distract from the content.
- Use variety in your charts, etc. – different types, colours, underlining, etc.
- If you draw on transparencies, use water-based pens, which can be rubbed out with a damp cloth – not those that require spirit for removal.
- Visual aids should stimulate interest and not simply provide a technical message.
- Check your pens or crayons in advance. Break up the script by using different colours. Make sure the lettering is large enough to be seen. Use

as few words as possible: for instance, do not say 'replaced by' – simply cross out whatever it is that has been replaced.

- Watch good school teachers using the blackboard, then transfer the techniques to your transparencies, slides or flip charts. They will ask their audience questions while they write, never remove their eyes from the class for more than a few seconds, and turn sideways when writing, never turning their back more or longer than absolutely necessary.

- Do not talk while you are changing transparencies or slides.

- If you show slides, try not to keep the room in permanent gloom while you talk – unless you would prefer not to know when your audience slide off into slumber. Maybe you can place yourself to one side or under a spotlight, or at least turn the light on when the slides are off.

- To avoid the blank spaces of darkness and silence between slides, you can now get what are called 'twin pair dissolve slides'. Operated with two machines, as one slide goes off the screen, another comes on it. However, these prepared slides have to remain in the same order and there is no way in which you can shuffle them. Inflexibility is a high price to pay for apparent slickness.

- Beware of over-preparation. An autocued, word-perfect script, the drama of music and lighting, the over-professionalism too often produced by specialists for the use of amateurs – avoid them all.

- To make the best of slides, overhead charts, etc., consider providing copies for your audience – as reference to save them writing, so that they can concentrate on your presentation; and for addition to their own notes. As in the case of all other documentation, consider carefully whether you would wish to supply this in advance (not generally recommended, because busy people seldom do their homework, and often forget to bring it with them on the day); and/or at time of presentation for use during its course; and/or at the end of the presentation, to take home.

The old-fashioned but worthy flip chart will never go out of fashion. At its simplest, it consists of a stack of newsprint attached to a board. With pens or crayons you illustrate your words, the sheets then being flipped over or torn off.

Or you may use and re-use prepared charts, again flippable. I use a helpful variant – a white-faced, steel board with magnetic lines, spots and dots and coloured, water-based pens that write and erase with ease.

Whatever type of chart or board you use, check the easel beforehand. Make sure it is firm the pegs are well in place, and it will not collapse with dramatic impact, creating havoc with your presentation and possibly injuring you in the process.

When pointing at a flip chart – as at a transparency – use your nearer hand or arm, so as not to have to twist your body and turn your back on the audience.

34   Notes

Some speeches are so important that they have to be read. Every word counts and the occasion is so fraught with peril that you cannot risk getting a word wrong. But read speeches are usually boring. (For the rules on reading, see Chapter 17.) Even Parliament, where some debates are an agony to endure, forbids the reading of speeches. Members may not turn exchange debates into a series of written essays, probably the product of the minds of others.

Remove the element of impromptu and the likelihood of the speech proving interesting recedes. As the audience know the speech is to be read instead of looking forward to hearing the speaker, they prepare for slumber and boredom. As soon as you start reading from a script, your audience begin to curl up – mentally if not physically.

To average, non-professional speakers the difficulty of constructing a speech as they go along is almost insurmountable. Even for the expert, preparation is a necessity, and the more complex the speech, the more essential it is to be reminded of its main points, so that none are left out.

The compromise, then? Notes. Have the skeleton of your speech (see Chapter 1) committed to paper, leaving you to clothe it with words, embellish it with new ideas and thoughts, and enliven it with wit as you go along.

What should good notes contain? The first sentence plus the last plus the skeleton. The flow of ideas. The thread of the speech. Brief phrases to indicate the contents of even lengthy paragraphs. Reminders of themes. Pegs on which to hang your thoughts. Bullet points.

You need brief headings for the eye, to direct the flow of speech but not to interrupt it. Except where you must quote, the shorter and clearer the note the better.

Divide up the note itself by using block capitals for the main headings and small script for subsidiary items. Underline in red, blue, green. Set the notes themselves into columns and lay them out so as to catch your eye, just as you seek to lay out your speech to catch the minds and imaginations of your listeners.

Notes are best on cards, preferably not larger than normal

postcard size. Each theme, each paragraph, each range of ideas can then be put on to a separate card. Use one side only. If you are operating from a desk, table, lectern or stand, this should be easy. Put your cards within easy view and reach or hold them. If not – as when you speak from the floor at a meeting – then you are not burdened by clumsy sheets, papers that slip through your fingers, scraps of notes that you lose at the crucial moment, sending you into that very fluster that the notes were intended to avoid. Return each card to the bottom of the pack as soon as you are through with it. In case you drop your notes, number each card cearly at the top right-hand corner, but be prepared to reshuffle them up to the very last moment.

Another advantage of the card system is that if you run out of time you can skip two or three of the least essential – or at least summarise them in sentences and turn them over at speed. They provide your guide without restricting you to an itinerary. They leave you room for manoeuvre, combined with the freedom to think on your feet.

35 How to read

The first rule in speechmaking is – don't read from a text. The second rule is – know how to handle exceptions to the first rule. This takes special skills.

You may be forced beyond notes for a variety of reasons:

- Because your words can be misinterpreted. Choose your words with care. Better still, record your speech, providing incontrovertible evidence against the twister, deliberate or careless.
- Because the content is so complex that word for word reading spells safety. An alternative is to provide documentation to put in the hands of your listeners, plus overheads and (perhaps) slides (see Chapter 33 on visual aids).
- Because you are giving a lengthy, commercial or academic discourse or lecture. Once again: are you sure that you cannot keep to the trail through preparation and notes, while holding the attention of your audience through visual aids?
- Because of a combination of two or more of the above – plus, perhaps, inadequate time for preparation, or lack of top-rate speechwriter and/or precise, fixed time for speaking.

36   Autocue – and invisible reading

Television newscasters read their scripts from the telecue – words that appear before them either on a still screen or, more likely, moving gently before their eyes. The words are invisible to the viewer, but to maintain the illusion, the newsreaders occasionally look down at scripts which they only actually use in emergencies.

If you make a video for your company or firm, you no longer have to memorise your script or otherwise ad lib and hope for the best. You can read the words while apparently looking straight at the viewers.

Now comes the autocue – the moving script, visible to the speaker, but not to the audience. Instead of appearing (as with the telecue) on a television screen, the words are flashed onto glass. The audience has the illusion of a speaker without notes.

37   Quotations

Your audience have come to hear you, but you may still pepper your speech with apt quotations from the thoughts of others. Quoting, though, is an art of its own. Perfect it.

Keep quotations short. To quote at length from memory is a form of showing off that is seldom appreciated. You are not engaged in stage soliloquy. To read someone else's words at length is rarely a good alternative to putting thoughts and ideas into your own words. The reading of speeches – or even lengthy parts of them – is usually an error. That error is compounded when you are not even reading your own original thought.

Quotations are only worth using if they are thoroughly apt. If your audience is flagging, it is sometimes helpful to 'drag in a joke by its ears'. This legitimate gambit may reduce strain, but the story must be apposite. It is a mistake to thrust an inappropriate quotation into your speech, merely because you have a fond feeling for it.

Attribute the quotation to its true author, if you can. If in doubt, you could try: 'Was it George Bernard Shaw who said . . .?' Or: 'I think it was Oscar Wilde who once remarked that . . .' Or if the attribution is to someone in your lifetime, you can seldom go wrong with: 'I once heard President Ford remark on television that . . .' or 'Did you read the saying, attributed to Mr Krushchev, that . . .' Who is to prove you wrong? Or maybe try: 'Was it not I who said . . .?'!

Make sure that your speech really is strengthened by putting the statement concerned in quotation marks – and as coming from the particular author. When trying to convince a British audience to adopt an American practice, it is sometimes better to adopt the transatlantic arguments without stating their origin. Conversely, for any non-American to express a preference for a candidate in an American election is to impose the kiss of death upon them. By all means use the foreigner's arguments, but if you must put them into quotation marks, try: 'A famous Marxist once proclaimed . . .' Quote Satan to condemn sin.

The best quotations come, of course, from the careless mouths of your opponents. 'Today, Mr Jones condemns amalgamation. But who was it who said, just two years ago – and I quote: "Our future depends upon achieving amalgamation. We cannot survive as a small independent unit"? None other than my friend, Mr Jones!'

Quotations from yourself should be avoided. 'Did I not say, six months ago, that . . .?' Or 'May I repeat what I said at our trade conference last month?' Unless a speaker has previously been accused of inconsistency, self-quotation is generally pompous and egotistical.

If you have something to say today, say it. Let someone else point to your marvellous consistency . . . to your wisdom before the event . . . to your status as a person whose advice should be taken. The best you can do is to make that insinuation. Self-quotation, like self-adulation, is proper only among consenting adults in private . . . as a solitary occupation.

38   Statistics

Mind how you use statistics. Everyone knows that they are in the same category as lies and damned lies. If your presentation is to succeed, your figures must at least appear to be accurate.

A queue of graduates applied for a job with a firm of city accountants. Each was asked: 'What is twice one?' Each replied: 'Two.' The applicant who eventually got the job replied: 'What number did you have in mind, sir?'

So when you present statistics, at least indicate their origin – assuming only that you are not ashamed of it.

Next, do not presume that others are as conversant with figures or accounts as yourself. I am constantly amazed by business people who cannot even read a balance sheet. So steer your way between the cardinal sins of talking down to your audience on the one hand and conferring undue knowledge on the other. If in doubt, explain.

Recognising that some human beings absorb by ear and others by eye, but most require a combination of both, and accepting also that your audience is far more likely to be innumerate that illiterate, supplement your words with paper – graphs and the rest – and, where appropriate, with visual aids (see Chapter 33).

39   Files and ideas

First-class journalists (especially freelancers with no access to newspaper files) keep their own careful files of clippings, cuttings, photographs and ideas which they can later incorporate into articles, features or books. Speakers should take a leaf out of their book.

Take jokes, for instance. There are books of allegedly humorous tales for every occasion. I sometimes wonder how anyone ever laughed at any of them. But then everyone has his or her own style and sense of humour. Do not be afraid to steal the tales of others. They will be flattered. Jot them down and file them. You never know when they may come in handy.

Then there is specialist material, which can be used time and time again. Most popular speakers are invited to talk on their particular specialities. The first time, research must be done, facts prepared, statistics unearthed and notes made. If those notes are carefully filed, next time will be a walk-over, though naturally they would have to be adapted for different audiences. The basic groundwork need not be repeated but updating is always advisable.

Some speakers favour a filing cabinet, others metal boxes with files inside. Still more make do with loose-leaf notebooks for stories and quotations, ideas and suggestions. The most modern store their gems on tape, or on word processors.

The object of it all is to reduce your homework to the minimum. You have no time to repeat your drudgery. So, however boring the keeping of files or notebooks may be, it is worth the effort in the present to reduce your work in the future.

Once again, the Retellable Tales in Book 3 should save you time and trouble and perhaps form the basis for your own collection, as it does mine.

40   Venues

Too often, speakers cannot choose their venue. The company meeting, organisational gathering or dinner party is held in a place selected and often paid for by others. Even there, they may be able to make the best of their surroundings, if they know what to look for. In other cases, they can influence (if not choose) the choice of venue.

First essential is to try to match the size of the room to the number of the audience. If the place is packed, an atmosphere should be easy to create and the speaker's task is made vastly simpler. Take 50 people and squeeze them into a home and you are likely to have a lively, happy meeting. Lose the same 50 in a hall and the evening is a failure before it has begun. So underestimate your audience. If a few get left outside, never mind. Next time they will come earlier. If some have to stand or perch on radiators, that cannot be helped. You must avoid the echoing emptiness of a partially filled hall.

If you do find yourself with a sparse audience, do not panic. Suggest to the organisers that they ask all those present to come right up to the front. People hate being at the front, preferring to tuck themselves away in a nook near the door, the better to make their exit if they get bored; and it is not only speakers who are sometimes shy. Still, a capable Chair can wheedle most people into 'helping our distinguished speaker'. If he or she is inexperienced, then (having obtained permission) you can ask your audience to 'gather round'.

It is often better to abandon the platform, draw the stage curtains and come down to your audience. If the formal gathering has failed to draw in the crowds, then at least ensure that you have an informal chat, so that your audience go home satisfied with their evening. It is most unlikely that they will be, if you regale them from above with an oration more suitable to a packed and cheering hall than to an empty room. Someone overestimated the audience in the first place and created your unfortunate situation. You must make the best of it.

Other suggestions? If the room is too hot, stop and ask for a window or a door to be opened. Your audience will bless you. If it is too cold, speak to the organisers and see whether they can warm the place. If they cannot, at least your audience will know that you are thinking of their comfort.

If there are aeroplane noises overhead, stop until they pass. To speak on regardless is a sure sign of inexperience. If a carpenter is banging next door, ask someone to use influence or pressure to get silence for you. Then wait.

Of course, it is far preferable to have these distractions dealt with in advance. If you get to a meeting early enough you can sometimes induce the organisers to rearrange the seating to suit your theme or your plans. You may want to avoid the use of a platform or to have the chairs arranged informally in a horseshoe, or conversely, to speak to your audience from a higher level.

Again, it may pay dividends to have the sound equipment tested before the audience arrives or the lighting adjusted to suit your requirements. No theatre audience expects to have these changes arranged in their presence. No audience for a speech or lecture, discussion or debate, likes to see them done after their arrival. Punctuality pays. If you wish to make a triumphal entry at a later stage, you can always disappear from the scene until the appropriate moment. If you hosts know their business, they will have organised some small room at the back for you to use for your coat and hat and for your refreshment.

So much depends on the occasion. As we shall shortly see.

41   Training in speechmaking

In Britain, speechmaking has always been regarded as an amateur art. Acquired through a combination of heredity and superior education, it finds no place in the curriculum of school, college or university.

Of course, 'the true Briton' learns to read, spell and count, but it is 'not done' to take lessons in speechmaking or in presentation. Which explains why both are so commonly done so badly.

The fact that you have bought or borrowed this book immediately places you in some peril – or have you put it into a plain, white cover?

As for lessons in speechmaking – they are for Americans and other foreigners, are they not?

There is, of course, neither educational rhyme nor reasonable logic behind this curious attitude. Speaking in private may come naturally; orating in public does not. It requires training and experience. Without the appropriate flair, no level of teaching can produce outstanding results. Without training, public speaking is likely to be a burden not only for speakers, but more especially for their unfortunate audiences.

So do not despise the lesson. If public speaking is a burden on you or on your hearers; if you need to practise in private, but with an experienced and critical audience; if you are prepared to learn from other people's mistakes, rather than from your own – then take lessons.

You do not need to advertise to your customers or clients, your friends or even your family that you are indulging in this particular form of masochism. Whether you are an experienced speaker in need of polish; an inexperienced performer, promoted to a position of prominence where self-expression becomes crucial; a presenter of your company's products or services, needing guidance in techniques and practice in their use; or especially, if you suffer from any form of speech impediment, a good teacher will enable you to avoid oratorical misery, and turn criticism into compliments.

The same principles apply to courses in speechmaking and presentation for your staff or your executives. Given even moderate material, the skilled teacher can produce marvellous changes.

How do you find your teacher or trainer? As usual, recommendation is the best guide. On the basis of horses for courses, others' gurus may suit their needs, but not yours. So experiment.

My colleagues and I organise presentational courses for individual executives – tailor-made for the individual group efforts, generally for a maximum of six; and large-scale, one-day presentations of basic techniques. Our delegates take their choice. (Details from: Effective Presentational Skills Ltd, Balfour Place, London W1Y 5RS.)

The more the training is angled at the needs of the individual, the greater its potential. Experience coupled with a video camera and monitor screen are our partners in perfection. The combination of seeing and criticising yourself, together with the vision and criticism of others – outsiders and, if you wish, your own colleagues, taking the same medicine – produces dramatic results in (we find) no more than two days.

If you are prepared to lavish resources on presentations; on estimates, tenders and quotations; on promotions and on product launches; on induction and promotional training; on employing consultants to advise you on everything from organisation and methods to time and staff management – why, then, do you underestimate the need to train for prowess in the marvellous art of the skilled speechmaker and the polished presenter?

Speakers in public may be amateurs at the art, but there is no reason in business or in logic for them to be untrained. If more speakers had more training, listeners would have a far more rewarding time – and speakers and presenters would reach for the stars.

42   Practice and perfection

All great speechmakers are nervous on mighty occasions or they would fail. So greet your 'butterflies' with respect and with courage – the speechmaker has nothing to fear but fear itself.

If you approach your speechmaking moment with trembling knees, take comfort. Your experienced colleagues may not show their discomfort, but they will feel it.

Skilled speakers will not twist their hat or their hair, chew their fingernails or tear up bits of paper. They have learned to dissemble their feelings. Speechmakers are actors who must normally write their own scripts. They must learn to cover up their apprehension.

So banish those terrifying fears that your throat will dry up, your voice crack, your mind go blank. Provided that you have prepared your speech, and that your notes are handy and steady and appropriate, and that you know your subject or can at least hide your ignorance, all should be well. Never panic or all will be lost.

The more your practise, the more your confidence will expand. So:

- If you attend a meeting, steal yourself. Ask questions.
- If you are offered the chance to propose a vote of thanks, accept. If a small group invites you to address it, agree.
- If you have been dealing with some new and interesting project, if you have gone on an unusual journey, or if you have something out of the ordinary to tell, then let this be known. Your club or organisation, charity, political group or trade organisation which has previously regarded you as a silent member will be delighted to invite you to speak to its members or to an interested section of them.
- Maybe you have a social function of your own: a dinner party, cocktail party, or company lunch. This time, tand up and say those few words of welcome, of thanks or of greeting. If the speech is to be of any length, then (whatever the social occasion) the rules in Chapter 43 (on after-dinner speaking) will provide you with some useful guides.

Remember, the higher you rise or aspire to in any field, the more vital it is to express yourself on your feet. The only way to gain experience is to get up on those feet. You will no longer fear becoming the centre of public attention. You will get used to the sound of your own voice, raised in public.

So speak. Your nervousness will fall away when your words emerge and your audience listens.

PART 5

Occasions

43   After dinner

A captive audience, well wined and amply dined, should be an orator's joy. Unfortunately more often than not speakers are too apprehensive to enjoy the food – and instead make a meal of the speech. Which is unnecessary, if they would only follow a few basic rules.

First, wait for silence. When you have it, look around amiably and begin: 'Ladies and Gentlemen . . .' or as the case may be. Those few words are useful. You discover that you have not lost your voice after all. Your audience (at that stage at least) is ready to listen – and to be entertained.

However heavy the dinner or the company, however important the occasion or mighty the listeners, no one wants a dry lecture on top of a wet repast. So however important your message, do your audience the courtesy of exercising patience. Start with a joke, a witticism, a story.

The best jokes are usually impromptu. A friendly reference to the chairperson, the restaurant, the food, or to the headline in the evening papers (those of the audience who have read it are delighted to be in on the joke). Otherwise, there are many good opening gambits such as:

- 'A few moments ago, the Chair turned to me and said: "Would you like to speak now – or shall we let them go on enjoying themselves a little longer?".'
- Not long ago, an after-dinner speaker was greeted by a woman, at the evening's end, who said to him: 'Mr Jones . . . that was a terrible speech!' He composed himself as best he could – and was then greeted by another woman who said: 'I'm awfully sorry about Mrs Brown . . . She has such a long tongue . . . and she's such an idiot – she hasn't got a mind of her own. She only repeats what she hears other people saying!'
- 'Thank you for your hospitality to my wife and to me. In the words of the proverb: Behind every successful man stands an amazed woman!'

However weak the wit, dry the humour or wet the joke, provided that you put it across with verve, courage or at least a friendly smile, you are on your way to establishing a rapport with your audience. They will settle back into their chairs, relaxed – and either be receptive to a continuation of merriment or, at worst, better braced for such message as you care to give.

Now launch into the speech. Keep it short. The lower down you come in the toast list, the greater the premium on brevity. So why do so many of the most nervous speakers find it necessary to be the most long-winded? Do they think they can make up with length for their lack of wit, their terror or their dearth of wise words? You may argue your bank manager into submission, stifle the opposition of your competitors by talking them into the ground, or exhibit superb salesmanship by making it clear that you are not going to leave until you get what you want. But all this is in private. Enter into the public arena in general, or the dinner table in particular, and you must be brief (see also Chapter 22 on time management).

As for the after-dinner speech itself, it requires the same careful construction as any other. It needs a flow of ideas as well as of words. The more the words are laced with wit, the more likely it is their wisdom will strike home.

Watch your audience. If they drop off to sleep, either tell them a joke or sit down. If they jiggle the cutlery, wind up your sermon. If you want to be asked again, do not outstay your welcome.

As you approach your end, remember what it is you have been called upon to do. If you are responding to a toast, you should start by thanking the person who made it and complimenting him or her on their wit and wisdom.

Finish where you began – by repeating, once again, your delight at having been asked . . . your pleasure at the privilege of responding to the toast . . . and your good wishes to the organisation which has asked you.

More important, if you are making the toast – do so. Nothing is more discomforting than for the Chair to have to say: 'And now, kindly rise and drink with me . . .'. That is *your* job. Do it.

The standard formula? 'Ladies and Gentlemen, I invite you to rise and drink with me a toast to the continued success and prosperity of . . . the health and happiness of . . .' or as the case may be. By all means vary it, but do not forget it.

One toast which should never be varied is that to: 'Her Majesty, the Queen'. If you are privileged to propose the loyal toast, then do so – in those words. No one wants a speech from you, extolling the beauty and majesty of the monarch – still less a defence of hereditary peerages, royal privileges and the like.

The presence of an ambassador calls for a toast, to the head of his or her state – but unless this is one of the non-formal variety, reserve your eulogy for some proper occasion.

No one should smoke until after the loyal toast and others of the formal, national variety. This explains why some hosts call on proposers of these toasts when the waiters are collecting the soup.

44   Funerals, feasts and epitaphs

You may be called on to 'say a few words' on festive or funeral occasions, involving family, friends or colleagues. In general, similar rules apply to those outlined for the after-dinner orator – and elsewhere in the book. But here are some special suggestions for particular occasions.

Funerals

There is no speech that is harder to make than a farewell. Nor is there any more worthy duty in the eyes of God or man than a salute to the departed.

If you face this responsibility, here are the key rules.

- From the start and to the end, you must never lose your composure. You must not break down under the weight of emotion. You must achieve detachment.
- Do not declaim. Speak slowly, clearly, simply.
- Avoid pompous and insincere language. Instead, choose short, simple, Anglo-Saxon words.
- As for content, remember that the only people who matter are the immediate family: the widow or the widower, parents and children. Friends come next, far behind.

So start by addressing the family by name: 'Mary, George, Richard . . . we have all come here today because we loved . . .'

On the principle that I am addressing the bereaved, I always ask them what they would like me to say.

Keep your speech structured and brief. Say what you are going to say. Start, 'With sadness but with pride, I pay the tribute of us all, to . . .'

Then say it. Set out your points in order. Try to catch the essence of the person, as you remember him or her and as their family would wish you to.

Then the family itself. 'We are also here because of our affection for . . . we admire them for their . . . we love them because they . . . we are with them in their grief, which we share.'

Then say what you have said. Sum up with your message. 'And so we shall remember . . . – with affection, with joy – and with thanksgiving, because we enjoyed and shared in the warmth of his friendship. We shall miss him.'

In your few moments, then, you must try to conjure up the happiest of memories of the deceased. Avoid platitudes and clichés. And if a touch of humour hits, use it. A whimsical, smiling recollection of a joy brought into your life by your friend . . .

Finally, remember that people eulogised may have had faults while alive, but they must have none visible.

There is an ancient Jewish tradition that someone must say good words at a funeral. So after David Cohen had been buried, the Rabbi asked: 'Who will perform this holy duty? I cannot do so because unfortunately I can think of nothing good to say about poor David . . .' Silence.

'Please, someone must find something to praise, in David's life?' Silence.

'I beg you . . . someone . . .'

'I'll do it,' said Sam. He came to the front, faced the audience, and said, "His brother was worse!" '

If you must pay your respects to the departed, you will certainly be able to do better than that!

Feasts

Happily, whilst every lifetime contains the seeds of its own sorrow, there are far more joyful occasions than sad ones. Births and baptisms, christenings, confirmations, barmitzvahs and first communions, engagements, weddings, anniversaries and birthdays: each is the occasion for a word of congratulation at the start of a meeting or speech – or for a celebration at which a speech is required.

Of the full-blown variety, the after-dinner speech may form the model (see Chapter 43). Perhaps the best advice of all is contained in the saying: 'The secret of talking to the public is the same as that of speaking to your spouse – keep your tongue in time with your thoughts; if either gets ahead, you are done for!'

45 Overseas speeches – and foreign customers

Isolationist business people are, or should be, as dead as the proverbial dodo. If you can export then you should, says every government the world over. If you must import, then do so – but at the most competitive prices. You must bargain with foreigners, eat with them, drink with them, even expense-account with them – and, ultimately, you may well be thrust into making speeches to or at them.

Naturally, if you are blessed with equal facility in the foreign language as you have in your own, your problems are minimal. You only have to follow the rules laid down in the rest of this book and all should be well. Subject, of course, to cutting your cloth to the style of your overseas audience, there is no essential difference between rousing, holding, interesting, convincing – or boring – an audience of English or French people, Russians or Greeks.

Melodrama goes over rather better in the United States than in Britain. The florid oratory that went out in Britain many years ago still thrives in some parts – and with some audiences – abroad. In general, if you play up to the image expected of you – if you give your audience a touch of urbane wit, rather than roistering slapstick – you are likely to come across best.

Stick to your style when in America and you have every chance of a friendly welcome. I once toured the United States, talking about Britain, the Welfare State, and even what they choose to call 'socialised medicine'. I met a certain surprise that this Englishman was not cold, reserved, humourless, upper crust and frosty. The image of the icy Anglo-Saxon who will only speak when introduced – and, preferably, when well warmed with alcohol – dies hard. So the friendly, humorous opening acquired an extra significance and importance. Establish a rapport and you are well away.

Once the overseas audience knows that you really do intend to entertain as well as to instruct – to talk across and not down – they are even more ready than your compatriots to give you a warm welcome. The best tip for heating the atmosphere? Use the language of your hosts.

Is English and American the same? In general, yes. Still, the idiom differs and so do the allusions. The American speaker in Britain who takes the trouble to look at the daily newspaper and to joke about the current crime wave, strike outbreak, political disaster or other local misery does well. When you are talking to overseas listeners, return that sort of compliment.

A simple, well-tried opening in the USA: 'You will be relieved to know that I am not about to launch into discussion of whether or not that which is good for General Motors is good also for the country as a whole . . . of the merits or otherwise of the political efforts of the Cabots, the Kennedys or [*here insert names of local politicians currently in the news*]. If I am asked whether I support the Yankees, the Redskins or [*here insert the name of the local baseball team*], I shall refuse firmly to enter into your local politics. We British have enough trouble trying to run our own affairs, without risking another Boston tea-party. No. I shall confine myself to a discussion of . . .'

Another invaluable story. 'I have been asked to comment upon your current commercial crisis. I must respectfully decline. You may know the tale of the dying man who was visited by his priest. "My son," said the priest, "do you renounce the Devil, now and for ever more?" "Oh, Father," said the dying man, "this is no time to be making enemies – anywhere!" Ladies and Gentlemen, as the solitary Englishman in your ranks, I wish to make no enemies anywhere – so I shall tell you about *our* troubles – rather than venturing to discuss yours.'

Once you have established friendly relations with the overseas buyers, suppliers or fellow traders, if you stick to subjects which interest them, all should be well. They are as anxious to pick up profitable tips from you, as you are from them. Provided that you assume a cloak of modesty, they will wish to hear of your achievements. After all, that is why you have been invited to speak. So do not be shy. Talk freely of your doings and the effort may prove more profitable than you had expected.

Now suppose that you are forced to launch into your speech in front of people for whom English is not the mother tongue. There are two main possibilities. Either you address them in English and hope that they will understand. Or you speak in the foreign language. The second is infinitely preferable, provided that you have a command of the tongue concerned.

If you are really talking business – putting across facts, figures, theories or ideas in respect of which words must be given their precise meanings; if what you say may create misunderstandings if the words are not used with their correct nuances; if shades of meaning matter – then you should stick to English and work through an interpreter if necessary. It is no tribute to your bravery if you venture into foreign seas without wearing a lifebelt.

On the other hand, it may be that this is an occasion when it would be worth preparing your speech beforehand and having it translated – and then reading it. Make a friendly, impromptu opening (or one which is apparently not read) and the audience will just have to put up with what may not be an oratorical masterpiece but which will at least be accurate. That will teach them to invite an overseas expert to speak to them!

In that case, you should do all you can to mitigate the misery by looking up from your speech, talking to your audience, whenever you can manage it, pausing from time to time, to throw in a joke in English – or an apology for having to read your script – and make sure that you do try to put it across in the accent of the native.

We have all heard Britons who speak foreign tongues as if they were their own. French words read in broad Scots, Yorkshire, Welsh or upper-crust Bath or Tunbridge Wells have a distinctly humorous flavour on the music-hall stage. To the foreign listener, it is just plain silly.

There is an exception. If you are going to make your speech in English, then you should always prepare a few words, right at the start, in your host's language – or, if you are the host, in that of your guests. It matters not how badly you mispronounce the words – that adds to the fun. Nobody cares if you make a hash of the grammar or even if you manage to make a ghastly boob which gives words their opposite meaning. What matters is that you make the genuine effort to speak to folk in their own tongue. You pay them the compliment of making what is obviously a brave attempt to be friendly – and in the most genuine possible way.

Start with your usual opening, in English. 'Ladies and Gentlemen, fellow workers in the – industry . . .' If you then break into the foreign tongue, you will produce just that element of surprise which should give rise to a very friendly reception. 'You did not know that I was learning Greek/Spanish/Hebrew/Chinese . . . did you?' (This, of course, in the language concerned.) 'After I'd met Mr . . . in . . . who speaks such marvellous English, I was shamed into trying. I am only sorry that my efforts have been, as you hear, so very unsuccessful. To avoid any future misunderstandings of what I have to say, I hope that you will forgive me if I return – very gratefully – to English!' All that in the foreign language. Memorise it if you can. Otherwise read it. The fact that you will have got the information and the translation from one of the nationals of the country concerned is irrelevant. The compliment you have paid your audience will undoubtedly be appreciated.

There is an alternative. You can launch right into the 'Ladies and Gentlemen . . . How are you? Welcome to Britain – we are very happy to have you and hope that you will have a very good time.' All that in the foreign language will delight your audience.

End with 'Farewell – and come back soon,' in the language of your hosts or guests. Then add: '*Jai Hind*' or '*Vive la France*' or whatever 'hail' is appropriate in their land. As usual, if you get the start and finish of your speech right, the rest will fall into shape.

Naturally, if your audience happens to be a mixed bag, then the above rules will have to be modified. I have heard a very successful opening: 'Ladies and Gentlemen, Messieurs, Mesdames, Señoras y Señores, Meine Damen und Herren . . . welcome to you all – and if I have managed to mispronounce even the few words in your language which I have ventured to speak, I know that you will appreciate why I am going to make the rest of my speech in English – I think it will be easier for us all.' Pause while the audience nod, smile, and chatter. 'Misunderstandings that are created by speakers – especially by politicians – who stick to their own tongue are only exceeded by those who have the temerity to create vast international misunderstandings by murdering the languages of others – and murder is a crime in every country in the world!'

46   Appeals and fund-raising

The art of extracting money from the listener requires careful thought and ready adaptation to the circumstances. The Chancellor of the Exchequer may have political problems, but at least he can enforce his financial requirements. Speechmakers seeking to raise funds for a pet charity, for a trade or industrial benevolent fund, or even for some less apparently altruistic outlet must win the cash, pound by pound. How? That depends on the audience and the cause. Here are some suggestions:

There are those who give out of pure kindness of heart. Guilt and self-interest are usually more powerful motives.

There are some who work hard for a charity – and others who do not. Even so, the latter may contribute the money they have earned whilst not striving for the good cause. In their own way, they can do as much for the needy as their more apparently energetic colleagues. Tell them so – by implication.

'There are those of us who are in the happy position of being able to spare time to work for this important charity. There are others who find it impossible to do so. May I make a special appeal to them? Give us the means and we will do the job. It is a job that desperately needs evey penny that you can afford to spare – and more . . .'

What, then, of enlightened self-interest? Maybe it is a question of insurance. The charity deals with the aged, infirm, ill or needy? And you are young, middle-aged or at least fit? That is now. What happens when you get dumped on the scrap heap . . . sacked . . . struck down by (Heaven forbid) some fell diease? You have a pension? Well, maybe the company will not be in a position to pay it or it will not suffice for the needs of the spouse you leave behind. So, now, when you are in a position to assure your future, do so.

This is seldom said. The better approach is this! 'I ask you to give as an expression of gratitude for the fact that you do not need to make use of this great trade charity for yourself. I hope that none of us will need at any time to occupy a bed in this convalescent home; to receive a payment from this fund; to rely upon the benevolence of others in the industry . . . But who knows?' Pause, significantly. 'And even if, as we all hope, we escape the need for help of this sort,

112

we can be proud that those who do require it can look to us. They have given good service; they have earned every penny that comes to them; they have been smitten by the ill-fortune that we have managed to avoid . . .' And so on. We all spend money on insurance, do we not? Well, this is a healthy and helpful form of outlet for the same, intelligent response to potential misfortune.

Consider always the best way to confer a bargain. This is generally done with the kind aid of the Revenue. If business people feel that they can lawfully and properly give more by paying less, you are far more likely to get your money, to have a bed endowed in the trade home, to acquire your 'Smith House' or 'Jones Hall'. So check on current covenant schemes, charitable trusts, and tax-deductible donations.

'Think of it, Ladies and Gentlemen. All those who pay income tax at the current standard rate can confer a benefit on this charity out of all proportion to the amount which they have to give up from their own spending. Here are some examples . . .' Then say how much a gift of £X or $Y per year will mean, gross, to the charity. Remember, of course, that when a charity receives covenants, these can provide good security for loans, if it needs the money at once. It is sometimes possible to get people to give a lump sum on the basis that it will be grossed up for tax purposes over the years. The charity's accountants should know the rules.

Then, remember that lawful blackmail is the charitable fund-raiser's most potent weapon. You phone your supplier. 'Jimmy,' you say, 'we've had such a tremendous call on our benevolent fund that we simply have to raise an extra £50,000. Can I count on you for a thousand?'

Jimmy groans inwardly. 'Certainly, Bill,' he smiles. 'Shall I send an advertisement for the Ball Brochure?'

Use the same tactic in public speech. Look at Jimmy when you ask for funds. He may turn away his gaze, but he may not dare to keep his cheque book closed. After all, when he came to the function or the meeting, he realised that the skinning knives would be unsheathed. Or, even better, corner him in advance. Find out how much he is willing to give. Announce it – as a bait for others, or to shame them into raising their donations to an appropriately announceable level. If you have goodwill, then use it for the benefit of the less privileged. No one will ever tell you of the resentment they feel. It's all in a good cause, is it not?

Of course, whether you can use this sort of direct attack or whether you have to be more subtle, whether you can announce donations at the meeting or have to let the word go round from mouth to mouth, whether you conduct a mock auction at inflated prices, a raffle, a tombola, all depends on all factors in the unhappy case. But one rule applies to nearly all: you cannot afford to be bashful, or to worry about rebuffs, if you are looking for money from the pockets of others.

The best time to attack those pockets is when the mind is weak through the stomach being overloaded or the heart touched by your words. If you have people in a happy, receptive and giving mood, then (literally) cash in on the situation. Either ask them for their donation at the time – and pass round the appropriate banker's order or covenant forms – or at least write to them the very next day saying: 'It was very good to see you last night . . . I enclose herewith a banker's order . . . I am sure that I can count on your further support . . .'

I reproduce with appreciation an interview in which a successful appeal-maker gave away some of his secrets:

'I know plenty of people who can make an excellent speech,' he said, 'but not an appeal. The technique is quite different. The man who makes a speech can create the right atmosphere for someone to follow in. The appeal-maker must not waste time making speeches. He needs a couple of minutes to say what it is all about. And, of course, an appeal-maker must never be satisfied with his audience. Whatever he says, he must have the people in a frame of mind when they want to give. He should know when to stop.'

An audience, then, should be like a 'juicy orange – you squeeze, but not until the pips fall out. When you stop is a matter of psychology or intuition.'

When you have finished your appeal, can you tell whether the audience is still with you?

'If they applaud you as loudly when you sit down as when you got up, you can be happy with the job done.

'An appeal-maker must never read a speech. What he has to say must be spontaneous. It must come from the heart. He must never embarrass people but make them feel happy about their giving and leave them in a good frame of mind, thanking him for a successful job. People recognise the sincerity of the appeal-maker. An appeal-maker must be somebody who sincerely believes in the cause he puts forward . . .

'Finally, the appeal-maker must set an example in giving.'

Give, and the world gives with you . . . the mean person is not an appealing figure, in any sense of the word.

47   In the open

The open-air speech is a comparative rarity. You should be prepared to make one, if necessary. Maybe it will be at the factory gates, at the dockside, or at some open-air trade show or speaking event. Perhaps it is only a vote of thanks at your local sports day or a talk or lecture on site, or maybe you have to speak at a rally in Hyde Park, Trafalgar Square or at your local war memorial? Wherever the place and whatever the circumstances, there are certain basic rules on open-air oratory that should help you succeed in any such appearance.

Human voices carry poorly in the open air. So the prime essential for the outdoor speaker is to be heard. If you have a microphone (see Chapter 32), use it. The chances of outdoor amplifying equipment going wrong are far greater than with their indoor brethren. The variety that hooks on to a motor-car battery is particularly vulnerable. Listen to the politicians next election time. Pity their attempts to be heard – especially when a crowd is all around them and the amplifying equipment points only to the front.

If you have a microphone, remember its outdoor limitations. For instance, if ever you have to speak in a moving vehicle – perhaps from the front of a car or the back of a truck – talk very slowly and distinctly and urge the driver to move as slowly as possible. People do like to hear what is being cried out at them from a moving object and they get aggravated when it darts past without giving them the chance to pick up the words – however banal or trite those words may be. Usually, there is time for a slogan only. 'Today's the day . . . come to the carnival . . . 12.15 p.m. at the park . . .' Then you are gone.

Most outdoor speaking is stationary. Mike or no mike, many of the indoor rules go out the window. For instance:

- The outdoor speaker can be far freer with movement and gesture.
- Old-fashioned oratory – rabble-rousing – is more effective and appears less insincere when out of doors.
- Instead of having an audience ready-made, you may have to collect it. Whereas indoors there is no point in speaking to yourself, outdoors you

may have no alternative, so the louder and more provocatively you rant, the greater your chances of an eventual audience.

Some rules of indoor speaking require special emphasis out of doors. For instance:

- Do not be afraid to pause . . . to wait . . . to give every possible indication of complete calm and confidence.
- Never panic, no matter what may be thrown at you – even if this is more than mere words. Remember always that the speakers on the platform have a vast advantage over their audience. If they are firm and refuse to be ruffled, they should win.
- Make certain that your voice carries. If you use a battery-operated hand megaphone, pull the trigger tight. As one famous Harvard professor used to say: 'Take your voice and throw it against the wall at the back of your audience and make it bounce off.' If you get hoarse as a result, do not worry. You have joined the professionals. Lose your voice and it will come back. Lose your audience, and it is gone forever.

48 Presentations and awards – as giver and receiver

The giver

You may view presentation or award speeches from two angles – that of the giver and that of the receiver. In either event 'a few words' will be expected of you; in either case, the keynote of the speech is sincerity.

Everyone likes to be honoured. The art of the well-turned compliment is appreciated more than almost any other. Flattery given freely and wholeheartedly is always welcome – but it must be given in moderation.

'Mr X is the most brilliant businessman, straightforward and sweet-tempered, a paragon of commercial virtue . . .' Rubbish. No one will believe it – not even Mr X.

Compare this: 'On the one hand, Mr Smith has been the head of a large and successful commercial concern. He has had to see that business became and remained thoroughly competitive. His has been the unpleasant duty of striking the hard bargain, ensuring that the business was tough and competitive, enabling the enterprise to survive and flourish in spite of the economic circumstances, the bitter and fierce rivalries within the trade, the battle for skilled staff and for shrinking markets.

'On the other hand, Mr Smith has sought to preserve the good name of the company and its good relations both with its suppliers, customers and competitors and with its own staff.

'That he has succeeded in building up the business without destroying the foundations of goodwill; that he has promoted the economic welfare of the business without demoting or undervaluing the honour and integrity of the Board; that he has earned such a warm regard not only for the company but for himself – those are the reasons why we are delighted to honour him this evening, and why we are so sad at his impending retirement.'

Or take the manager, the foreman or the operative leaving after long service, or receiving an award for distinguished, long-term conduct.

'We were thinking of presenting Mr Jones with a watch. But we do not believe our staff really want to know the time just when it has become least important to them. And so we felt that this electric tea-maker would be more appropriate and much more useful. It comes with the thanks and admiration of the company – and its gratitude.

'It is also given with the affection and goodwill of his fellow members of staff. They have contributed towards it and I know they hope, as much as I do, that it will remind him – and his wife and family – of the affection and esteem in which we all hold him, and of our thanks to him for his loyal service. We wish Mr Jones, together with his charming wife, a long and happy retirement, blessed with the very best of health. And we hope that he will visit us often. He will always have the warmest of welcomes from all of us, his colleagues and friends.'

No flowery insincerities. No 'schmaltz', no overdone compliments, just straightforward, sincere and sensible words, bound to be appreciated by the person concerned.

Sometimes the presentation of an award is really an excuse to encourage people to come to a dinner or other function, knowing that they would not wish to offend the recipient by being absent. With this sort of award or presentation it is expected that the toast to the recipient will be coupled with a eulogy of the organisation he or she represents – and/or of the virtues represented by the organisation which is conferring the award. This sort of excuse for an oratorical jamboree is becoming increasingly common, and is a not always altogether welcome transatlantic importation. The public relations people have created a new vehicle. If it comes your way, be prepared to steer it.

'In the new and expanding sauna industry, we are proud of our pioneers. This dinner is in honour of Ms Finn, whom we are all delighted to welcome to England.' Hear, hear!

'Ms Finn has helped to put our industry onto the British map. Close on the heels of the central heating boom has come the realisation that sauna treatments bring health and true family relaxation. Whilst no public authority should be without one, there is an immense, untapped demand for them in the larger private homes throughout the country.' (The press start scribbling.) 'What better occasion could there be than this to launch the great new drive for British-built saunas – we shall create a home demand so as to build up an economic export potential . . . And we wish to express our admiration and thanks to our honoured guest, Ms Finn, to whom I am delighted to present this gold pin, in the shape of a sauna, as a token of our respect and gratitude.' Loud cheers. The audience rises. Flash bulbs pop.

This is only a slight exaggeration of the sort of award occasion that occurs somewhere, every day. If you are the presenter, the more fatuous the occasion, the less deserving the recipient, the bigger the publicity hoped for, the more your sincerity becomes vital – if the occasion is not to deteriorate into sickening slush.

How do you appear sincere, even when you are not? By playing down. By avoiding exaggeration. By excluding melodrama, theatricals, tears in the eyes or choking in the throat. 'I am so moved that I can scarcely speak . . .' Then don't. 'Ms Jones is fabulous, fantastic, magnificent . . .' Superlatives are seldom either sincere or accurate. A few, quiet words of praise are worth paeans of exultation.

The receiver

With luck, you may be at the receiving end of an honour, an award, a presentation or a toast. Praise may be heaped on your receptive shoulders. How do you cope with it?

'I am very grateful to Mr Smith for his most generous obituary,' said Adlai Stevenson.

'There is one difference between a speech of this kind heaping praise on the living, and a funeral oration, extolling the dead,' said Israel's first President, Chaim Weizmann. 'In the former case, but not the latter, there is one listener who is ready to believe in the truth of all that was said.'

More common: 'I would first like to thank Mr Jones for his very kind references to my wife and myself. We are very grateful – and only wish that half of it were true.' Or: 'I am deeply grateful to you, Chairman, for the very generous way in which you have referred to my organisation and to myself. We shall do our best to live up to your high regard.'

Just as it is vital for the maker of the speech of praise to be patently sincere, so the recipient must be clothed in decent modesty. It would be ungracious and insincere to say: 'It's all true . . . you shouldn't have said those things . . .' You could hardly say: 'Every word is an understatement . . .' You may be immodest about your wife: 'All that has been said about my wife is true. I am very proud of her – she's a gem!' But then you must go on: 'I only wish that I could believe the same of the words about myself. Nevertheless, I am most obliged to Ms Smith for having spoken them. Maybe she convinced my wife of their truth, even though she left me in doubt.'

The next stage is to return the compliment by speaking well of the individual or organisation that has had the good sense to honour you. 'I have been very lucky to serve this company over so many years . . . It has been a privilege to work with you all . . . I shall miss you . . . I hope that we shall meet again, very often . . .'

Or: 'Whilst this fraternal organisation has been good enough to make an award to me, I should in fact have been making a presentation to the organisation. The honours are flowing in the wrong direction. I shall try to redress the balance a little by saying why it is that I regard the work of this organisation to be of such enormous significance, especially in the present state of . . .'

Or: 'It was very good of Ms Smith to speak so well of me. As everyone here knows so well, most of the virtues that she was kind enough to attribute to me were in fact her own. This company is fortunate to be led by a woman of her calibre . . .'

Sincerity and the nicely turned compliment should not be the sole prerogative of the giver.

Finally, the conclusion. 'And so my speech – like my time with the company – has drawn to its close. Thank you, Ms Smith, once again for your very kind words. Thank you, my colleagues, for your goodness to me – and for your most generous gift. My wife and I will treasure it always – as we shall the memories of our association with you. Good luck to you all.'

Or: 'And so, in accepting this award, I thank you all for the compliment you have paid to me – and through me to my organisation. My colleagues and I are all happy to have been able to carry out our work – and we undertake to attempt in the future to exceed our past achievements which have caused you to honour us in the present. Our thanks to you all.'

The sentimental anecdotes you have slipped into the body of your speech; the reminiscences, memories, tales with a moral – all of which go down so well in this sort of situation – these are all rounded off with a final word of thanks. End, where you began, with your gratitude. It has been a fine occasion – and an excellent speech.

49 Votes of thanks

The formal vote of thanks to the speaker is a mark of courtesy as necessary as the word of gratitude to the hostess at the end of the evening. You may not have enjoyed your meal. The company may have been excruciatingly dull. Unlike the fabled hostess who was said to have made her guests feel at home even when she fervently wished that they were, Mrs Black may have made you thoroughly ill at ease. You will still thank her as you leave – and no doubt compliment her warmly on the excellence of her cooking and the pleasure you have had in the company of her other, well-chosen guests. Because the compliments are apparently unrehearsed, they may be believed. Anyway, they must be given.

So it is with guest speakers. They must be thanked. In America, it is normal to make handsome payment to those who lecture, even to Rotary Clubs, friendly societies or business or charitable organisations. The guest speakers are given appreciated thanks, in tangible form. In the UK, the audience considers that it is doing the speaker a favour by listening to them!

When your guest says: 'It was very kind of you to invite me to this splendid, peaceful Highland resort', he or she probably means: 'I wish I could have thought of some way to refuse your invitation to trek up to your God-forsaken, Arctic, barren development area slum!' So at least bathe him or her in the warmth of your thanks.

Incidentally, have you remembered to offer to pay your guests' expenses? They would probably be too embarrassed to ask for them and may even refuse your offer. But to beg for and receive the benefit of the time of busy speakers and then to expect them to pay for fares or accommodation is a typically British stupidity. All speakers know the wretchedness of being dragged many miles for a few minutes of speech to a minute audience. That is one of the hazards of the trade. When they do so entirely at their own expense, in money as well as in time, their irritation is understandable.

What, then, of the vote of thanks itself? How do you best put it across?

Sincerity is the key. This rests on a genuine (if possible) and topical (certainly) assessment of the positive and helpful aspects of the visitor's speech. Refer to his or her wit and wisdom . . . to the

121

full and frank way in which they dealt with the subject . . . to the particular interest that you had in that portion of the talk which dealt with . . . Elaborate on a point or two, to show that you have really taken it in – or that *you* have been taken in, as the case may be. Do not use the occasion to launch into a tirade of your own. Your job is to thank. Do it.

A vote of thanks is a mini-speech. The general rules apply, in abbreviated form.

Write out your first sentence and the skeleton of the speech (see Chapter 34 on notes). To have the whole speech written in advance is a travesty. 'We have all been extremely impressed with the wise words of Mr Stout,' the speaker reads from a typed card. 'He gave us a very clear exposition of the subject. We have much to think about as a result.' Terrible – an effort not worth the paper it was written on. Of all the speeches which should never be written out in advance, votes of thanks head the list.

'We are very honoured to have had Ms Slim with us this evening. We realise and appreciate how far she has come. We know and understand the effort that it has cost her. And I know that I am expressing the feelings of everyone here when I tell her how deeply grateful we are to her.' Pause for applause. If you rush on, your audience will not know what is expected of them. There will be a few embarrassed hand-claps and the speaker will not be complimented.

'We listened with great interest to Ms Slim's views on . . . I was especially impressed with the concept of . . . If my own company does not take steps to put this system into effect, it will not be through any lack of enthusiasm on my part, nor any failing on the part of our distinguished speaker. She has paid us the compliment of laying out before us in the clearest terms the essence of the organisational method which she has distilled through years of trial, error and experience.

'The greatest tribute which can be paid to our guest will be through our adoption of her ideas.' All speakers like to feel that they have sown good seed on fertile ground. Treat their words as pearls and they will not think of you as the proverbial swine.

'Perhaps our greatest delight has been in the way in which Ms Slim has succeeded in bringing her somewhat recondite subject to life. She has proved that to tell a tale of . . . need not be dull. She has enlivened our evening with wit and humour.

'And so, in thanking Ms Slim for her good words this evening, I can only hope that we shall have an early opportunity of hearing her again. We wish her every success. Thank you, Ms Slim, very much indeed.'

Thank you, too, for a terse, appropriate, sincere, friendly and well constructed vote of thanks. Just to think that the audience inwardly groaned when you were called upon to speak, worrying in case you were about to make the late hour even later, cause them to miss the last bus or train or lose the services of their aggravated drivers – or, possibly, embarrass them by saying that they really thought about their guests. So they were pleasantly surprised – and are likely to invite you to perform the same service again. Or maybe they knew all the time that you would perform this underrated chore with aplomb, which is why they asked you to do it. In that case, their trust was not misplaced. Thank you, indeed.

50   Brains trusts

Curiously, even prominent people are prepared to take part in so-called 'brains trusts'. The audience gets at least two views for the price of one evening. The speaker – who might otherwise resent the competition and the feeling that the audience really should be satisfied with an evening of him or her – perhaps agrees to participate out of delight at not having to prepare any set speech. Some or all of the speakers are often fooled into accepting because they think that the others on the panel have already done so, or they turn up because they have been asked by someone whom they cannot refuse.

Whatever the circumstances, most speakers have to perform at brains trusts at some time or another. So here are some suggestions.

The organisers should provide each speaker with a pencil and pad. They often fail to do so. You should never arrive at any meeting without pen and paper, least of all for a brains trust.

When a question is asked, jot it down. Alongside it, put your random ideas. If you have none, indicate to the Chair that one of your colleagues should open the batting. Something will come to your mind whilst your colleague answers. If it does not, then say: 'I agree', or 'I'd rather not comment on this one, thank you.'

There are questions that may provoke all sorts of possible answers, none of which you wish to give. Do not be browbeaten into words you may later regret.

Each answer you do give should be a small, neat speech. It should have a beginning, a body and an end. It must be concise; and precisely because it is extempore, you may find it considerably more difficult than the ordinary, set effort. There is an art to brains trusting.

You may have to cope with interruptions from your colleagues or from the chair. Take them in your stride. React to the informality of the occasion. Do not be afraid to break your train of thought – or, if you cannot return to it, say: 'Now, where was I, before Mr Brown's witty intervention?' Someone will remind you.

Conversational informality is the key to a successful brains trust performance. You are performing at a dinner party, with an audience to play up to. Make use of your powers of showmanship.

React to your audience. Fish for applause and laughter. Relax and enjoy yourself and your audience will do the same.

Well-chosen brains trust panels include people with different backgrounds, viewpoints and ideas. Speakers engage in gentle teasing. Jokes against yourself will be appreciated. Smart retorts to points made by other speakers seldom go astray. The tradition is still that of the dinner party and not of the political tub-thump. Aggressive and unfriendly rejoinders, rude or unkind rebuttals, personal remarks to or about other speakers which hurt (whether or not they are calculated to do so) are all to be avoided. The object is to demonstrate your brains, not to tear out those of the other panellists.

51 Conferences and seminars

Business and professional people are often dragooned, shamed or enticed into presenting themselves and their wares at conferences or seminars. To this also there is an art.

Your approach to success depends upon the purpose of the occasion. Is yours, for instance, a promotional exercise, designed to introduce new clients or to stiffen the loyalty of old ones? Do delegates come to learn, from those who are trained and qualified to teach? Either way you are in show business.

There is absolutely no excuse for a dreary conference. However dull the subject, it can be enlivened by visual aids (Chapter 33), relaxed by wit and brought to life by enthusiasm.

Individual speakers should follow the usual rules of good presentation. In particular, they should know and prepare their material, communicate with and according to their audience, and speak with style and demonstrate with skill.

Whether dealing with a small-scale, teaching seminar or a larger assembly or conference, the best presenters will respect their audience. If they wish to return, they will also entertain them.

The fact that so many conferences are dull and disastrous is a denunciation of those who organise and who address them. They not only harm their own cause, but they also spoil the market. They forget that while schoolchildren are tied to their desks and to their classrooms, conference delegates can opt for the bar. Hence the new and musical disease of 'conference syncopation' – staggering from bar to bar!

The presenter's success depends to a vast extent upon the conditions created by the conference or seminar organisers. Check these in advance, preferably before you agree to take part. If, for instance, the room is to be vast and the audience small, the acoustics echoing and the amplification minimal, or the delegates crowded and unhappy and the food inedible, then do not attach your good name to their bad feelings.

Otherwise and in any event, arrive early enough to check your atmosphere and your apparatus, your audience and your audibility.

Pay special regard to the following:

- Is the stage, platform and/or table as you like or need it?
- Stuck as *you* are with the amplification arrangements as *they* are, how can you make the best of them? For instance, will you be able to remove, adjust and/or stroll with the microphone, or is it fixed – and if so, is it at your height or at that of a pygmy or a giraffe?
- Is the overhead projector or other equipment for your visual aids in proper order and position? If you need assistance, perhaps in the showing of slides, is it available?
- If you need arrangements for your comfort and convenience, will you get them? These may range from water for a dry throat, to (in my case) somewhere quiet for a lunchtime nap and battery recharge. The same applies to the provision of pre-meal drinks or intermission tea or coffee.
- If you are to be paid a fee for your presentation, are the arrangements clear, recorded or confirmed in writing and followed through? If these are to any extent on a commission, bonus or other basis that depends upon the success of the event, then how will you find out what you are owed, and will you need to send an account or invoice?
- Should you require smokers to remain at the back or to one side, or do you want to mix the chimneys with the abstainers?
- Always try to fill up seats from the front. If you are not sure whether the room will be filled, can you insist that no one sits in the back rows until front and centre are full?
- Will you avoid interruptions from the clatter of crockery and cutlery, before and after breaks? Separate reception and coffee rooms will help, but thin partitions destroy the best of plans.
- How will you achieve a climax at the end, so that your delegates/audience leave happy?
- If you are to be introduced has the introducer adequate and correct details for the purpose? Who will introduce or sell your products or services? Have you made arrangements for details, samples or goods – or order forms, brochures or other documents – to be properly and prominently displayed?

52   Ceremonial and commercial

With a roll of drums and a fanfare of trumpets, the Chair marches to the centre of the platform. Behind, high on a screen in the darkened room, flash the name and logo of the company. Speaking from invisible notes on the autocue, the executive tells his or her story, proclaims the company's successes, acclaims winners of awards, and presents greetings, salutations and gifts to the worthy.

With every cost lavished, the Chair has become part of a modern spectacular, of an audio-visual experience, professionally produced and royally rendered. If it is properly prepared and well delivered, the speech is the centre of the message. The rest is vivid illustration. If it is delivered in an embarrassed monotone, its deficiencies are exaggerated by their unhappy contrast with the brilliant audio visual effects. Conversely, many an excellent speech has been ruined by inadequate, unsuitable or inappropriate slides, by over-amplification or too obstrusive music, or by visuals that are intended to aid but in fact hinder.

If you must make a major presentation of this kind, then it is not enough to hire in top experts. You must prepare yourself and them, check on all their materials as well as your own, and work for a balance.

As the speechmaker and major presenter, you are both soloist and conductor. In your first role, you must both stand out and be outstanding – which means: neither allow yourself to be cast into darkness nor your words into the background. In the second, you must ensure that your Light and Sound show is co-ordinated, so that the ears and the eyes of your audience combine to transfer your message to their emotions and to their intellects.

You have renounced the simplicity of the simple speech for the complication of the staged production. You are in the world of show business and will need producers, directors, light and sound engineers, machinery and equipment to work in harmony.

Cost apart, this sort of modern speechmaking should either be well prepared and expertly performed, or avoided completely.

For example, a top City financial institution invited clients, actual and potential, to a presentation and dinner. I was one of over a hundred who accepted.

The opening cocktail reception went well. The victims were then duly herded into the dining room and seated at their tables, one host executive at each. The presentation was horrific. We endured a series of speeches, read by the Chair and two of his colleagues, to the background of lush, logoed slides.

Our hosts should have asked four questions:

- Who are my audience?
- Why are they here and what do they want from us?
- What is our message – what do we want to put across to them?
- How do we drive home that message?

They had answered question three. They wanted to show us the size, strength and structure of their set-up – to convince us of its heritage of excellence. They had decided to spread their message orally, by their top people, and visually, by modern techniques. They had answered question one: they knew who we were, and how to attract us. Question two, which is the most important, they had totally forgotten.

After all, why should such a large number of legislators wish to spend an evening with them? We would all enjoy a good meal and most would happily swallow a few drinks. But few of us were totally undernourished or dehydrated.

What we wanted was to tune in on our hosts' view of the economy, their explanation for past events, their vision of the future. We wanted our questions answered, even if they went unasked. Instead, we were served up with a droning monotony of voice, to a background of well-produced irrelevancies. Not one of us cared about their pyramid of management strength, the growth in turnover, the monumental architecture of their new premises.

So the opportunity and the money was wasted. Modern technology destroyed the communication, the presentation and the speeches.

By contrast, I enjoyed a brisk presentation by an hotel company. Drum rolls, fanfare, name and logo, flashes of hotels – all were there, along with a succulent buffet. Both speakers were spotlighted; they spoke well, voices and eyes raised.

The Minister of Tourism spoke briefly and clearly. He presented flags to the hotel managers. The three 'Es' flowed through the event – Energy, Excitement and Enthusiasm.

The combination of classic speechmaking and technological miracles can produce high impact. Misused, it can destroy.

Our City hosts would have done much better to stand on the stage; to ask what questions we wanted answered; then to field them, with skill and authority. Instead, they killed off their occasion. Learn, please, from their mistakes.

53 Postscript – pastimes whilst others speak

Part of the price of the pleasure of hearing your own voice is the need to endure the speeches of others. You may, of course, be lucky. If you are the sole guest speaker you will have only the introduction and vote of thanks to sit through. During the former you will be thinking of your speech and – if you take the advice given in this book to heart – trying to find something in the words of your introducer to quote, adapt or answer, and so establish a rapport with your audience. During the vote of thanks, you must simply try to believe that the words spoken of you are true. You need exhibit no false modesty to yourself.

Inevitably unlucky is the after-dinner speaker, no matter what his or her place in the toast list. The Chair of a committee may be able to regulate the speeches of others, but the rest must put up with them. If you happen to be a Member of Parliament, you may be able to escape from the function after you have spoken, perhaps blessed with a three-line whip. ('Mr Jones must now return to his Parliamentary duties. We appreciate all the more that he has spared some of his most valuable times to be with us.') Heaven help anyone else who leaves before the other speeches are complete.

So the art of enjoyable listening is worth careful cultivation.

In private, the good listener is generally credited with fine powers of perception, intelligence and even eloquence. In public, to fall asleep whilst others speak is the height of bad manners. How to avoid it?

Every practised speaker is a skilled doodler. One handwriting expert is alleged to make his living largely by interpreting the doodles of the famous. Much more constructive is the writing of those neglected letters.

The dinner is dull? Too bad. You must try to get your neighbours to talk about their speciality and you may find that they are more interesting than you had realised. The after-dinner speeches are a misery? Then use the back of the menu, toast list, guest list or brochure. Take out your pen and write your correspondence. Look up every now and again at the speaker. No one – least of all the

speaker – will suspect that you are doing anything other than paying them the compliment of noting their words. My relatives in Australia always know when I have been cursed with dull speeches to hear. They receive missives on agendas, minutes, jotting-pads . . . anything that happens to be handy.

Of course, you could instead be jotting down notes for the current work which you have in hand. In the unlikely event of the speaker sparking off a constructive chain of thought, make a note of the idea before it flees for ever. If you hear a good story, write it down. If all else fails, and you can fight off slumber no longer, then you must do your best to organise your forty winks so as to attract the least possible suspicion.

An acquaintance has, through long years of experience, learned how to sleep whilst sitting bolt upright and with his eyes open. Most of us must be content with the head rested on the hand, the elbow on the table. Alternatively, the head droops forward and the notes, brochure or agenda are in front of you so that it may (with luck) appear that you are reading – or at least engaged in deep thought.

Speakers should learn to amuse themselves during the unamusing speeches of others, without any appearance of flagging attention or lagging concentration. Spare a thought for diplomats and the royals, who must do it all the time.

54   Radio – the sightless wonder

Ask any experienced radio producer or interviewer which are the best and the worst categories of performer. Odds on the answer will be the same. The best? Professionals, like most actors or politicians – especially politicians, because they are skilled at making up their own scripts as they go along. The worst? Executives – industrialists and business people. Believing that their success in commerce qualifies them for harnessing sound without sight, they mumble, ramble and prevaricate and make the worst of themselves and their case.

So if *you* must make a radio appearance, how can you avoid joining the ranks of the awful? I offer a concise victim's guide.

Start by arriving on time. If you are late, you will either miss the show or never be asked back.

The ultimate in reporters' lateness provided me with one of my few and cherished chances to enter the *Guinness Book of Records*. I had arrived my customary few minutes early for a local radio recording session. The reporter was late. After half an hour of waiting, I made my revolutionary proposal to the man in charge: 'Let me interview myself!' I suggested. I promised to ask myself only the nastiest and most probing questions. 'You can dub in the reporter's voice when he turns up!' To my delight, he agreed.

I carried out the interview with immaculate courtesy, but dug away at my own weak points, being sure of course to supply succinct and appropriate answers. When the interviewer turned up, with the judicious use of the razor blade he duly dubbed his voice into the questions.

Next, approach radio with a touch of paranoia. Whether you are asked questions by telephone ('down the line') or in the studio, unless you are certain that your words will not be broadcast, take care.

President Reagan was to make a crucial 'state of the nation' broadcast. The producer said to him: 'Now, Mr President, please will you say something so that we can have some sound level. Tell us what you think about our United States economy?'

'I must tell the nation,' said the President, 'that our economy is in one hell of a mess!' Unfortunately for him, the studio had already been linked up to loudspeakers in the White House and Press Room. Despite the frantic efforts of the President's advisers, his words were beamed around the world, to the huge delight of all those who take pleasure in someone else's awful mistake.

So concentrate. Ignore the interviewer sipping coffee, news flashes on a monitor screen, people through the glass in the control room, or busy 'cutting' tapes in the next studio. Allow your mind to move off your subject and you invite disaster.

The best help to concentration is posture. Sit up.

If your piece is recorded, do not worry if you 'fluff'. 'Sorry,' you say. 'I'll repeat that.' Then do – and leave it to the interviewer or editor to slice out your initial and muddled effort. They will not hold that against you. They have too many miseries of their own to correct and they are professionals.

Do not be bullied. A good interviewer asks questions and lets the victim get on with answering them. If you do not get fairness, complain. If you need time to think out the answer to a question, ask to have it repeated. If you cannot properly reply, say so.

Sincerity is vital. Only your voice can convey it. Be concise and relevant. Answer the questions you are asked – briefly, accurately and to the questioner's point.

Brighten your broadcast with stories and analogies. Talk to the interviewer as though you were engaging in ordinary chat with no one listening. Concentrate on him or her and forget your audience.

Take care what you wear, for the sound it may make. Radio broadcasters are heard and not seen. A young woman deafened listeners with a crackling roar, every time she breathed. A particularly sensitive directional mike picked up and magnified the sound of her new underwear rustling!

Avoid noisy bangles, beads or leather jackets. Do not click ballpoint pens or fiddle with paper clips. Above all, avoid the rattle of paper. If you work from a script on separate sheets, do not turn them over. Lift each gingerly and silently from the pile.

Avoid drinking too much 'hospitality coffee' before committing yourself on air for any length of time. Mother Nature has often destroyed the best of discussions. Keep off alcohol. Many careers have been ruined by that most hazardous marriage of broadcast and booze.

Nothing is more daunting in prospect, more challenging in reality or more lasting in memory than a broadcast confrontation. If your interviewer gets nasty, keep cool. You lose control of yourself and of your audience at the same moment. Lose command of yourself and you cannot command the argument.

If they want to turn you into a human sacrifice, don your armour. If they wish to make a meal of you, ensure that you are thoroughly indigestible.

Remember, an interviewer's job is to produce good radio. So if you suspect trouble, try threatening to 'dry' if your interrogator is unfair.

If you are faced with guest opponents, battle for your fair share of precious time. And always try to commandeer the ending.

After a particularly bloody radio confrontation, a supporter of mine said: 'You did well – but not well enough. How *could* you let that (*expletive*) get the last word?'

So be courteous and firm. Find out in advance how long your piece will last. Is it to be pre-recorded, in which case your 'fluffs' can be removed but also your best arguments edited out? Or will you go out 'live', so that your errors cannot be erased?

If offered an invitation to speak ill of some other person, as opposed to criticising their opinions, remember that broadcast defamation is libel. Keep awake and take care.

Finally, make sure you are off the air before you relax and speak your mind. Many a good broadcast and the reputation of its maker have been ruined at this injudicious moment. As 'Uncle Mac' once said at the end of *Children's Hour*: 'Well that will hold the little bastards for another day . . .'! At least your livelihood does not depend on your radio excellence – so relax, follow the rules and pray for good luck. You'll need it!

55   TV – your head on the box

Television is every other sort of presentation writ large. It is the ultimate challenge for the speechmaker or other presenter, with (in general) a maximum audience for exploitation and error alike. Add the dimension of sight to sound and errors pile high.

Every TV second counts and must be cherished. Compare the cost of buying, say, a 10-second 'plug' on commercial radio as opposed to the same moment on TV. The higher cost of television reflects its potential power and impact.

Every peril in radio presentation is concentrated, condensed and made visible. Politicians and business people alike are made and broken by the oblong screen. So if you are given the chance to project yourself, your company or cause on the box, here is a victim's guide.

- Keep calm. Arrive early; check the venue; and if your stomach heaves, remember that adrenalin sharpens the mind.
- Prop up your nerves with alcohol and you invite disaster with the same certainty as the drinking driver. So eat well but drink little.
- The make-up person will take charge of your face, but you should adjust your own dress. Remember that the box magnifies the most minor blemishes. Tie askew; white label sticking up from the back of dark jacket; dandruff on the shoulders; dangling shirt tail, drooping socks, laddered tights . . . If you must look slovenly, do it at home.
- Dress in clothes suitable to the image you wish to present and in colours and patterns that do not move, shimmer or 'strobe' on the screen. Checks or narrow stripes on jackets or (especially) dresses, suits or ties are major culprits. Avoid 'flashy' jewellery, in either sense of the word. Best colours are pastel shades; worst, black and white.

Your face may be your fortune, but put it on television and it emerges transformed – probably much for the worse. So relax and hope for the best – and follow some basic rules.

- Fix your gaze on the interviewer or at your fellow gladiator, thrown into the same ring for the pleasure of the public. Eye expression is crucial for contact, confidence and conveying sincerity.
     Victims who surreptitiously swivel their eyes – perhaps for a glimpse of

136

the audience or the clock, or a peep at the monitor screen – are done for. Immediately by chance or by malicious design, the camera switches to them and they look shifty, cunning, wicked . . .

If you are to be interviewed in a separate place or studio from your interviewer, ask for an 'eye-line'. Find out where to look so that you appear to be fixing your eyes in line with your interrogator.

- Keep gestures to the minimum. The rarer and the more sparing, the greater the effect. Watch amateurs on the screen – the unconscious scratchers, twitchers, lip-lickers and nose-pickers, the finger-waggers, arm-wavers and (even more disastrous) pounders of fists and strummers of fingers.

Sit up. Animation should come from your face, eyes and speech, and not from your body.

- Treat your interviewers with kindness and – as they are probably human – they may return the compliment. As a distinguished colleague told me when he was about to face a particularly notorious interviewer: 'The key words for him are *re*spect and *sus*pect!'
- Smoking will probably be forbidden in the studio and is in any event inadvisable on the screen.
- At the start of the interview do not smirk. Instead, stare straight ahead.
- Then keep still. A distinguished cleric who is a most relaxed and brilliant TV performer once reached down into his briefcase, nestling against his leg, with such speed that he went totally off screen – to the huge delight of his friendly viewers but to the misery of the studio.

Intelligent cameras flash on and off, red lights blinking – when the light is on, so is the camera and so are you.

- If you read from a prepared script, you will be helped by an autocue. Be not afraid. It is controlled by the performer and the operator will go at your speed.
- Do not look at the clock. The studio manager – probably the person who led you to your seat – will stand within view of the interviewer and relay time signals.

The time to dive in with your capture-the-last-word summary is when the 'come to a close' hand windmill signal starts. If it means interrupting someone else – courteously but firmly – go ahead.

To succeed on the screen, you must project your personality, radiating relaxation without relaxing, confidence without appearing smug or superior and sincerity without gush: the same qualities, in fact, that apply to personal presentations, but with far greater tact.

So how do you achieve these evidently desirable aims? Take training. Watch yourself on a video screen. Get as much practice as the media will allow you.

You cannot practise for an interview, but you can follow the crucial rules. Listen to the question; have it repeated if you do not understand – or if you want extra time to think; then reply to that question, not to some other one that you would have preferred to hear.

A Cabinet Minister was lost while driving through the countryside. He stopped at a village and wound down his window. 'Where am I, please?' he asked a passer-by.

'You are in your car, sir', he replied, unhesitatingly.

'That,' replied the Minister 'is a perfect Parliamentary answer. It is brief, accurate – and adds nothing whatever to the sum total of human knowledge!'

So try to add a touch of information, a spice of wit or a modicum of common sense or your TV presentation is hardly likely to sparkle. But do so by way of addition or rider. 'The answer to your question is . . . But perhaps we could ask a different question?' Or: 'The answer is yes – but please remember that . . .' First answer, then add.

In a confrontation or debate keep calm. Do not underestimate your opponent. If you are defeated, then announce that you will fight back. Or flick away the defeat like a fly from your shoulder, hoping that it does not matter.

If interrupted say: 'May I finish my sentence, please . . .'; or 'If you don't mind, I'll just finish this point then give way . . .' Then wrap up your argument as swiftly as you can.

Above all, concentrate. Forget the hundreds of thousands of viewers. A moment's distraction may spell disaster. Lose concentraton and you lose all.

Follow instructions, and if you mess up your performance then at least it may be someone else's faulty!

The joy of television is that everyone both hears and sees you and trouble can only be a fraction of an error away,

PART 6

The Chair

56   The Chair as compère

When you chair a meeting – any meeting – you set the tone. If you are dull, the meeting will be boring. If you are in a lively or contented mood, the meeting will be of good cheer. If you are long-winded, members of the audience not bound to stay will disappear. If you are angry, aggravated, tactless or unkind, this will soon be reflected in the atmosphere. Not for one moment dare you be off your guard. You are the compère, the life and soul of the gathering – or its death and decay.

Consider the ordinary variety programme. The compère is the link holding the show together. The same applies to anyone in the chair.

To keep a meeting in good humour, here are some suggestions.

- Do not allow yourself to get aggravated. The more difficult the gathering, the more important it is for you to keep your self-control and your pleasant manner.
- Set the tone before the meeting begins. Try to do your colleagues or your audience the compliment of arriving on time. Spare a few minutes before hand, if you can, to iron out difficulties and to prevent personal affronts.
- If the meeting is a small one, try not to ignore people who come in late. 'Good evening. Thank you for coming': worthwhile words to make a guilty latecomer feel at ease – and obliged to you.
- There is no need to take too literally the old warning: 'Stand up, speak up and shut up.' But do try to let others do as much of the talking as you can. Time them beforehand, if possible. Introduce them, invite them to speak, ask what they think. Link the speakers together and provide the channel through which they communicate. But as for yourself – talk only when you must.
- Let your audience feel that they have had their say. Do your best to allow time for adequate questions.
- Cajole your speakers into brevity and into agreeing to answer questions at the end. The audience that has its questions answered is almost always satisfied.
- Where the session is a small one – a committee or board meeting, for instance – the same principle is even more vital. Let the others put their views before the gathering. Try not to choke off discussion before it comes to an end. Wait until you get the feeling of the meeting that the time has come for the particular debate or argument to be wound up.

141

- Let everyone feel that their presence is appreciated. One way is by saying so: 'We are delighted to have you all with us.' When the meeting is small enough, make sure that everyone has said something. 'What are your views about this?' The quiet person may have more valuable advice to give than the garrulous soul who monopolises the discussion. The timid participant may be more expert than the exhibitionist. If talent is available, make sure it gets used.
- Do not be afraid to season the proceedings with laughter. A few moments spent on a friendly joke may be more worthwhile than ten times as long devoted to argument. Try to avoid the unkind cut. Round the meeting off with appropriate words of thanks – and set the atmosphere right for the next time.

Most of these suggestions could be grouped under one word: tact. You are running the meeting. But (except in case of disorder) you should try not to let it be too obvious. The horse knows when it is mounted by a skilled rider who does not have to keep tugging at the reins or hurting the animal's mouth. The best leaders give their followers the maximum feeling that they (the followers) are running their own show. The top compères keep the programme going and ensure that everyone stays contented and awake. The finest Chairs are those who rule through good humour, quiet tact and gentle persuasion.

57   Controlling the audience

Whether you are dealing with a committee of three or a crowd of 3,000, when you are in the chair you must be in control. Except for those who have arrived with the intention of breaking up the proceedings, your audience have given up their time for a constructive purpose. They may wish to advance the company's business and hence their own prospects. They may be seeking knowledge or entertainment. They may wish to extend the work of their trade or charity. Whatever the reason, they wish the business of the meeting to be done. Then they will want to get back to their offices or, at the end of the day and with even more fervour, to their homes. Those who control the audience and hence the business of the meeting from the chair are much appreciated.

So do not be afraid to put your foot down (metaphorically) or (literally) to tap with the gavel. You were elected or appointed Chair to keep order. Do so and you will have the meeting on your side.

Do not shout. A firm 'Order please, Ladies and Gentlemen'; 'Will you please give Ms Black a fair hearing'; or 'I must insist on quiet for our speaker, please' – these are courteous and successful gambits. Occasionally, you might need: 'I'm afraid that if those who are attempting to break up the meeting will not desist, I shall have to ask the stewards to have them evicted.' Much more common is the 'Thank you, Ladies and Gentlemen', addressed to those of your colleagues whom you hope to thank for their future silence.

You must know precisely what you are doing. You must understand the basic rules of procedure. If you do make a mistake, then you have two alternatives, and one or other must be grasped as firmly as possible. Either you stand by your error or you smile and apologise.

Alternatively: 'It is clear that the meeting would, in fact, like to discuss the matter. So be it.' Or: 'You are quite right., Mr Jones. I should have allowed the discussion to go further. Please do carry on.' A graceful retreat. You are being decisive even about your indecision.

Still, it is 'the sense of the meeting' that usually matters. You

143

must be able to judge what people want. You must employ tact so as not to override the wishes of those who have seen fit to put you in charge of their proceedings. Whilst not pandering to the inevitable mischief-maker – that abrasive irritant and aggravating nuisance which nearly every organisation, body or community seems to contain – you must nevertheless give even such persons (who may be right on occasion and who have a certain acid usefulness) the opportunity to let off steam. When the meeting has had enough of them, you will know. So will the aggravators. Sense your meeting – and run it. That is your job in the Chair.

To some extent, speakers can and must control their own audience. They must command attention. They must know how to deal with their own hecklers. If necessary, they must be prepared to tongue-lash those who will not heed their words. But if speakers fail, the Chair must step in. It is part of your task from the chair to ensure that the speaker gets a hearing.

Once again, in most cases, a smart rap with the gavel and a command of 'Order' should suffice. If you have no gavel, a smart rap on the table with a coin, pen-knife or lighter will probably do the trick. It is also both more effective and more dignified than a pounding of the fist, which may, in any event, prove painful.

If disorder breaks out, you must know precisely how to handle it. The main rule, of course, is to handle yourself with restraint, calm and dignity. You must never lose your head, or you will have failed. With luck, you will have the secretary sitting beside you, to guide you on procedures, but knowing the rules in advance breeds the confidence you need. The secretary should know them, too. So here they are.

58   Debates and procedure

If you take the chair you must study the rules of debate. Your duty is to enforce them. Speakers must know the rules, either to follow them or to attempt to evade them.

When you are in the chair your are in charge. You have been elected or appointed to your position and you are expected to guide and control the meeting.

When you stand, everyone else is expected to sit and to be silent. If you cannot obtain order by rapping your gavel and demanding silence, you may have to adjourn the meeting. Unless the meeting is closed, your are entitled to speak whenever you wish – and to prevent anyone else from doing so unless you wish. You decide the order of speeches. You will have the agenda but you may vary it.

You should rule by consent. For instance, if you decide to change the order of business, you should explain your reasons. If the bulk of the meeting objects to the change, then you should revert to the original order. You are not a dictator. If you forget this you can expect rebellion.

Normally, each item of business should be discussed separately. If there are steps to be taken – or even if it is to be resolved that there be no action on the matter – a resolution or motion will be 'put'. This can be done informally, where there is either no opposition or a general consensus. If after discussion has taken place there is no agreement, there should be a vote.

Where the formalities are being preserved, a motion will be proposed and seconded. It will then be thrown open to the meeting for discussion – and the Chair will attempt to call on someone to oppose the motion. After the matter has been sufficiently ventilated, the proposer will normally exercise the right of reply. Then a vote may have to be taken.

If the motion or resolution is not on the agenda, the proposer should be asked to phrase it as concisely and clearly as possible. The Chair who has to put a resolution which even the proposer has not put into sensible English (and into words that can be put into the minute book) is in a bad way. The motion should be clearly stated either by the proposer or by the Chair before it goes forward for debate.

The length and number of speeches will depend on the Chair. But anyone may 'move the closure'. A show of hands will indicate whether those present have had enough of the subject or whether they wish to debate the matter further. If the Chair is in doubt as to whether or not the debate should be closed – or if it would appear partisan to terminate it – then it is easy to test the feeling of the meeting, if necessary by asking whether anyone wishes 'to move the closure'.

If it is agreed that the question 'be now put' – then that is what happens. The motion is voted upon.

If a motion is carried that the meeting move on to 'next business', then no vote is taken on the motion. It is often better not to reveal the split in the ranks. Or all sides may prefer to avoid a vote that no one is really confident of winning.

Some organisations allow the moving of 'the previous question'. The effect of this being passed is that the discussion on the current topic terminates and all reference to it is expunged from the minutes. No vote is, of course, taken on the matter in question. There are times when people feel that it would have been better for the organisation or meeting had the discussion not taken place at all. 'The previous question' is a useful procedure.

Again, someone may move that the entire meeting be adjourned. It is not only the Chair who can terminate the proceedings. If those present at the meeting wish to put an end to it, they may normally do so. But, of course, there may be debate 'on the adjournment'.

While a debate goes on, there may be interruptions. One common device is a 'point of order'. Anyone is entitled to raise any point concerning the order of the meeting, at any time. In theory, a participant is only free to query whether the procedure in hand, what the speaker is saying, or the Chair's ruling . . . is 'in order'. No one should stray away to deal with side issues or use the occasion to deal with substantive issues. Skilled interrupters, though, can often disguise their disruptive attacks as 'points of order', and so insinuate extra speeches where none would otherwise be allowed.

In some meetings, the custom is for speakers to give way on 'points of information' – but generally, it is a matter for them (the speakers themselves) to decide. The Chair cannot force them to give way, or take any step if they decline to do so. But if the Chair addresses the speaker, the latter may remain standing but (like anyone else at the meeting) must accord the Chair the right to speak – and while he or she does so, must remain silent.

The speaker, then, must 'obey the Chair's ruling'. No one who 'has the floor' may occupy it in the teeth of objection from the Chair.

If all motions were proposed, seconded, opposed and voted upon as they stood, the job of the Chair would be moderately easy. Too often there are amendments to be considered. In general, motions to amend a resolution must (if seconded) be allowed. They should be considered individually and voted upon if necessary. If accepted (whether or not after a vote) they become incorporated into the original motion, which must then be put, as amended. If rejected, they die. An amended motion, once put, can then be the subject of further amendment, with the procedure as before.

Often a skilled Chair can induce the mover of a resolution to vary or extend its terms so as to incorporate the amendment. A peaceful meeting is a Chair's delight.

If an amendment is really no more than an effort to kill the resolution, the Chair may rule it out of order and require the proposer of the amendment to put forward his or her views in opposition to the substantive motion.

The Chair must ensure that everyone is given a reasonable opportunity to express their views, but should not allow a minority to dominate. The Chair is entitled not only to select the speakers but also to sort out the resolution and the amendments, so that the feelings of the meeting may be tested in the fairest way.

Once the meeting has had a reasonable opportunity to express its view, the Chair may – with the consent of the meeting – close the debate and put the motion to the vote.

Some additional points:

- Unless a Company's Articles (or the constitution of the organisation in question) require motions to be seconded and/or submitted in writing, neither is strictly necessary.
- No one has any right to speak more than once on any motion or amendment – although the proposer of an original motion (but not usually of an amendment) will generally be given the right to reply.
- Once a motion has been defeated, it should not be allowed back before the meeting under some other guise.
- No amendment can be proposed after the original motion has been passed or rejected.
- An amendment cannot be proposed or seconded by those who

performed that service for the original motion; but they can, of course, accept (or speak on) the amendments proposed by others.

• If you wish to frame an amendment, usually the best way to do so is by moving that the words you have in mind be added to, omitted from, or inserted into (as the case may be) the motion of resolution.

Meetings are usually governed by consent and common sense. Keep your head and never panic. Speakers should help you, unless you have shown yourself unwilling to act impartially. In that case, the battle is on.

59   The company chairman

Some of the duties of a Chairman* are prescribed by law. In the United Kingdom, company Chairmen should be referred to the Companies Act, 1948, in particular to Sections 58, 134 and 141. More importantly, they should read with care the Company's own Articles of Association, which lay down most of their powers and duties in the conduct of the meetings of the organisation concerned.

In so far as the law and the Articles are silent, the meeting may itself decide on its own conduct. As Lord Russell pronounced in 1937:

> 'There are many matters relating to the conduct of a meeting which lie entirely in the hands of those people who are present and constitute the meeting . . . It rests with the meeting to decide whether accounts, resolutions, minutes or notices and such like shall be read to the meeting or be taken as read; and when discussion shall be terminated and a vote taken; whether representatives of the Press, or any other persons not qualified to be summoned to the meeting, shall be permitted to be present, or if present, shall be permitted to remain; and whether the meeting shall be adjourned. In all these matters, and they are only instances, the meeting decides, and if necessary a vote must be taken to ascertain the wishes of the majority. If no objection is taken by any constituent of the meeting, the meeting must be taken to be assenting to the course adopted.'

In practice, if you can keep the meeting with you, you win. If you lose its support, you fail.

So what of people who come to break up your meeting? From the chair, you have the right to order their removal; or you may adjourn the meeting until 'the disorderly element' has gone.

At a company meeting, you need an experienced company secretary at your side. At any other, seek a wise and experienced colleague to advise on points of order and procedure.

---

* I have tried in this book to use terminology equally applicable to men and to women. However, 'chairman' is used throughout business law. I have therefore adopted this usage.

60   Introducing the guest

However well you know the person you are about to introduce, have his or her name written clearly down in front of you. The chances of your mind going blank are remote. But it happens. The most famous occasion? During the 1970 UK General Election when a local Conservative party chairperson was introducing Mr Edward Heath: 'In the short time since our guest of honour has become leader of the party,' she thundered, 'his name has become a household word. I am proud, honoured and delighted to introduce to you our next Prime Mnister, Mr . . . er . . . er . . . er . . .' Calamity!

Or: 'The name of our guest is a household word in the trade. Ladies and Gentlemen, Mr er . . . er . . . er . . .'

Or: 'Our guest needs no introduction . . . without further ado, I am pleased to introduce to you Sir Robert . . . er . . . er . . . er . . .'

My son Daniel once introduced an unknown and undistinguished MP to the Cambridge Union thus: 'Mr Smith's name is a household word – in his own household!'

The harm done by forgetting a name cannot be undone. It may be the result of inadequate preparation. Those abysmal words 'our guest needs no introduction' generally mean that the introducer has not bothered to find out anything about the speaker. Let your secretary dip into *Who's Who*, *The Wine Producers' Year Book*, *The International Dictionary of Great Millionaires*, or whatever the appropriate reference book happens to be.

Alternatively, get someone to phone up your guest's assistant or secretary or manager and get details. Even better, hunt around for a personal and friendly anecdote. The less it appears that you had to do research the better, but the more research you do, the more effective your introduction is likely to be.

If the speaker arrives and you have no information about him or her do not despair. Speakers appreciate being asked. Take your guest on one side and say quietly, with your pencil in hand: 'I am to have the pleasure of introducing you to our audience. Which of your many offices would you like me to mention? How would you like to be introduced?'

Every speaker has foibles. He may not want you to say that he is an ex-president of the Undertakers' Society – he may have been defeated in a recent and bitter election contest. She may prefer to forget that she was the author of a book that resulted in a libel action. On the other hand, he or she may especially wish you to remind the audience that they are an ex-president of the Oxford Union . . . former secretary to James Director . . . a champion golfer, as well as a prominent industrialist or trade union leader.

Or suppose that you are introducing a woman who has really fought her way up the ladder. Maybe she would like you to refer to her humble origins. Or perhaps she would rather repress them. Unless someone has given you the tip off, you cannot know.

At a recent dinner, a famous, generous and charitable businessman was introduced to his audience as the man who 'not only conceived the idea of the . . . School, but had personally raised the very large sum needed to establish it.' Unfortunately, the Chair had omitted to check on how the school was going. Had he done so, he would have discovered that there were only eight applicants for the 120 places and that the entire venture was a flop which the guest of honour was not anxious to recall.

The mixture of embarrased silence and delighted laughter that greeted this *faux pas* reflected in no way upon the affection which the audience had for the gentleman concerned, whom everyone knew to be a first-class man. But it made the audience feel sorry for him – and for the Chair. The fact that the Chair was another voluntary worker in good causes and a popular man of business in no way excused an error that could so easily have been avoided.

If you are too busy to prepare your introduction, get someone else to do it (either the preparation or, if necessary, the introduction itself) for you. There is no law to prevent the Chair from saying: 'I shall now ask his ex-mentor/disciple/managing director (*or as the case may be*) to introduce our guest to you.' It does not happen very often – which makes it all the more delightful when it does.

So speak of your guests' known achievements. By all means couple this with friendly or flattering references to their firm or forebears. Avoid:

'We are very pleased to have Mr Jackson with us tonight. His father is a very famous figure in the industry and we know that, in listening to his son, we shall have a treat awaiting us . . .'

Little better is: 'Mr Bloggs is the distinguished son of famous parents . . .'

Much worse (but often committed in practice):

'Lord Bloggs is unfortunately unable to be with us tonight. But we are pleased that Lady Bloggs has consented to speak to us. Without further ado, I introduce Lady Bloggs.'

Lord and Lady Bloggs could have been complimented on their splendid and happy partnership. But the disappointment at the absence of the original guest must not be made apparent. Anyway, has Lady Bloggs herself nothing to commend her other than her good taste in husbands? The Honourable James Bloggs inherited his courtesy title, but surely he has done something with his life which the Chair should explain? The guests will be curious to hear something of the background of their speaker. Heredity is not all.

Try this: 'Ours is an industry which is proud of its family connections. Many of us are old colleagues and friends of William Harness. We have been delighted to see the active part taken by his son, Roger, in our great charity. Naturally, we honour him because he is the son of our old and distinguished friend. But he is invited to speak to us tonight in his own right. His achievements are many. He is . . . He was . . . And we are confident that he will be a leader in our industry for many years to come. Ladies and Gentlemen, Mr Roger Harness . . .'

Or: 'Tonight, we are honoured by Lady Bloggs. It is true that her husband was to have addressed us. I will not repeat the gaffe of the chairman who once introduced the wife in circumstances such as these by saying: "Sir William's misfortune in being ill is our good luck. We are indeed happy to welcome his wife in his place." We are delighted that the reason for Lord Bloggs' absence is that he is busy selling his goods in the USA and hence keeping up his company's magnificent export record. We are fortunate that he has been good enough to leave his wife behind in England – and to entrust her to our company this evening. She is . . .'

If (as so often happens) the speaker is a last-minute substitute, do not apologise for the fact. 'We were to have had Mr Hodge to speak to us, but he has let us down at the last minute. We are grateful to Mr Black, his assistant, for stepping into the breach. Ladies and Gentlemen, Mr Black.' There are two decent alternatives. Ignore altogether the fact that Mr Hodge has let you down. Everyone will know it. The word will have gone around; and it may be much less embarrassing if nothing is said. Alternatively, make a virtue out of necessity.

Thus: 'Ladies and Gentlemen. I know that you will all have been very sorry to have heard that our proposed guest, Mr Arthur Hodge, has been struck down by the flu. But equally, you will be pleased to learn that he is making a good recovery. He sends his greetings to us all – I have a telegram from him here.' (That was intelligent of Mr Hodge, incidentally.) 'It wishes us every good fortune. And I know that you will want me to reply, on behalf of us all, wishing him the most speedy recovery.

'I cannot tell Mr Black how grateful we are to him for having agreed to come to us at such very short notice. His readiness to speak today is just one indication of his loyalty to our organisation, and another reason why he has earned the affection of all his colleagues . . . He is . . . He was . . . He will be . . .'

Or: 'Our good friend and proposed guest, Mr Arthur Hodge, has, alas, been called abroad on urgent business. We know that he would never have let us down had there been any possible alternative. We wish him success in his venture – may he bring home the bacon – or, to be more precise, may he have every success in exporting his prize pigs. And we are very much obliged to him for having on our behalf asked Mr Robert Rook to address us in his place.

'Mr Rook is already well known to us. He is . . . He was . . . He will be . . . We know the pressure of work on Mr Rook and we are extremely grateful to him for honouring us by joining us this evening. Ladies and Gentlemen, Mr Rook . . .'

There are, of course, occasions when the speaker should not be introduced. For instance: 'I shall ask our chairman, Edward Smith, to propose the loyal toast.'

Or: 'Thank you, Mr Hodge. I am pleased to ask our treasurer, Richard Bright, to propose the vote of thanks.'

From the chair you set the tone and call the tune. You have many important duties, one of the most vital of which is the introduction of the speakers. Treat this job seriously. Apply the same rules to brief speeches of introduction as you would to longer efforts. An introduction needs a beginning, a body, and an end. The opening and closing sentences matter. Careful preparation (which, as usual, must be as unobtrusive as possible when the speech is actually made) is important. A bad introduction can ruin a good speech – and a potentially fine meeting.

61 · Handling the speaker

No area of the duties of the Chair is so potentially hazardous as handling the guest speaker. Here are a few hints:

- If you are not sure how your guest pronounces his or her name, ask. If it is to be put in a programme, toast list, brochure or other document, check the spelling. People are very sensitive about their names.
- Find out in advance as much as you can about the speaker. Members of the royal family are renowned for their splendid memories. They come into a room and promptly recognise people and even remember where they last met. This is partly because they are blessed with good memories, but mainly because they do their homework. The best way to flatter your speakers is to remember all about them. The surest way to antagonise them is to be indifferent to them and to their past achievements.
- If they have incurred expenses, remember to ask them to let you know.
- Remember to say thank you – and to write and repeat your thanks afterwards. You can never express gratitude too often.
- While trying to ensure that the speaker gets a fair hearing, be careful not to interrupt too often. Competent speakers can handle their own audiences and prefer, where possible, to do so. The Chair should exercise authority with moderation.
- Prime speakers on the length of time you want them to speak, and ask them whether they would like to be reminded when they are a few minutes away from the appointed end. Most speakers will gladly agree, and will not then resent a reminder. If necessary, push a note in front of the speaker, with '5 minutes please', in large letters. Do this without pre-arrangement and you may upset them.

Much of the Chair's job is done before the meeting actually begins. If you read this book beforehand, you should do better at the time. Otherwise, bring it with you.

So all that remains is to wish you – in the role of speaker or in the Chair – the very best of luck. However experienced and able you may be, however carefully you follow the rules I have given, whatever the occasion, there is no substitute for good fortune. May you be blessed with luck, skill and success on your feet!

BOOK 2

Draft Speeches

PART 7

Model speeches for various occasions

62   Openings

Prominent people are frequently invited to declare functions or occasions open – from trade exhibitions or fairs to sales conferences, from new premises to the same old annual garden fête run by the local church or by the trade benevolent society.

The opening pronouncement may be one of two varieties, which must be carefully distinguished from each other – the formal opening and keynote speech. Either way, you may be asked to speak because of your eminence; because of past usefulness or benevolence; in hope of future service or cash; or because of a mixture of all of them. If you want to be asked again, though, you must do a good job this time.

The following are examples of brief openers, plus skeletons of key-note speeches. By their nature, these presentations are expected to be longer and fuller, and likely to provoke thought or action rather than an atmosphere of generalised goodwill.

Opening a trade fair

Ladies and Gentlemen,

Some ancient peoples had disgusting habits – like examining the entrails of animals to see whether the auguries were satisfactory for some proposed enterprise. I have taken a much shorter and pleasanter route – to the greater oracle of this organisation, Mr . . . He tells me that the preparations for today's gathering have been carried out swiftly, in harmony and without a whiff of industrial ill-will; that advance orders already total half as much again as those received at this stage last year; that we are expecting one of the biggest gatherings in the history of the trade.

What a delight it is, then, for me to sound the tocsin and to proclaim in advance the value, the importance and the success of this year's vital exhibition.

On your behalf as well as my own, I thank our organisers, Mr . . . and Mrs . . . and Miss . . ., as well as . . . and their staff. If the arrangements look smooth and simple, it is because the organisers have worked so hard.

Now – in anticipation of good companionship, top sales and a continuation and ending to the fair which will be as successful as its inception – I have the greatest pleasure in declaring the fair – open.

Opening an industrial exhibition

Madam Chairman*, Ladies and Gentlemen,

We are not as wasteful in this industry as our colleagues who build ships. We will not smash and spill good champagne on the side of our machines (*or furniture or equipment – or as the case may be*). Instead, we will use the wine to drink a series of toasts.

First, we salute the prosperity of our trade/industry/company. Today's effort is of vast importance to it and so to us all.

Second, we salute the health of those whose efforts have created this exhibition – from our chairman/chief executive/organiser (*etc.*) at the top of our trees, to the carpenter, the electricians and the cleaners who have firmed down its roots. Our warmest thanks to them all.

Third, we salute the future of our great new product, the . . . (*here give details*).

This is an exhibition of machinery/equipment/furniture (*or as the case may be*). It is designed to exhibit products – and to help design exhibits. Its success depends on orders and cheques, not on words – however warm or well meant.

Symbolically only, then, I am proud to launch this exhibition. By its end, I hope that at dinner tonight we shall drink a toast to the beginning of a new era of prosperity for our trade/industry/company.

Madam Chairman, Ladies and Gentlemen – I declare the exhibition open.

Opening a new building

Ladies and Gentlemen,

Like most of us here, I have survived many happy, successful but hideously cramped, cribbed, cabined and confined years in our old premises. It is therefore with delight that I can declare this new building open.

Think what we can now do. Each of us can swing as many cats as we wish; turn around in our chairs without being accused of

---

* Horrid? Yes, but still common. Better yet, use the Chair's name: 'Mrs Brown . . .'

indecent assault; drink a cup of coffee without worrying whether we have swallowed our neighbour's sustenance.

Seriously, we can now expand our business and, inevitably I hope, our profits – so bringing delight to our bank manager, to our shareholders and to all of us who are a proud part of our enterprise. We hope that we will pack our custom-built building with more and more satisfied customers. Certainly we shall be able to do our work not only with greater economy and speed but also in greater comfort – and that is important because the environment of our workforce has taken priority in the plans for our new structure.

Ladies and Gentlemen – this is a time for building. The bricks, the mortar, the cement, the steel – all is in place. We must now build the business – and have done with the words, mine or anyone else's. I thank the architects, Messrs . . .; I thank all of you for putting up with the inevitable discomfort involved in the move; I thank those who have organised this reception and, in particular, our own Miss . . . I most happily declare this new building – open.

Opening an old people's home

Friends,

A sage once divided charity into categories of merit. At the bottom came gifts where the donor was known to the recipient and the recipient to the donor. At the top were those where neither knew the other. This old people's home has been created by the generosity of the trade/industry – individuals, firms and companies – each giving so that others may enjoy their old age.

There is far too much clap-trap talked about old age, isn't there? Autumn years . . . senior citizens . . . well earned years of pleasurable rest . . . Well, that's how they should be. Unfortunately, they are too often years of loneliness and poverty.

But not for the residents of this home. Here they will have privacy in their own rooms, companionship in the communal rooms, relaxation in the gardens, peace when they want it but kindly supervision and help when they need it.

Your committee has had more trouble in selecting residents than it has had even in the raising of the money for the building. With hundreds in need, how do we select the tens who get help? Who are we to select who are to live here in happiness and who to die alone? All have served the trade/industry; all deserve service from us.

So my function is two-fold. First, I join you in looking back with

161

pride and thankfulness to what has been achieved – and in thanking those responsible. Our special gratitude to . . . and . . . and . . .

Second, we must now service and expand the home.

I once went to a very rich man and asked him for the money to create a building for a certain charity. He replied: 'How are you going to run it . . . to staff it . . . to pay for it once it is opened? I am tired of giving buildings and then having the same people come back to me and saying: "What's the good of giving the building without the running costs?"

Well, we have the building – given not by one person but by many – our thanks to them all. We have enough to keep the place going for . . . months. Did you know that it costs about . . . to pay for each resident for each year?

So in thanking you all for your kindness and generosity . . . for your presence here today and for your presents to this home in the past – I ask for your support in the future. We close one era when we open another.

It is with the greatest of pride – and in the hope and confidence that this home will provide a great comfort and joy to its residents – that I declare the building open.

Keynote – sales conference

This Company lives through sales – and we all live through the Company. It is by building the sales that we can ensure a prosperous future not only for the organisation but also for each one of us here. We are part of the same enterprise. This conference has been carefully designed to help us all in our work.

I am happy to introduce to you not only the conference but also our new season's range/tremendously successful line/new equipment, specially designed for our market by . . . (*or as the case may be*).

(*Description and explanation of product/service, etc. follows.*)

The key to this conference, then, lies in expanding our territory and our sales – but with the help of our new lines/products/ equipment (*etc.*).

My introduction marks the beginning of two/three days/weeks of intensive discussion/instruction/conference – which I am confident will herald the start of a year of distinction and prosperity.

The conference will also enable us to get to know each other socially and to enjoy that good companionship that is so much part of the atmosphere of this organisation. On behalf of your board/

directors/chairman, I wish you good days and fruitful discussions – followed by brisk and burgeoning sales and continuing success for the company and for all of you. I am happy to declare this conference duly opened. Good luck to you all.

Opening an exhibition

We are honoured to be holding in our shop/factory an exhibition of paintings by Martha Smith and of sculpture by Roger Jones, drawing their inspiration from our trade/industry.

You will all have seen the brochure/catalogue, designed by our own Walter Brown. One half, read from the top, sets out the work of Martha Smith; the other half, reading from the bottom of the page, lists the sculpture of Roger Jones.

I know that our two guest artists will not be offended if I say that the hanging committee felt a little like the brochure – not quite sure which way up to hang some of the pictures or to stand some of the sculptures. No matter. The shapes are glorious and the colours superb.

You will, I am sure, be as delighted as I was to learn that each of the artists has offered to donate one work to our trade charity. This is immensely kind of them and we are very grateful.

I am told it took Martha Smith about a week to create each painting and Roger Jones took nearly as long with his larger sculptures. Still, it is not the time that matters but the spirit.

Many years ago, when a pound was twenty shillings and worth a sovereign of gold, the painter Rex Whistler claimed £500 for a portrait in oils, commissioned by a client. No price had been agreed and he sued on a *quantum meruit*, claiming that £500 was reasonable and right.

Counsel cross-examined him on behalf of the client. 'Mr Whistler,' he said, 'how long did it take you to paint this portrait?'

'Three days,' the artist replied.

'Then are you asking my client to pay £500 for three days' work?'

'No,' retorted the painter. 'I am claiming £500 for a lifetime of work which enabled me to paint this portrait in three days.'

It was not the time that was taken by our generous artists which is the dominant matter – it is their lifetime of skill which has made each of them predominant in his or her own sphere. They are giving us of their own best work. I offer them on behalf of all of us our warmest thanks.

The time has now come, then, for each of us to browse, to look and to learn. There may be some of you who are capable artists – I have trouble in drawing a circle with the help of a compass. A cynic remarked: 'He who can, does; he who can't, teaches.' We might say: 'He who can't visits exhibitions and admires those who can.'

We have an exhibition now and here. I thank the artists for bringing that collection together and enabling us to enjoy it at our leisure. I have much pleasure in declaring the exhibition – open.

63   Guests of honour

To the disabled

Some people are obviously disabled because they are missing a limb
. . ., because parts of their body do not work properly. But I know
plenty of people whose bodies are in excellent shape, but who never
use their heads. I congratulate this organisation on its work because
it helps disabled people to make the best possible use of their assets
– and encourages people here, who have absolutely excellent heads,
to use them, and to compensate for their physical disabilities.

We must each make use of the assets we have. This organisation
helps its members to recognise and to exploit them to the full.

Far too many disabled folk are left bored and lonely at home.
You help to get them out into society, so that they are part of the
world, making their contribution and enjoying doing so.

Your committee are themselves disabled – but by their work they
have not only brought new and vigorous life to others, but have – I
know and they know – enriched their own lives in the process.

I congratulate the committee for their efforts; I welcome so many
members here today; I am delighted to be your guest of honour –
and to give any impetus I can to your efforts, today and every day –
and I thank you very much for inviting me.

Now, my friends – on with the party . . .

*Note: This approach is, of course, designed for the physically
handicapped. A variation for the mentally handicapped follows.*

For the mentally handicapped

Our object must be to enable each member of our society to make
the best of his or her assets.

When I went into the Army, many years ago, my closest friend
was a postman's son. We had sat our aptitude tests together.

I found the verbal reasoning and intelligence test easy. The first
question sticks in my mind: 'The sun is blue, yellow, green – cross
out the answers which do not apply.'

Dick managed the first couple of dozen questions without too
much difficulty, but he then came to a dead halt. His vocabulary
was limited.

Next came technical aptitudes. I spent the first half hour trying to assemble a lock and the second a bicycle pump. I failed totally on both. Dick performed all 10 puzzles swiftly and without difficulty.

Regardless of our intellectual or mental ability, we all have different talents, and the handiwork done by members of this club and on exhibition here today shows how much pleasure they can give to others – and at the same time, to themselves. They have a right to develop their talents to the full – and I congratulate the committee and organisers of this club for the work they have done to enable the members to enjoy their lives.

This place is full of happiness, isn't it? People have the odd idea that where human beings are not blessed with the same degree of mental aptitude as themselves, they are necessarily less happy. I congratulate you all on the measure of happiness which this organisation brings not only to its members but also to those who love and care for them.

Thank you, then, for inviting me to be your guest of honour, you, the organisers and committee and your members. I am at your service and proud to be here among you. The very best of luck to you all.

Note: This speech is essentially aimed at the organisers. You must always decide to whom you are going to speak. If you are addressing a school audience, never mind the parents, talk to the youngsters. Thus:

School celebration

Teachers, Parents, Boys and Girls,

I am here as a Governor of the school. Unlike the Governor of a prison who is top boss, a Governor of this school is only one of a group – all of whom work together with the Head and the staff to help you, the pupils, to make the most of your time here.

Why, then, is this school different from others? Why should I and my fellow Governors be proud to be associated with it?

First . . .

Second . . .

Third . . .

Well, I expect you know the story of Henry VIII – and what a happy time he had, didn't he? I say to you – as he said to each of his wives in turn: 'I shall not keep you long!'

Didn't he say that? Unfortunately many of the best historical tales are not necessarily accurate. Like the one about Oliver Cromwell. Charles II definitely did dig him up, lift off the lid of his coffin, chop off his head and put it on a pike on the roof of Westminster Hall for six years – that is the ancient Hall of the Palace of Westminster, the only part of Parliament which is still standing almost as it was when it was first built.

What cannot be proved is the old story that when the head was on the pike on the roof of the Hall, it dripped blood onto the flagstones for six years. Then one night there was a terrible storm and the head blew down with a horrible thud. A huge cat ran out of the crypt, grabbed the head in its teeth and was rushing off towards the door when the Serjeant-at-Arms – our sort of Head Prefect – drew his sword, speared the cat and grasped old Cromwell's head.

The next part is true. The head was then taken up to Sidney Sussex College in Cambridge and duly buried. It is there to this day.

I do not recommend that you use that story in your history essays – but I do hope that someone will take you to Westminster Hall one day. If you look carefully enough, you might even find Oliver Cromwell's blood still on the flagstones.

Anyway, before my blood is spilled for taking up too much of your time, I will simply wish you well . . . congratulate you all on a tremendous year of success . . . wish you happiness for the holidays . . . (*or as the case may be*).

Good luck to you all.

Note: An imaginative tale enlivens any speech. Draw from your own experience or from anyone else's – but do not talk down to your audience, whatever its age.

At prize-givings, avoid telling children how badly you did when you were young – even if it was true, they will not believe it. Do by all means remember the children who get no prizes. Skip the tale of how dreadfully Winston Churchill did as a boy – and try something like this:

Prize-giving

Mrs Green, Parents, Boys and Girls,

It's marvellous being top of the class, head of the school, a prefect or a monitor, isn't it? Even being in the top form gives you status. You are a senior character, looked up to by the new pupils.

Unfortunately, no sooner do we reach one pinnacle – no sooner do we get to the top of one mountain – than we slide right down again and, once more, become new boys and new girls – 'freshers' as they call them in college.

All you leavers will be feeling a bit nostalgic today. When you start your new school, university or college – at your work – you will be back down at the bottom again.

Naturally, those of you who have won prizes today – and I congratulate you all – will treasure them as a memento of a happy and successful occasion. Still, you will be no higher on the ladder than those of your friends who will be joining you at your work without prizes. And next time, it may be their turn.

In many ways it is a pity that we have to have prizes at all isn't it? Many people here, I know, will have worked very hard and done extremely well but will not be getting rewarded. Never mind. Your turn may come.

Just think of all the successful politicians and scientists – and teachers – whom everybody congratulated and who won all the rich prizes in civilisation. Ten years later, where are they? Where is the businessman . . . the captain of industry . . . the big boss . . .? They retire and are forgotten about and that is the end of them. Well, you are not retiring, any of you, are you?

Apart from presenting your prizes, which I shall look forward to doing, my task is simply to wish you all well – wherever you are going, whatever you do. I hope that your ambitions will be fulfilled.

As for those of you who remain – I hope that you will have very happy times ahead. Next year, some of you will reach the top. Enjoy it. Jimmy Durate, the famous American comedian, once remarked:

'Be nice to people you pass on your way up because you will pass them again on your way down!'

To all of you who are going up or down, and even to a few who are staying still, the very best of luck to you – and thank you for inviting me to be with you today.

Note: Never mind the parents. They will enjoy your talking to the children. Adapt your words according to the age of the youngsters. Chat to them as if they were your own. A child can see through pomposity or insincerity far better than an adult. You may be elevated onto a platform – but pretend that you are in and amongst them. Indeed, it is sometimes possible to climb off the stage. On great state occasions, the dignities and proprieties have to be maintained. But when talking to children, I try to perch on the edge 'of a table, to walk down among them, or even to remove my jacket and hang it on the back of a chair – that almost always breaks the ice.

A beginning that I was taught by a member of the Magic Circle – and which requires a certain sleight of hand that I have enjoyed acquiring – goes like this.

Magic opening

Good Morning,

I am sorry that you are all looking so sad. I promise you that I am not going to bore you. So you can relax. There's a chap sleeping at the back – I can see you.

What's this . . . (*holding up a coin in left hand*).

It's an ordinary coin, isn't it? (*vanish coin*).

Now where is it? (*inevitable gasps and cries of 'It's in your pocket . . . It's up your sleeve . . .'*)

No, it's just gone, but you are not going until I have finished talking to you, so you might just as well relax . . .

Note: At one famous school, there was a long pause before proceedings began. It was a small room, with about 50 restless youngsters in it. I said: 'I am sorry to keep you. We shall be starting soon.' 'I shall say when we begin,' the Headmaster reproved me, publicly and rudely. This sort of treatment of a guest is unusual – but one reproof of that sort is too many. Always consult the organisers, chief citizens or bosses of the place or occasion before opening your honoured mouth.

Equally you must choose your opening – and, for that matter, tailor your speech according to the nature and dignity of the occasion. If in doubt, relax.

There are those who regard too informal an approach as a slur – as not recognising the importance either of the occasion or (worse) those present. Tread warily on the dignity of others.

A charitable occasion

Ladies and Gentlemen,

Some regard homes as chattels to be bought and sold. Others – including everybody here – consider a home to be part of a person's entitlement. So is it not scandalous that so many people are so shockingly housed?

I am delighted to be with you today because you are working to provide roofs for the homeless – and more, to help those in homes to put down their roots and to cope.

These are the twin challenges. First, there is the physical worry of providing a place for people to live in decent happiness and contentment. Second, there are many in our civilisation who cannot cope with life, even when they have a home to live in.

It is this second category that provides so many of our most underprivileged and deprived. They are inarticulate; they have no Members of Parliament, because they are on no register; they drift rootless through a world that prefers to disregard them.

Just as those who know no medicine tell the chronically depressed to 'snap out of it', making matters infinitely worse – so those who are able to cope with life tend not to understand the troubles of those who are inadequate.

This organisation . . . (*set out its objectives*).

This organisation . . . (*set out its successes*).

This organisation . . . (*set out its remaining problems and how people can help to solve them*).

To this organisation and all who struggle for it – and to those whom it seeks to help – my warm and affectionate greetings. If my colleagues and I can be of help to you, we shall be pleased – meanwhile, we are delighted to be associated with your work.

Trade association

Dear Friends,

We are all part of the same trade/industry aren't we? Some of us are more fortunate than others – and those of us who are here today are certainly very lucky.

It has not all been smooth sailing, has it? We can all remember difficult days when we might have been toppled into trouble.

I know some people here who have fought their way back to the top, after slithering into great difficulty, usually through no fault of their own.

However, this benevolent association of ours is designed to help those who have not been fortunate enough to make success a permanence – who need broad shoulders to lean on.

The association has many achievements . . . (*outline them*). The association has great plans . . . (*outline them*).

This gathering today is designed to . . . (*set out objectives of meeting*).

My colleagues and myself are honoured to be part of your work. I am delighted to be your guest/Chair – and I can assure you that I will do everything in my power to help. There but for the Grace of God goes any of us, in our great industry.

64 Introductions, greetings and thanks

To the Minister

Secretary of State, Ladies and Gentlemen,

We are all very grateful to the Minister for joining our family (*or the family of our trade, industry or as the case may be*) when he could so easily and comfortably have been with his own. We appreciate not only what he has said, but the fact that he has snatched the time to be with us today.

I once asked a friend who is a safety officer how he defined his job. 'Oh,' he replied, 'I'm in charge of accidents!' By that token, the Minister is in charge of illness, deprivation and disease (*or unemployment, or as the case may be*). He deals with our problems and his own with admirable calm – and for the sake of us all, we wish him success.

For our part, we recognise the acute dangers created for our society by any condition of unrest. When people regard all politicians with equal distaste, democracy is in danger. A statesman was once defined as a dead politician. We are glad that there are live statesmen like our guest, concerned with the affairs of our land.

(*Then refer to one or two points made by the guest.*)

So once again I thank the Minister for giving this event the accolade of his lively presence – and I ask you to join me in expressing to him our warmest appreciation.

Apologies for a small audience

There is nothing in the speaker's world more embarrassing than bringing a prominent guest to speak to your organisation, membership or club and then to find that – for whatever reason – the audience is pathetically small. How do you handle the situation?

- Make your apologies as best you can – relying on the foul weather, apparent trade disputes or any other excuse that seems reasonable.
- If possible, transfer to a smaller room: a few people in a small room make a fine audience, while a small crowd is lost in a huge hall.

• Adapt your introduction to the occasion. Thus:

Distinguished Guest, Ladies and Gentlemen,

I know that we will all be sorry that the weather (*industrial action or as the case may be*) has kept so many people away. We are to have the treat. We are the fortunate few. I am reminded of a story: Mr Brezhnev and Mr Kosygin were discussing the problems of the Jewish minority wanting to emigrate. Mr Brezhnev said: 'Why don't we let them go?'

Mr Kosygin replied: 'Once you let them out, you will have to release the Ukrainians, the Armenians, the Baptists, the Uzbeks . . . and after that, I will go . . . You will be the only person left . . .'

Mr Brezhnev replied: 'No. I shall not be alone. The Soviet Union will be empty!'

We are far from empty this evening, we have here among us the most distinguished members/some of our top industrialists/some of the most famous executives in our trade/industry.

We have gathered here because we know of the work of our guest – and on behalf of us all, I welcome him to . . .

(*Then give details of the guest's work.*)

Ladies and Gentlemen, I present Mr . . .

Livery dinner: response on behalf of guests

(*Court Night of Armourers and Brasiers Company, Armourers Hall, January 1987. Seventy members and guests, all men. Guests of Honour: The Lord Mayor of London and the Sheriffs. Response on behalf of guests.*)

On behalf of all of your guests, Master, I thank you for this glittering and convivial evening. We enjoyed dining with you by candlelight in this splendid old hall and we much appreciate your hospitality.

I am especially grateful because I have special leave to be away from my parliamentary barracks. My Chief Whip decided, on balance, that it would be sensible for a Labour M.P. to know something about insider eating.

Which reminds me of the story told by that most genial of Welshmen, Lord Elwyn Jones. He swears that he was in court in the West Country while the jury was being sworn in. One of the jurymen asked to be excused from jury duty. 'What is your reason, Mr Brown?' the judge enquired.

'Well, My Lord,' he replied, 'my wife . . . is about . . . to conceive!'

'I don't think that's what you mean, Mr Brown,' said the judge, 'I think what you mean is that your wife is about to be confined. But whether I am right or you are right, I do agree that you should be there!'

My Chief Whip thought that I ought to be here and I salute him for his good nature.

When you invited me, Master, you made it quite plain that I was to be short. But you need not have seated me in front of an hourglass, however ceremonial!

It is a special joy for me to be here with your other guests. Gunner Janner of Larkhill found himself seated beside this gentleman in his gold braid. I asked him: 'And what do you do?' He replied: 'I look after the Royal Navy!'

To sit alongside the First Lord of the Admiralty and Chief of Naval Staff is indeed a treat. I wish that I, too, had (in the words of W. S. Gilbert in *H.M.S. Pinafore*) 'polished up the handle of the big front door' – so that I might not be a mere Labour backbencher.

As for Lord Delisle and Dudley, I salute his House – also known as life after death. I wonder if you were at a recent Labour Party Conference, My Lord?

['Only in spirit,' the Tory peer answered.]

Then your spirit would have enjoyed with me the sight of wonderful Lord Manny Shinwell, aged 94, the only person in the room to support your House and win a standing ovation by saying: 'With so much unemployment in the country, why do you want to take away my job? Haven't you got better things to do with your time?'

Manny would have enjoyed this evening. Like me, he would have appreciated the pleasures of your good company.

As for your ceremony of the loving cup, what a marvellous idea that is. Where I work, of course, everyone loves each other. So much, in fact, that some of us are said to be stabbing each other in the front. Just imagine the loving cup being passed down the two front benches, before Prime Minister's Question Time.

So, in thanking you, may I finish on a serious note. Looking around this magnificent hall tonight, I was thinking of my grandparents, all four of whom came to this country to escape from pogrom and from persecution. They did not take for granted that marvellous freedom which enables us to come here to differ in convivial friendship, about the way in which the country is run, or even the best way in which it should be defended. They treasured our freedom. And they taught their children and their grandchildren that when you have the good fortune to live in a great and free land like Britain, you must take pride in putting back into the country some of that which it has given to you.

This evening, you have been kind enough to invite me – a man who differs much from many of you – as your guest, to enjoy a happy evening in your good company. Tonight I thank you on behalf of all your guests for your hospitality. Together we must hope that the arms and armour which are on the walls of this hall will, like their modern equivalents, be on show and not in use. May your ancient company flourish in a land of both freedom and peace.

Retirement

Mr Chairman, Colleagues and Friends,
It will seem strange to attend a meeting of the . . . without Arthur Jones presiding over it. In the past . . . months/years, he has established himself as the epitome of all that is best in our trade/industry/organisation. There is much to thank him for.

First, I thank him for the kindly way in which he has referred to me. He has been warm, generous and extremely accurate . . .

I can therefore say with equal accuracy that his qualities of . . . and . . . have enlightened his period of office and helped him to create a vibrant organisation.

Most of us here are forthright individualists – or we would not be doing this job. We may disagree as to the best way to serve our customers/clients/firm's business interest. We argue, we debate and we dispute. But we are united in our admiration for Mr . . .

Let me list some of his achievements during the past . . . (*expand on his achievements*).

And now that his period of office is over, we know that we will receive the same unassuming, kindly and affectionate welcome – and the same help – from him as a fellow member of our . . . as we did when he held the highest office and honour that we could give him.

Thomas Mordaunt wrote:

> Sound, sound the clarion, fill the fife
> Throughout the sensual world proclaim

> One crowded hour of glorious life
> Is worth an age without a name.

Our friend, and mentor, Arthur Jones has enjoyed his very crowded hour – and he has put glorious life into our proceedings/company/ organisation. We thank him – and we wish him well.

Distinguished guests

In the unavoidable absence of our President, I have been asked on behalf of the guests to thank our hosts for the splendid austerity lunch (*smoked salmon sandwiches*). I would wish this sort of austerity on all business people everywhere.

In particular, I thank our two guests for joining us – and for their enthusiastic words. How they adjust – physically and mentally – to their eternal round of the world is a mystery. Maybe it is due to the sustenance provided by the international smoked salmon sandwich.

One of our guests is a lawyer, the other is a financier. When justice and money come together on the same platform, then indeed we have found common cause.

We have listened with immense care to their speeches – and I can assure them that we are happy to associate ourselves with their work. (*Then a few sentences about that work*).

We are involved – and we are all grateful to our guests for increasing that involvement. We look forward to seeing our guests back with us again very soon – and next time for a much longer stay.

65   Business speeches

State of the industry

I am happy to have this opportunity to review the state of our industry – and to appeal on behalf of all of us for government understanding and help. We have honourably adhered to governmental guidelines and advice. We have – as Ministers have sometimes unhappily put it – cut away the fat. But we are becoming extremely and dangerously lean. First, the dangers. They are many.

We face increased competition from countries where employees are paid miserably low wages. We contend with the dumping of goods by suppliers who – directly or indirectly, lawfully or otherwise – are heavily subsidised by their governments. And no government appears ready to help us to meet this unfair competition.

We are against neither competition nor imports. We recognise the need of others to sell. And we must export to live. We know that if we place undue restriction on our imports, then we must expect the same treatment from others to whom we must export. We are against *unfair* competition . . . *unfair* imports . . . *improper* dumping . . . *wilful* subsidy by others, unmatched by governmental aid to our ailing industry.

Add to these overseas miseries, over which we have no control whatever, the results of our own recession; the state of the currency; the weakness of our economy; the problems of overseas demand matched by the collapse of our market – and the reasons for my anxiety are clear.

So let us plan and plot, organise and lobby, work together for the preservation of our industry. Let us learn from the unions that individually we are weak, but if we fight and use our unity, then these times of trouble will have brought great lessons for us all.

Remedies

The diagnosis for our trade is clear – cure the recessional misery. That cure requires capital and investment – but above all, hope and confidence.

The time for cutting each other's industrial throats has passed.

We must now work together for the survival of . . ., recognising that collapse for one is a signal of tempest for all.

So my colleagues and I are proposing the following specific steps, to draw our plight to the government's attention and to take constructive help for our problems – not least in preserving employment in this key area of our industry.

First . . .

Second . . .

Third . . .

I commend these proposals to you. I ask you to accept them unanimously. We need more confidence and you need leadership, which we have now united together to provide.

66   Unions and colleagues

Never talk down to anyone – least of all to trade unions or to your colleagues or workforce. I have watched speeches collapse into ruin at school prize-givings, company occasions, debates at universities and conferences of trade unions – nearly always because the speaker made it plain that he or she regarded the audience as inferior for some reason. Conversely, nearly all the most successful speeches shine because the listener is treated as a colleague, a partner, an equal.

Trade unions are especially sensitive to apparent condescension, even when it is in fact a mask for shyness or apprehension. You only fool your unions once. They will not trust you again. Nor will they accept your invitation to share with them the miseries of recession if you do not also let them benefit in times of profit. Provided that their accounts will not reach the eyes of their creditors, employers are always glad to show the miseries to their workforce. But in days of gloom, the accounts only emerge after due provision has been made for the pension reserve fund and other receptacles for profits that are better unseen.

So the key to a successful speech to employees – and especially to those with the combined strength provided by a well-run union – is: the sharing of information, anxieties and hopes, with sincerity and frankness. Or to use a useful American phrase: 'Level with them . . .'

Disclosure

Mr Chairman, Ladies and Gentlemen,
Thank you for agreeing to meet me today. I would like to explain to you very briefly the position of the company and our plans and hopes for the future. Then I shall be glad to answer your questions.

Our company secretary, Roger White – who is, of course, here with me – has just provided your board with our latest figures. I have provided a summary for each of you, and when I have concluded this introduction, Roger will be glad to join me in answering your questions on these accounts. They provide management with a guide to liability and prospects. And they will give you an indication of the state of business which, of course, provides a livelihood for us all.

Remembering that the period covered is the year/six months/three months from . . . to . . ., let me summarise for you:

First, the turnover during this period increased/decreased from . . . to . . .

Second, our workforce grew/diminished from . . . to . . .

Third, working days lost through illness rose/fell from . . . to . . .; and from industrial action rose/fell from . . . to . . .

Fourth – and do please treat this information as entirely confidential – in broad terms, at the start of this period we had enough orders on our books to keep us busy/on full-time working for a period of . . . weeks/months. We can now see confidently ahead only until . . .

Our plans for the future are as follows.

We shall make every effort to retain our present workforce. If unfortunately we do have to reduce numbers, we shall try to do so through natural wastage – that is, not replacing employees who leave us. If redundancies do become inevitable – and I repeat that we hope and believe that this will not occur – we shall consult with all unions concerned; and we shall try to arrange redundancies with the minimum of hardship.

Anyway, I repeat that I hope that this situation will not arise. It is certainly the determination of your board and of all the management team to scour the countryside/the world for orders and to take any steps within our power to keep our organisation – with all its skills, experience and comradeship – together. We know that you know the problems – and how much we appreciate your partnership and help. We believe that together – all of us together – we can survive this miserable recession. Thank you – and now please do ask your questions. We shall try to answer them all, frankly and in the confidence that you recognise that we are all working – together – for the future of this, our works/business/undertaking.

Note: The redundancy sections of this speech sets the tone for misery and, of course, should not be used unless that misery is at least in prospect. If you have any alternative joy to offer, then by all means do so. Alternatively, you could use the redundancy section to form a major part of an even more unhappy speech, if redundancies really do become inevitable.

Similar principles apply to speeches to management, thus:

To management colleagues

I appreciate greatly your coming together today. I know how far some of you have had to travel and the difficulty that some of you have had in leaving your work/departments. But it is essential that we confer together on how to meet the current emergency/make the best of the present opportunity/avoid (*or as the case may be*).

First let me refer to the background paper which has been provided to you all. I must emphasise the following points:

1 . . .
2 . . .
3 . . .

The board consider that the following steps should now be taken – but before making any decision irrevocable, we are seeking your views. Our proposals are:

1 . . .
2 . . .
3 . . .

I look forward to hearing your comments and any counter-proposals. We shall value your constructive criticism and your ideas – as we do your comradeship, your partnership and your assistance – without which this business could not survive in such excellent shape.

Note: Accounts (as in the previous example); a background paper (as in this) or some other document, prepared carefully in advance, will avoid waste of time; provide the basis for discussion; and reduce the length of your speech.

Sales team talk

I have asked you – our sales team – to join me today so that we can together plan for the future of the entire business. In the past customers have come to us. In these troubled times, we must go to them – and arrive well ahead of our competitors.

I shall now ask our colleague, Bill Black, to present to you our new product – which will lie at the centre of our effort for the coming year. Bill . . .

(Mr Black then introduces and explains the product – with appropriate diagrams, charts and/or visual aids.)

Now you have seen the product and you know the plans. So how do we beat the competition, sell well, and justify the skill, brilliance and the enterprise of our colleagues in research and development? How do we make the most of this great new opportunity? If we succeed, then the company will flourish. Failure is unthinkable – for the company, and for us all.

Note: Visual aids are vital – as a supplement to speech (see also Chapter 33). They are indispensable in (a) explaining complicated ideas or machinery; (b) punctuating a lengthy speech or brightening a shorter one; and (c) feeding other people's talents into your talk. (See also Janner on Presentation.)

PART 8

Classic speeches

'Our next speaker needs no introduction from me. . . .'

67 David Lloyd George: 'Limehouse Speech'

Extract from Lloyd George's address to over 4,000 people at Limehouse in 1909.

. . . Now unless I am wearying you, I have got just one other land tax, and that is a tax on royalties. The landlords are receiving eight million a year by way of royalties. What for? They never deposited the coal there. It was not they who planted these great granite rocks in Wales, who laid the foundations of the mountains. Was it the landlord? And yet he, by some divine right, demands – for merely the right for men to risk their lives in hewing these rocks – eight millions a year!

Take any coalfield. I went down to a coalfield the other day, and they pointed out to me many collieries there. They said: 'You see that colliery there. The first man who went there spent a quarter of a million in sinking shafts, in driving mains and levels. He never got coal. The second man who came spent £100,000 – and he failed. The third man came along, and he got the coal. But what was the landlord doing in the meantime? The first man failed; but the landlord got his royalties, the landlord got his dead-rents. The second man failed, but the landlord got his royalties. These capitalists put their money in. When the scheme failed, what did the landlord put in? He simply put in the bailiffs. The capitalist risks at any rate the whole of his money; the engineer puts his brains in, the miner risks his life.

Have you been down a coal-mine? Then you know. I was telling you I went down the other day. We sank down into a pit half a mile deep. We then walked underneath the mountain, and we did about three-quarters of a mile with rock and shale above us. The earth seemed to be straining – around us and above us – to crush us in. You could see the pit-props bent and twisted and sundered until you saw their fibres split. Sometimes they give way, and then there is mutilation and death. Often a spark ignites, the whole pit is deluged in fire, and the breath of life is scorched out of hundreds of breasts by the consuming fire.

In the very next colliery to the one I descended, just three years ago, three hundred people lost their lives in that way; and yet when the Prime Minister and I knock at the door of these great landlords and say to them, 'Here, you know these poor fellows who have been digging up royalties at the risk of their lives, some of them are old, they have survived the perils of their trade, they are broken, they can earn no more. Won't you give something towards keeping them out of the workhouse?' they scowl at you. And we say: 'Only a ha'penny, just a copper?' They say: 'You thieves!' And they turn their dogs on to us, and every day you can hear their bark. If this is an indication of the view taken by these great landlords of their responsibility to the people who, at the risk of life, create their wealth, then I say their day of reckoning is at hand.

The other day, at the great Tory meeting held at the Cannon Street Hotel, they had blazoned on the walls: 'We protest against the Budget in the name of democracy, liberty, and justice.' Where does the democracy come in this landed system? Where is the justice in all these transactions? We claim that the tax we impose on land is fair, just, and moderate. They go on threatening that if we proceed they will cut down their benefactions and discharge labour. What kind of labour? What is the labour they are going to choose for dismissal? Are they going to threaten to devastate rural England while feeding themselves and dressing themselves? Are they going to reduce their gamekeepers? That would be sad! The agricultural labourer and the farmer might then have some part of the game which they fatten with their labour. But what would happen to you in the season? No weekend shooting with the Duke of Norfolk for any of us! But that is not the kind of labour that they are going to cut down. They are going to cut down productive labour – builders and gardeners – and they are going to ruin their property so that it shall not be taxed.

All I can say is this – the ownership of land is not merely an enjoyment, it is a stewardship. It has been reckoned as such in the past, and if they cease to discharge their functions, the security and defence of the country, looking after the broken in their villages and neighbourhoods – then those functions which are part of the traditional duties attached to the ownership of land and which have given to it its title – if they cease to discharge those functions, the time will come to reconsider the conditions under which land is held in this country.

No country, however rich, can permanently afford to have quartered upon its revenue a class which declines to do the duty which it was called upon to perform. And, therefore, it is one of the prime duties of statesmanship to investigate those conditions. But I do not believe it. They have threatened and menaced like that before. They have seen it is not to their interest to carry out these futile menaces. They are now protesting against paying their fair share of the taxes on the land, and they are doing so by saying: 'You are burdening the community; you are putting burdens upon the people which they cannot bear.' Ah! they are not thinking of themselves. Noble souls! It is not the great dukes they are feeling for, it is the market-gardener, it is the builder, and it was, until recently, the smallholder.

In every debate in the House of Commons they said: 'We are not worrying for ourselves. We can afford it, with our broad acres; but just think of the little man who has only got a few acres'; and we were so very impressed with this tearful appeal that at last we said: 'We will leave him out.' And I almost expected to see Mr Prettyman jump over the table and say – 'Fall on my neck and embrace me.' Instead of that, he stiffened up, his face wreathed with anger, and he said: 'The Budget is more unjust than ever.' Oh! no. We are placing the burdens on the broad shoulders. Why should I put burdens on the people? I am one of the children of the people. I was brought up amongst them. I know their trials; and God forbid that I should add one grain of trouble to the anxiety which they bear with such patience and fortitude. When the Prime Minister did me the honour of inviting me to take charge of the National Exchequer at a time of great difficulty, I made up my mind, in framing the Budget which was in front of me, that at any rate no cupboards should be barer, no lot should be harder. By that test, I challenge them to judge the Budget.

(*Reprinted, by kind permission of Caxton Publishing Co. Ltd, from* The Book of Public Speaking, *Volume 3, edited by C. Fox-Davies.*)

68   King Edward VIII: 'Abdication Address'

Edward VIII's abdication address, which he broadcast to Britain and the world on 11 December 1936.

At long last I am able to say a few words of my own. I have never wanted to withhold anything, but until now it has not been constitutionally possible for me to speak.

A few hours ago I discharged my last duty as King and Emperor, and now that I have been succeeded by my brother, and Duke of York, my first words must be to declare my allegiance to him. This I do with all my heart.

You all know the reasons which have impelled me to renounce the throne. But I want you to understand that in making up my mind I did not forget the country or the empire, which, as Prince of Wales and lately as King, I have for twenty-five years tried to serve.

But you must believe me when I tell you that I have found it impossible to carry the heavy burden of responsibility and to discharge my duties as King as I would wish to do without the help and support of the woman I love.

And I want you to know that the decision I have made has been mine and mine alone. This was a thing I had to judge entirely for myself. The other person most nearly concerned has tried up to the last to persuade me to take a different course.

I have made this, the most serious decision of my life, only upon the single thought of what would, in the end, be best for all.

This decision has been made less difficult to me by the sure knowledge that my brother, with his long training in the public affairs of this country and with his fine qualities, will be able to take my place forthwith without interruption or injury to the life and progress of the empire. And he has one matchless blessing, enjoyed by so many of you, and not bestowed on me – a happy home with his wife and children.

During these hard days I have been comforted by Her Majesty my mother and by my family. The ministers of the Crown, and in particular, Mr Baldwin, the Prime Minister, have always treated me with full consideration. There has never been any constitutional

188

difference between me and them, and between me and Parliament. Bred in the constitutional tradition by my father, I should never have allowed any such issue to arise.

Ever since I was Prince of Wales, and later on when I occupied the throne, I have been treated with the greatest kindness by all classes of the people wherever I have lived or journeyed throughout the empire. For that I am very grateful.

I now quit altogether public affairs and I lay down my burden. It may be some time before I return to my native land, but I shall always follow the fortunes of the British race and empire with profound interest, and if at any time in the future I can be found of service to His Majesty in a private station, I shall not fail.

And now, we all have a new King. I wish him and you, his people, happiness and prosperity with all my heart. God bless you all! God save the King!

69   Winston Churchchill:
'Blood, Toil, Tears and Sweat' – 1940

I beg to move,

> That this House welcomes the formation of a Government representing the united and inflexible resolve of the nation to prosecute the war with Germany to a victorious conclusion.

On Friday evening last I received His Majesty's Commission to form a new Administration. It was the evident wish and will of Parliament and the nation that this should be conceived on the broadest possible basis and that it should include all parties, both those who supported the late Government and also the parties of the Opposition. I have completed the most important part of this task. A War Cabinet has been formed of five Members, representing, with the Opposition Liberals, the unity of the nation. The three party Leaders have agreed to serve, either in the War Cabinet or in high executive office. The three fighting Services have been filled. It was necessary that this should be done in one single day, on account of the extreme urgency and rigour of events. A number of other positions, key positions, were filled yesterday, and I am submitting a further list to His Majesty tonight. I hope to complete the appointment of the principal Ministers during tomorrow. The appointment of the other Ministers usually takes a little longer, but I trust that, when Parliament meets again, this part of my task will be completed, and that the administration will be complete in all respects.

I considered it in the public interest to suggest that the House should be summoned to meet today. Mr Speaker agreed, and took the necessary steps, in accordance with the powers conferred upon him by the Resolution of the House. At the end of the proceedings today, the Adjournment of the House will be proposed until Tuesday, 21st May, with, of course, provision for earlier meeting, if need be. The business to be considered during that week will be notified to Members at the earliest opportunity. I now invite the House, by the Motion which stands in my name, to record its approval of the steps taken and to declare its confidence in the new Government.

To form an Administration of this scale and complexity is a serious undertaking in itself, but it must be remembered that we are in the preliminary stage of one of the greatest battles in history, that we are in action at many other points in Norway and in Holland, that we have to be prepared in the Mediterranean, that the air battle is continuous and that many preparations, such as have been indicated by my Hon. Friend below the Gangway, have to be made here at home. In this crisis I hope I may be pardoned if I do not address the House at any length today. I hope that any of my friends and colleagues, or former colleagues, who are affected by the political reconstruction, will make allowances, all allowance, for any lack of ceremony with which it has been necessary to act. I would say to the House, as I said to those who have joined this Government: 'I have nothing to offer but blood, toil, tears and sweat.'

We have before us an ordeal of the most grievous kind. We have before us many, many long months of struggle and of suffering. You ask, what is our policy? I will say: It is to wage war, by sea, land and air, with all our might and with all the strength that God can give us; to wage war against a monstrous tyranny never surpassed in the dark, lamentable catalogue of human crime. That is our policy. You ask, what is our aim? I can answer in one word: It is victory, victory at all cost, victory in spite of all terror, victory, however long and hard the road may be; for without victory, there is no survival. Let that be realised; no survival for the British Empire, no survival for all that the British Empire has stood for, no survival for the urge and impulse of the ages, that mankind will move forward towards its goal. But I take up my task with buoyancy and hope. I feel sure that our cause will not be suffered to fail among men. At this time I feel entitled to claim the aid of all, and I say, 'Come then, let us go forward together with our united strength.'

(Reprinted, with kind permission of HMSO, from Hansard, *Fifth Series, issue No. 1096, volume 360, 13 May 1940, col. 1501 to col. 1502.)*

70 Jawaharlal Nehru: 'A Glory has Departed'

Nehru, first Prime Minister of independent India, addressing the Constituent Assembly at New Delhi on 2 February 1948, three days after the assassination of Mahatma Gandhi.

What then can we say about him except to feel humble on this occasion? To praise him we are not worthy – to praise him whom we could not follow adequately and sufficiently. It is almost doing him an injustice just to pass him by with words when he demanded work and labour and sacrifice from us; in a large measure he made this country, during the last thirty years or more, attain heights of sacrifice which in that particular domain have never been equalled elsewhere. He succeeded in that. Yet ultimately things happened which no doubt made him suffer tremendously though his tender face never lost its smile and he never spoke a harsh word to anyone. Yet he must have suffered – suffered for the failing of this generation whom he had trained, suffered because we went away from the path that he had shown us. And ultimately the hand of a child of his – for he after all is as much a child of his as any other Indian – a hand of the child of his struck him down.

Long ages afterwards history will judge of this period that we have passed through. It will judge of the successes and the failures – we are too near it to be proper judges and to understand what has happened and what has not happened. All we know is that there was a glory and that it is no more; all we know is that for the moment there is darkness, not so dark certainly because when we look into our hearts we still find the living flame which he lighted there. And if those living flames exist, there will not be darkness in this land and we shall be able, with our effort, remembering him and following his path, to illumine this land again, small as we are, but still with the fire that he instilled into us.

He was perhaps the greatest symbol of the India of the past, and may I say, of the India of the future, that we could have had. We stand on this perilous edge of the present between that past and the future to be and we face all manner of perils and the greatest peril is sometimes the lack of faith which comes to us, the sense of frustration that comes to us, the sinking of the heart and of the spirit that comes to us when we see ideals go overboard, when we see the great things that we talked about somehow pass into empty words and life taking a different course. Yet, I do believe that perhaps this period will pass soon enough.

He has gone, and all over India there is a feeling of having been left desolate and forlorn. All of us sense that feeling, and I do not know when we shall be able to get rid of it, and yet together with that feeling there is also a feeling of proud thankfulness that it has been given to us of this generation to be associated with this mighty person. In ages to come, centuries and maybe millenia after us, people will think of this generation when this man of God trod on earth and will think of us who, however small, could also follow his path and tread the holy ground where his feet had been. Let us be worthy of him.

A glory has departed and the sun that warmed and brightened our lives has set and we shiver in the cold and dark. Yet, he would not have us feel this way. After all, that glory that we saw for all these years, that man with the divine fire, changed us also – and such as we are, we have been moulded by him during these years; and out of that divine fire many of us also took a small spark which strengthened and made us work to some extent on the lines that he fashioned. And so if we praise him, our words seem rather small and if we praise him, to some extent we also praise ourselves. Great men and eminent men have monuments in bronze and marble set up for them, but this man of divine fire managed in his life-time to become enshrined in millions and millions of hearts so that all of us became somewhat of the stuff that he was made of, though to an infinitely lesser degree. He spread out in this way all over India not in palaces only, or in select places or in assemblies but in every hamlet and hut of the lowly and those who suffer. He lives in the hearts of millions and he will live for immemorial ages.

(*Reprinted, by kind permission of Dover Publications, New York, from* The World's Greatest Speeches [*second revised edition*], *edited by L. Copeland and L. Larner.*)

71 Harold Macmillan: 'The Winds of Change'

Addressing the South African Parliament in 1960 on the theme of emerging third-world nationalism, Prime Minister Macmillan opened his speech as follows.

Sir, as I have travelled round the Union I have found everywhere, as I expected, a deep preoccupation with what is happening in the rest of the African continent. I understand and sympathise with your interest in these events, and your anxiety about them. Ever since the break-up of the Roman Empire one of the constant facts of political life in Europe has been the emergence of independent nations. They have come into existence over the centuries in different forms, with different kinds of government, but all have been inspired by a deep, keen feeling of nationalism, which has grown as the nations have grown.

In the twentieth century, and especially since the end of the war, the processes which gave birth to the nation states of Europe have been repeated all over the world. We have seen the awakening of national consciousness in peoples who have for centuries lived in dependence upon some other power. Fifteen years ago this movement spread through Asia. Many countries there of different races and civilisations pressed their claim to an independent national life. Today the same thing is happening in Africa, and the most striking of all the impressions I have formed since I left London a month ago is of the strength of this African national consciousness. In different places it takes different forms, but it is happening everywhere. The wind of change is blowing through this continent, and, whether we like it or not, this growth of national consciousness is a political fact. We must all accept it as a fact, and our national policies must take account of it . . .

(Reprinted, by kind permission of Macmillan London Ltd, from Pointing the Way 1959–61, *Volume 5 of Macmillan's Biography.)*

72   Martin Luther King: 'I Have a Dream'

Martin Luther King's evocative black masterpiece of hope – 1963.

I have a dream that my four little children will one day live in a nation where they will not be judged by the colour of their skin but by the content of their character.

I have a dream today.

I have a dream that one day the state of Alabama, whose governor's lips are presently dripping with the words of interposition and nullification, will be transformed into a situation where little black boys and black girls will be able to join hands with little white boys and white girls and walk together as sisters and brothers.

I have a dream today.

I have a dream that one day every valley shall be exalted, every hill and mountain shall be made low, the rough places will be made plain, and the crooked places will be made straight, and the glory of the Lord shall be revealed, and all flesh shall see it together.

This is our hope. This is the faith with which I return to the South. With this faith we will be able to hew out of the mountain of despair a stone of hope. With this faith we will be able to transform the jangling discords of our nation into a beautiful symphony of brotherhood. With this faith we will be able to work together, to pray together, to struggle together, to go to jail together, to stand up for freedom together, knowing that we will be free one day.

This will be the day when all of God's children will be able to sing with new meaning 'My country 'tis of thee, sweet land of liberty, of thee I sing. Land where my fathers died, land of the pilgrim's pride, from every mountainside, let freedom ring.'

And if America is to be a great nation this must become true. So let freedom ring from the prodigious hilltops of New Hampshire! Let freedom ring from the mighty mountains of New York! Let freedom ring from the heightening Alleghenies of Pennsylvania!

Let freedom ring from the snowcapped Rockies of Colorado!

Let freedom ring from the curvaceous peaks of California!

But not only that; let freedom ring from the Stone Mountain of Georgia!

Let freedom ring from every hill and mole hill of Mississippi. From every mountainside, let freedom ring.

When we let freedom ring, when we let it ring from every village and every hamlet, from every state and every city, we will be able to speed up that day when all of God's children, black men and white men, Jews and Gentiles, Protestants and Catholics, will be able to join hands and sing in the words of that old Negro spiritual, 'Free at last! Free at last! Thank God almighty, we are free at last!'

(Reprinted, by kind permission of George Allen & Unwin Ltd, from What Manner of Man: a Biography of Martin Luther King *by L. Bennet.)*

73   Hugh Gaitskell:
'Fight and Fight and Fight Again'

Speech delivered at the 57th Annual Conference of the Labour Party, Scarborough, 1960.

. . . There is one other possibility to which I must make reference because I have read so much about it – that the issue here is not really defence at all but the leadership of this Party. Let me repeat what Manny Shinwell said. The place to decide the leadership of this Party is not here but in the Parliamentary Party. I would not wish for one day to remain a Leader who had lost the confidence of his colleagues in Parliament. It is perfectly reasonable to try to get rid of somebody, to try to get rid of a man you do not agree with, who you think perhaps is not a good Leader. But there are ways of doing this. What would be wrong, in my opinion, and would not be forgiven, is if, in order to get rid of a man, you supported a policy in which you did not wholeheartedly believe, a policy which, as far as the resolution is concerned, is not clear.

Before you take the vote on this momentous occasion, allow me a last word. Frank Cousins has said this is not the end of the problem. I agree with him. It is not the end of the problem because Labour Members of Parliament will have to consider what they do in the House of Commons. What do you expect of them? You know how they voted in June overwhelmingly for the policy statement. It is not in dispute that the vast majority of Labour Members of Parliament are utterly opposed to unilateralism and neutralism. So what do you expect them to do? Change their minds overnight? To go back on the pledges they gave to the people who elected them from their constituencies? And supposing they did do that. Supposing all of us, like well-behaved sheep, were to follow the policies of unilateralism and neutralism, what kind of an impression would that make upon the British people? You do not seem to be clear in your minds about it, but I will tell you this. I do not believe that the Labour Members of Parliament are prepared to act as time servers. I do not believe they will do this, and I will tell you why – because they are men of conscience and honour. People of the so-called Right and so-called Centre have every justification for having a conscience, as well as people of the so-called Left. I do not think they will do this because they are honest men, loyal men, steadfast men, experienced men, with a lifetime of service to the Labour Movement.

There are other people too, not in Parliament, in the Party who share our convictions. What sort of people do you think they are? What sort of people do you think we are? Do you think we can simply accept a decision of this kind? Do you think that we can become overnight the pacifists, unilateralists and fellow travellers that other people are? How wrong can you be? As wrong as you are about the attitude of the British people.

In a few minutes the Conference will make its decision. Most of the votes, I know, are predetermined and we have been told what is likely to happen. We know how it comes about. I sometimes think, frankly, that the system we have, by which great unions decide their policy before even their conferences can consider the Executive recommendation, is not really a very wise one or a good one. Perhaps in a calmer moment this situation could be looked at.

I say this to you: we may lose the vote today and the result may deal this Party a grave blow. It may not be possible to prevent it, but I think there are many of us who will not accept that this blow need be mortal, who will not believe that such an end is inevitable. There are some of us, Mr Chairman, who will fight and fight and fight again to save the Party we love. We will fight and fight and fight again to bring back sanity and honesty and dignity, so that our Party with its great past may retain its glory and its greatness.

It is in that spirit that I ask delegates who are still free to decide how they vote, to support what I believe to be a realistic policy on defence, which yet could so easily have united the great Party of ours, and to reject what I regard as the suicidal path of unilateral disarmament which will leave our country defenceless and alone.

(Reprinted by kind permission from the Labour Party Report of the 57th Annual Conference.)

74 Aneurin Bevan: 'Socialism Unbeaten'

Extract from Bevan's speech to the Labour Party Conference following Macmillan's General Election victory of 1959.

What are we going to say, comrades? Are we going to accept the defeat? Are we going to say to India, where Socialism has been adopted as the official policy despite all the difficulties facing the Indian community, that the British Labour movement has dropped Socialism here? What are we going to say to the rest of the world? Are we going to send a message from this great Labour movement, which is the father and mother of modern democracy and modern Socialism, that we in Blackpool in 1959 have turned our backs on our principles because of a temporary unpopularity in a temporarily affluent society?

Let me give you a personal confession of faith. I have found in my life that the burdens of public life are too great to be borne for trivial ends. The sacrifices are too much, unless we have something really serious in mind; and therefore, I hope we are going to send from this Conference a message of hope, a message of encouragement, to the youth and to the rest of the world that is listening very carefully to what we are saying.

I was rather depressed by what Denis Healey said. I have a lot of respect for him; but you know, Denis, you are not going to be able to help the Africans if the levers of power are left in the hands of their enemies in Britain. You cannot do it! Nor can you inject the principles of ethical Socialism into an economy based upon private greed. You cannot do it! You cannot mix them, and therefore I beg and pray that we should wind this Conference up this time on a message of hope, and we should say to India and we should say to Africa and Indonesia, and not only to them, but we should say to China and we should say to Russia, that the principles of democratic Socialism have not been extinguished by a temporary defeat at the hands of the Tories a few weeks ago!

You know, comrades, parliamentary institutions have not been destroyed because the Left wing was too vigorous; they have been destroyed because the Left was too inert. You cannot give me a

199

single illustration in the Western world where Fascism conquered because Socialism was too violent. You cannot give me a single illustration where representative government has been undermined because the representatives of the people asked for too much.

But I can give you instance after instance we are faced with today where representative government has been rendered helpless because the representatives of the people did not ask enough. We have never suffered from too much vitality; we have suffered from too little. That is why I say that we are going to go from this Conference a united Party. We are going to go back to the House of Commons, and we are going to fight the Tories. But we are not only going to fight them there; we are going to fight them in the constituencies and inside the trade unions. And we are going to get the youth! Let them start. Do not let them wait for the Executive, for God's sake! Start getting your youth clubs, go in and start now! Go back home and start them, and we will give all the help and encouragement that we can.

75 Brian Sedgemore:
'A Long Streak of Spit'

On 8 March 1988, the Commons debated whether a Guardian journalist should be reported to the Committee of Privileges. He had made derogatory remarks about MPs. During the subsequent debate, Brian Sedgemore, Labour MP for Hackney South and Shoreditch, made a classic contribution.

Mr. Brian Sedgemore: I begin by declaring an interest. I drink and I have been known to take a catnap in the Library. Indeed, when I once appeared as a barrister before the Lord Chief Justice of England, he said to me, 'I can see you are doing your incompetent best, Mr. Sedgemore.'

Nevertheless, I hope that we will take the motion seriously. It is serious for *The Guardian*, that radical newspaper——

Mr. Dennis Skinner (Bolsover): What?

Mr. Sedgemore: A radical newspaper, which is not only short of money and a decent layout artist, but if I may paraphrase Swift, is in danger of dying by swallowing its own lies. Having said that, I want to defend *The Guardian* and the right of journalists to abuse hon. Members.

All my life I have had the misfortune to be laughed at. You will understand, Mr. Speaker – well, perhaps you will not, because perhaps no one has ever laughed at you – that it hurts. The position became unbearable when I was at the school debating society one year and one of my opponents described me as 'a long streak of spit'. I thought, 'Well, this cannot go on.' I was lying in the bath and I had a brilliant idea. I said to myself, 'I know what I'll do to stop it, I'll become an MP. Then I'll get the protection of the all-powerful, all-party Committee of Privileges. No longer will anyone in this life be able to hold me up to hatred, ridicule and contempt.' Imagine my surprise when only last week, as a result of something that I said during proceedings on the Education Reform Bill in Committee, a journalist who is sitting in the Reporter's Gallery described me as 'Derek Jameson's voice coming out of Kerry Packer's body.'

I do not know how hon. Members can worry about 200

Members of Parliament being called 'incompetent, lazy drunks' when a tender, delicate soul like myself is being likened to Sid Yobbo.

I am not claiming that Andrew Rawnsley is entirely innocent. I am not sure how I am supposed to respond, as a paid-up member of the National Union of Journalists, when he argues in his column, as he argues every day, that politicians are even more odious than journalists.

You will be aware, Mr. Speaker, that I am not one of those hon. Members who believe in vulgar, personal abuse – [*Interruption*]. I prefer to leave such abuse to the right hon. Member for Chingford (Mr. Tebbit) and I am sorry that he is not in the Chamber. I understand that at this very moment he is seeking to raise the standards of artistic appreciation in our country by trying to persuade *The Sun* to set up a Kelvin MacKenzie room at the Tate gallery to house a permanent collection of nipples. That is the kind of abuse that we could do without. If the right hon. Member for Chingford had not become a Member of Parliament, I am sure that he would have become a PPE – not a graduate in politics, philosophy and economics, but a purveyor of pornography extraordinaire.

I believe that my hon. Friend the Member for Newham, North-West (Mr. Banks) will agree that we should judge political abuse by three standards. First, abuse in politics must be treated as an art. Secondly, abuse is at its best when it is in thoroughly bad taste and finally, and this was the only point that my hon. Friend the Member for Newham, North-West picked up himself, abuse should at some stage hint at reality. That is where poor little Rawnsley up there in the Press Gallery, the fearless scribe from Farringdon road whose goolies are about to be tweaked today, got it wrong.

Mr. Speaker: Order. Will the hon. Gentleman seek to use language that is more parliamentary?

Mr. Sedgemore: You are absolutely right, Mr. Speaker. I am getting carried away. Obviously Mr. Rawnsley came to the House and was hard-pressed, like the rest of us, to earn a crust. He did not have a story, and the classic story to make up in the Reporters' Gallery is the 'empty Chamber' story.

Before I finish, I want to ask my hon. Friend the Member for Newham, North-West two questions. I want my hon. Friend to consider some of the best abuse down the ages and I want to give one example from cross the Atlantic and one from this side. When my hon. Friend replies and withdraws his motion I want to know how he would respond to such abuse.

How would my hon. Friend have responded to these comments made by Harry Truman?

'Richard Nixon is a no good, lying bastard. He can lie out of both sides of his mouth at the same time and if he ever caught himself telling the truth, he'd lie just to keep his hand in.'

Also, how would my hon. Friend have responded to the classic 18th century argument between Lord Sandwich and John Wilkes?

''Pon your honour, Wilkes, I don't know whether you'll die on the gallows or of the pox.'

To which Wilkes replied:

'That must depend, my Lord, upon whether I embrace your Lordship's principles or your Lordship's mistress.'

A serious point is involved. It is important to preserve the freedom of the press, and that necessitates the freedom of journalists in the Press Gallery to abuse hon. Members down here on the Floor of the House.

'And before leaving I would like to express my thanks to all those at Fire Station 37, Beryl on the switchboard, Chief Officer Hargreaves, Driver Jenkins. . . .'

BOOK 3

Compendium of Retellable Tales

Introduction

A lively story is to a good speech as spice is to a fine meal. A touch of wit, a flash of humour, a shaft of laughter, each is appreciated by every audience. Everyone likes a good story – whatever his, her or its age. The best tales are like wine. They mature with the years.

As I have sat through millennial miseries of meetings and dinners, many of them extremely boring, I have jotted down on menus, notepads and scraps of assorted paper the best of the story-teller's crop. To create this section of the book, I have now raided piles of files, deciphered scrawl and shorthand, rejected some tales, too blue or too terrible to retell – and brought together the mixture that now follows.

Each tale – be it a joke, an aphorism, an illustration, a wisecrack or an unwise gaffe – has been well-used and much appreciated. I have sorted the accumulation into rough sections – although many stories could fit just as well into several of my groupings. Anyway, if you wish to pick out a story for a special purpose, the index should help. Or maybe you will just enjoy browsing your way through a quarter-century of tales which – told or retold – have brought me much pleasure. Use them in good health, in good voice – and with that good fortune that is the essential prerequisite and precursor of every standing ovation.

A tale is only as good as its teller. Bad workmen blame their tools, poor comedians their scriptwriters. Still, tools and scripts must be selected with care, to suit both user and occasion.

Some of these Retellable Tales will suit you, others will not. Most can be adapted.

Sometimes, I have suggested possible changes, in brackets or footnotes. Do not hesitate yourself to change the material to suit your occasion or your audience.

Naturally, it is unhelpful to misattribute a quotation, though, we may all be prepared to accept the paternity of wise words, fathered off on us by affectionate quoters. Misquoted ideas are the source of many a libel suit.

So use and enjoy these tales with pleasurable care. They should serve you well.

76 Presentations, speeches and stories

Opening gambits

As Henry VIII said to each of his wives in turn: 'I shall not keep you long . . .'.(*Lord Janner*)

Like the time the toastmaster said: 'Ladies and Gentlemen . . . pray for the silence of Mr Greville Janner . . .'.

The last time the Chair introduced me and was told to be brief, he began: 'The less said about Mr Greville Janner, the better . . .'.

Your Chair has just said to me: 'Would you like to speak now – or shall we let them go on enjoying themselves a little longer?'

Why me first?

I have been asked to speak before Mr . . . because I have several dates in (*naming two months hence*) which I wish to keep. (*Bob Monkhouse*)

Short cut

Guest speaker to Chair: 'How long should I speak?'

Chair: 'As long as you like. But I must be away by five.'

Civic slip

I have to address a lot of conferences. Indeed, last week, somebody said: 'Would you please address a meeting of 150 co-operative women'. (*Mayor of Harrogate addressing conference opening session.*)

Royal introductions

Presenting a stream of notables to the Queen at a reception, I remarked that it must be a strain meeting so many strangers all at one time.

'It is not as difficult as it might seem,' came Her Majesty's deadpan reply. 'You see, I so seldom have to introduce myself – they all seem to know who I am!'

Compliments	Mark Twain once said: 'I can live for two months on a good compliment.' You have given me enough compliments for several years. . . (*Useful response to flattering introduction. GJ*)
AGM	Chair: 'We now come to another annual meeting – after an interval of a year . . .'
Audience	I asked your chairman for details of the people I would be speaking to today – numbers, broken down by age and sex – and he replied: 'Yes, they are . . .' (*Clement Freud*)
Sleep	A new pastor arrived in a country parish. He noticed with dismay that each week during his sermon, the senior churchwarden dropped off to sleep. He put up with this until one week the man snored. After the service he went up to him and said very gently: 'I am sorry to mention this, but it does set a very bad example when my senior churchwarden sleeps during the sermon.' 'Not at all,' replied the Elder. 'It just shows that I trust you!'
Foot in mouth	Conservative MP Andrew Mackay tells of his introduction by the chairperson at a local Tory women's meeting. 'We offer an especially warm welcome to Mr Mackay tonight, since he has refused to accept any payment for his appearance. This means that next time we will be able to afford a proper speaker!'
Off the record?	'How did your speech go?' 'Marvellous. Even the journalists put down their pencils and listened . . .'
Quote	'War has devastating results', as Lenin said. And it would be true even had *he* not said it . . . [*Translatable to, from, or for anyone else. GJ*]
Applause	If they clap before you speak, that is faith; if they clap during your speech, that is hope; if they clap at the end, that is charity!

208

Presentations, speeches and stories

Jokes by numbers   At a jokesters' conference, everyone knew each other's stories so well that they simply used numbers. A man got on the stage and said: '75'. Silence – except for two men who were rolling about in the aisles. When asked why they were laughing, one said: 'I like the way he tells it'; the other said: 'I haven't heard it before.'

Golden silence   Business people must first learn when to make speeches. Then they get wise and learn when not to make them.

Pronunciation   An American tourist was crossing Westminster Bridge. He stopped a passer-by and said: 'Sir, could you please tell me. Is this river pronounced "Thems" or "Tems"?'

'Thems,' the man replied.

"Gee, I'm surprised,' said the American. 'I always thought it was pronounced "Tems". Are you quite sure?'

'Yeth,' answered the man. 'I'm thertain!'

Preferred position   Addressing a large meeting, a politician was worried in case his microphone was not working.

'Can you hear me at the back?' he called out.

'I can't hear you,' cried a voice from the rear.

'I *can* hear you,' shouted a man from the front row. 'Would the man at the back like to change places with me?'

To inattentive listener   'Can you hear me? That's good . . . I can hear you too!' (*David Berglas*)

If . . .   There is no end to the oratorical use of the word 'if' – nor to the stories which may embellish it. If (there we go) you decide to use Kipling's poem, please ladle on your vocal melodrama. The best 'if' story is a reversed chestnut:

'How was the dinner?'

'If the chicken had been as fresh as the waitress . . . if the waitress had been as young as the wine . . . if the wine had been as mature as the jokes . . . it would have been a lovely evening!'

209

Or there is the French saying: 'If my aunt had wheels, she would be a bicycle!' (*Si ma tante avait des roues, ce serait une bicyclette* – in case you use it to a French-speaking audience.) *If any reader would care to submit an original 'if' story that I can use in the next edition of this book, I shall be glad to provide a reward. Meanwhile, please do not think that because a joke or a story happens to be known to your audience, they will reject it. GJ*

Vote of thanks   At least Macbeth knew that when the dreadful banquet was over, he would not be the person required to return thanks.

77 Epigrams and definitions, proverbs and laws

Anger   A sage who is angry ceases to be a sage. (*Talmud-Pesahim*)

Argument   My father told me never to argue with an angry man . . . (*Nahum Goldmann*)

Average man   A defendant in a negligence action pleaded that 'anyone with average intelligence' would not have suffered damage. With shattering accuracy, the judge replied: 'You should perhaps bear in mind that something like one half of the people in this country are below average intelligence!' (*See also* Public opinion.)

Balance   Churchill once remarked that there is nothing more difficult than holding up a wall leaning towards you except kissing a girl leaning away from you.

                   People in our industry are well balanced – we have a chip on each shoulder! One chip is provided by Revenue, the tax man . . . the other by (*the Government, Customs and Excise – or what-have-you*).

Change   The UK Government was considering switching its vehicles to driving on the right-hand side of the road. Anxious about a transitional change-over period, the Department of Transport suggested effecting the alteration 'by stages . . . starting with heavy goods vehicles'.

Company   A man is known by the company which he thinks no one knows he is keeping.

Corroboration Never lie alone. (*Janner's Law.*)

Cranks   Crank – A man with a new idea until it succeeds. (*Mark Twain*)

211

Danger from fools   Any fool can throw a stone into a lake; but a hundred wise men cannot get it out. (*Greek proverb.*)

Democracy   Democracy – national or corporate – requires the enlightened balance of satisfied self-interest. (*Janner's Law.*)

Deterrence   Deterrence requires existence of power; willingness to use it; and knowledge by the adversary that it will, if necessary, be used. (*Abba Eban, Israeli statesman and orator.*)

Discretion   If I know something you do not know, then you know that I cannot tell you; and if I do not know anything that you do not know, you will not want to hear me anyway!

Education – and training   The difference between education and training? If your daughter comes home and says that she has been having sex education at school, you will doubtless rejoice. But if she says that she has been having sex training, you would have due cause for alarm

Enemies   Choose your enemies with care. Make sure that they are important. Your importance depends upon theirs. (*Founder of World Jewish Congress, Nahum Goldmann – who maintained that he was unknown until he was publicly attacked by the redoubtable Rabbi Abba Hillel Silver.*)

Fatherly boast   I have never raised my hand to my son – except in self-defence. (*Lord Janner*)

Friends   The Prime Minister left tonight for a tour of all our friendly European countries. She will be back within a couple of hours.

Friendship   The Greeks say of a true friend: 'I have taken bread and salt with him.'

Genius   A Rabbi visited a kibbutz on the edge of the desert. He said: 'You kibbutzniks are so clever . . . You know how to settle where the trees are!'

Helpful A driver stopped at a crossroads in a village. 'Excuse me,' he said to a passer-by, 'but does it matter which of these roads I take to get me to the next town?'

'Not to me it don't', replied the villager.

Holes First law on holes – when you're in one, stop digging! (*Denis Healey*)

Ideas A friend once said to Einstein: 'When I have a good idea, I do not want to forget it. So I keep a notebook by my bed. What do you do?'

Einstein replied: 'I do not understand your question. I have only had two or three good ideas in my life.'

Intolerance We *should* not endure intolerance; but we *must* not endure tolerance. (*Chaim Weizmann, first President of Israel*)

Isolationism A man once sat in a boat, boring a hole under his seat. 'Don't worry, shipmates,' he said to his fellow travellers. 'It's only under *my* seat, not yours . . .' (*Talmud*)

Knowledge Everything I know about this subject would fit into a nutshell and still leave plenty of room for the nut. (*Lord Mancroft*)

Legislation The effect of a statute is in directly inverse ratio to the amount of noise made during its passage. (*Janner's Law.*)

Life? Confucius says: 'I am asked why I buy rice and flowers? I reply: I buy rice to live and flowers so that I have something to live for.'

Litigation Litigants fight cases – lawyers win them. (*Janner's Law*)

Men Men who try too much to be macho do not amount to mucho. (*Zsa Zsa Gabor – quoted by Michael Foot, with reference to Dr Owen, October 1983.*)

213

Opinions	A Russian Jew was asked whether he didn't have any mind of his own on political affairs. He replied: 'Yes, of course I do. I have my own opinions. But I don't agree with them.'
Optimism	An optimist says that the bottle is half full – a pessimist that it is half empty.
Paranoid?	Remember that just because I am paranoid doesn't mean that I ain't got enemies. (*Henry Kissinger*)
Photographs	The road to political oblivion is paved with good photographs.
Plagiarism	Copy from one book and that is 'plagiarism' or breach of copyright. Copy from two or more books and that is 'research'.
Power	Power is wonderful, absolute power is absolutely wonderful.
Public opinion	There was once a Russian doctor who bustled into the ward and said: 'I'm in a terrible hurry. Please give me the average temperature of all the patients . . .' (*Shimon Peres*) [*Useful when asked: 'What is the feeling in the UK about . . .? GJ*]
Quietude	Chinese proverb: May we live in uninteresting times.
Quotes	UN Resolution 242 is like most sacred texts – more often quoted than read. [*May be applied to most of its kind. GJ*]
Recession, depression – and recovery	Recession is when your neighbour is out of work; depression is when you are out of work; recovery is when the government is out of work . . .
Resignation	Never resign – unless a better job awaits. (*Janner's Law.*)
Resolutions	The road to political ruin is paved with excellent resolutions. [*See also* Photographs.]

Success	Mark Twain bemoaned that he had not seen the Niagara Falls, so they made up a special party to take him there. Afterwards his hosts said: 'What did you think of it?' Mark Twain paused: 'It's certainly a success,' he said.
Successors	Nothing succeeds like a successor.
Survival	The porcupine may be less attractive than the rabbit but it has a greater chance of survival and much less chance of being digested.
Systems	A system is only as good as those who attempt to deceive it.
Temptation	Do not blame the mouse – blame the hole in the wall. (*Talmud*)
Tolerance	Tolerance is the ability to put up with opinions which bother us little.
Secrets	The vanity of being known to be entrusted with a secret is generally one of the chief motives to disclose it. (*Samuel Johnson*) If you want to preserve your secret, wrap it up in frankness. If you want another to keep your secret, keep it yourself. (*Seneca*)
Tradition	It is a long-established tradition . . . as Lord Denning (*or anyone else you are to name*) would say when he has a new idea . . .
Victory and defeat	'What a glorious thing must be a victory, Sir.' 'The greatest tragedy in the world, Madam, except a defeat.'
Wisdom	Just as the bee gathers honey from all flowers, so the wise man gathers knowlege from all men. (*Indian proverb.*)

78   Insults

Churchillian

I don't just give offence, I take it. (*Churchill*)

Churchill described Prime Minister Attlee as: 'A sheep in sheep's clothing'; and said of Christian Socialist Chancellor of the Exchequer, Sir Stafford Cripps: 'There but for the grace of God goes God.'

Book reviews

From the moment I picked up your book until I laid it down I was convulsed with laughter. Some day I intend reading it. (*Groucho Marx*)

An author wrote to the perpetrator of a fiercely offensive review: 'I am sitting in the smallest room in the house. Your review is before me. It will soon be behind me.'

Prejudice

I believe I have no prejudice whatsoever. All I need to know is that a man is a member of the human race and that is bad enough for me.

Lady Astor was the first woman MP. She once said to Churchill: 'If you were my husband, I would flavour your coffee with poison.' He replied: 'Nancy, if I were your husband, I would drink it!'

On another occasion, Nancy said: 'Winston, you are very drunk.
  He retorted: 'Nancy, you are very ugly, but in the morning I shall be sober.'

The late Will Paling, MP, once called Churchill 'a dirty dog'. The Tory benches erupted with cries of: 'Withdraw, withdraw . . .'
  The old man rose to his feet. 'Not at all,' he said. 'I do not invite the Honourable Member to withdraw. On the contrary, I invite him to repeat what he has said outside this Chamber.

And I will then show him what a dirty dog does to a paling!'

No comment   Churchill once tried unsuccessfully to get Lord Catto to make a statement on a particular issue. He got no results and complained: 'Alas – Lord Catto is lying doggo . . .'

Death wish   President Johnson attended the memorial service in Australia for a Prime Minister, recently drowned. He was asked by the press what he would do for peace. 'Anything,' he replied.

'Mr President,' came a voice from the back. 'Would you take a swim?'

Fence sitting   An American Senator described King Hussein as 'Forever Amber'. [*Could be used for anyone else who cannot make up his mind whether to stop or to go, on a particular issue or generally. GJ*]

Accountants and politicians   Aneurin Bevan coined a marvellous phrase for a heartless human being. Many wrongly believe that he applied it to the austere Sir Stafford Cripps. In fact it was used in rage when he was beaten by Hugh Gaitskell for the Treasurership of the Labour Party. Without naming his target, he said: 'The right kind of leader for the Labour Party is a *desiccated calculating machine* who must not in any way permit himself to be swayed by indignation . . . at suffering, privation or injustice . . . for that would be evidence of the lack of proper education and absence of self-control.'

[*'You sir, are – as Bevan once said – a desiccated calculating machine!' is a spendid insult, especially when aimed at an accountant or a politician.*]

Worst enemy   Herbert Morrison was once quoted as saying that he was his own worst enemy. 'Not while I'm alive, he ain't', Ernest Bevin retorted.

Feminists   I myself have never been able to find out precisely what feminism is. I only know that

217

people call me a feminist whenever I express sentiments that differentiate me from a doormat . . . (*Rebecca West, 1913*)

Compliment or insult?

One day, when Chancellor of the Exchequer David Lloyd George was making an important speech, a Conservative from the Opposition benches kept interrupting him. Eventually, Lloyd George exclaimed: 'I should think that the argument would be plain even to the colossal intellect of the Honourable Member.'

The Tory leapt to his feet. 'Is it in order, Mr Speaker,' he asked, 'for the Right Honourable Gentleman to refer to my colossal intellect?'

'Well,' replied Mr Speaker Lowther, very softly. 'I think it is not only in order, but is rather complimentary than otherwise!'

Disaster *v.* calamity

'If Gladstone fell into the Thames, that would be a misfortune; and if anybody pulled him out, that I suppose would be a calamity.' (*Disraeli*) [*This one is capable of innumerable variations, directed towards your current pet hate. Thus: 'If the Prime Minister/Leader of the Opposition/ managing director of main competitors, were to fall out of an aircraft, that would be a misfortune – if his parachute were to open, that would be a calamity.' GJ*]

Young parent

If you are faced with an inexperienced and youthful opponent, try the insult aimed by US Interior Secretary Harold Ickes at the then young Thomas Dewey, Republican candidate for President: 'Dewey has thrown his diaper into the ring.'

Lying

I do not accuse Mrs Thatcher of lying. She merely has what psychologists call 'selective amnesia'. (*Denis Healey*)

Plagues

I was recently at a charity dinner, with my wife on my right, and a very persistent lobbyist on my left. During the first three courses, he regaled me with horror stories of the way that politicians of all parties had ruined his business and how no country could really survive its treatment by those of us elected to office. Finally, my wife said to him: 'But surely you do make *some* distinction between the policies of the two parties?'

'There's no difference between you,' he retorted. 'I say: A plague on all your houses.'

My wife smiled across at him. 'When the plague comes to our house,' she said, 'you *must* come and visit us!'

Memories   I always smile at Mr Smith's jokes. First at their elegant wit, and then again with nostalgia.

Mindless?   Mr Smith didn't say a word till he was ten. His mother didn't know whether he was dumb or just speaking his mind.

Repetition   . . . we were all glad to hear his speech again.

Speechmaking   Mrs . . . has proved the theory that the brain is a wonderful organ that never stops functioning from the moment of birth until one rises to speak in public.

Sleeptalking   Mr . . .'s speeches always do the audience some good; they either go away stimulated or wake up refreshed.

Non-contribution   He makes the same contribution to commerce (*or to the subject under discussion*) as Cyril Smith* does to hang-gliding . . . [*Or any other well known man of huge build. GJ*]

Libraries   Mr Brown's library was burned down. Both books were destroyed. And one of them he had not even finished colouring in. [*This one can be used for your favourite ignoramus. GJ*]

Genius   The chairman (*Foreign Minister, director or whomever-you-will*) was a man of few words which were quite adequate to express the full range of his ideas.

Unbiased assessment

No one thinks more highly of Mr Smith than I do – and I think that he's not very bright.

One nation

Some Americans say that Yankees from the North are like haemorrhoids. If they come down and then go up again quickly, that's not too bad. But if they come down and stay down, that is a pain in the rear . . .

Manchester (or any other grimy city)

Manchester (*Pittsburg – or where-have-you*) is the place where the birds fly backwards so as not to get grit in their eyes.

Prizes

The first prize for the raffle was one week at Yarmouth-on-Sea. The second prize was two weeks at Yarmouth-on-Sea. The third prize was a month at Yarmouth-on-Sea. (Or anywhere else.)

Thanks

At her husbands's request, a wife gave him a plot of land in the local cemetery as his birthday present. The following year, she refused to give him a birthday present at all.

'Why no present darling?' he asked.

'Because you haven't used last year's yet,' she replied.

79   Works, trade and management

Perks

Our staff reckon that they can only take the company's property off our premises at certain times . . .

Welcome

When the Pope landed on a ceremonial visit to the UK, he knelt and kissed the soil.

'I wonder why he did that?' an astonished onlooker exclaimed.

The man beside him retorted: 'You would too, if you'd flown Alitalia and landed safely!'

Fringe benefits

On 'cabbage' (*the rag trade term for material offcuts*): We usually sell cabbage to our staff — if they don't pinch it first . . .'

Working hours

Alistair Cooke passed a country station and found the stationmaster tending his roses. 'How many hours a day do you work?' he enquired.

'Eight hours, sir. Five days a week.'

'Always eight hours? Always five days a week?' said Mr Cooke.

'Yes, always the same.'

'Why always the same?'

'Because if I worked less than eight hours, I wouldn't have enough money to buy roses. And if I worked more than eight hours, I would not have time to tend the roses . . .'

Short-time?

Employer: 'Did you work a full week last week?'

Employee: 'Yes — but I don't want any publicity . . .'

Occupational illnesses

Three well known diseases: *Plumbi pendulosis* — swinging the lead; *Haemophraemia* — bloody mindedness; and *Non digitus extractus* — failure to pull out the finger . . .

Tell-tale twitch

A man applied for a job as a television

221

announcer. Unfortunately, he suffered from a very severe twitch of his right eye. His interviewer said: 'Wouldn't you be better off applying for a job with the radio?'

'No,' the man replied. 'I take one of my special pills and I'm all right for a couple of hours.'

'In that case,' said the interviewer, 'you'd better take one now and let me see how it works.'

The man fished in his pockets and pulled out a packet of contraceptives . . . then another . . . then a third . . . then a whole pile of them, before finally producing a bottle of aspirin.

'I understand the aspirin,' said the interviewer. 'But why the contraceptives?'

'The interviewee looked at him sceptically. 'Have you ever tried going into a chemist's shop and saying: "I'd like a (*wink*) bottle of (*wink*) aspirin, please"?'

Job description   Fred answered an advertisement, offering £1,500 for a man prepared to sleep with a gorilla. He asked whether he could have time to pay.

Unemployment   A miner applied for a job at a Rhondda pit. The manager told him to 'come back in the spring'.

'What do you think I am,' asked the man, 'a ruddy cuckoo?' (*Speaker George Thomas, now Viscount Tonypandy*)

Warning   The managing director of a great engineering company invited school classes to see round the works. One of the teachers was overheard at the end of the morning saying to his class: 'There you are, lads and girls. You have now seen where *you* may end up, if you don't do well in your O-levels!'

Passing the buck   An Ordinary Seaman was applying for promotion. He was asked to correct the following statement: 'It was me what done it.' He wrote: 'It was *not* me what done it.' [*Legend has it that*

222

he was immediately promoted to Rear Admiral! GJ]

Trade unions

A trade union is an island of anarchy in a sea of chaos. (*Aneurin Bevan*)

'Differentials' and 'anomalies'

If I earn more than you do, that is a 'differential'. If you earn more than I do, that is an 'anomaly'.

Management – and industrial disputes

The latest argument at a works renowned for its management problems got senior executives so upset that they began to stab each other in the front. [*Also useful to describe feelings in the Cabinet, Shadow Cabinet, boardroom – or where-you-will. GJ*]

Pay day?

A son asked his father for a loan until pay day. His father asked: 'When is pay day?'

The son replied: 'I don't know. You tell me. You're the one who's working . . .'

Leadership

There are two types of leadership. One is where you go in front and lead from there. The other is where you wait to see where people are going and then run around to the front and take over. (*Julius Berman, then Chairman of the Conference of American Jewish Organisations*)

Explanations

A personnel director was having great trouble in inducing an employee to sign up under a non-contributory pension scheme – which was in fact far better for him than the current contributory pension scheme. He refused to sign.

Eventually, the personnel manager sent the man to the managing director. 'Alex,' said the MD, 'You must sign. I know that you have been with us for 30 years without causing trouble, but that is no reason for not signing . . .'

Alex: 'I refuse.'

Managing director: 'Alex, you must sign – or I will give you the sack!'

Alex signed.

The next time that personnel manager saw Alex, he said: 'Why did you sign when the managing director asked you to – but you always refused me?'

Alex: 'Well, no one explained it to me properly before . . .'

Supervisors   Supervisory staff can do no right. They can only mitigate their wrong. (*Lord Goddard*)

Self-service   Two foremen were arguing over whether sex was a pleasure or a chore. The first, a married man with eight children, regarded it as a chore. The second, a bachelor, thought it was the greatest delight in life. To settle their argument, they called over young Fred, the apprentice. 'So you tell us, Fred,' they said. 'Is sex a chore or a pleasure?'

'It must be a pleasure,' said the boy.

'Why?'

'Because if it was a chore, you fellows would make me do it for you!'

Up yours   A worker removed the guard from a machine and lost two fingers on his right hand. He only noticed his loss when he said good night to the foreman!

Once a failure   A man was sacked for trying to kill his foreman. His shop steward begged the employers to give him a second chance.

Never resign   Frederick the Great intended to dismiss one of his Generals. The General wrote to him: 'After the battle, my head is yours. Meanwhile, I intend to use it to best effect on your behalf.'

Dismissal   The chairman of a large company called in his directors, one by one. Eventually, only the newest and most junior director was left outside the chairman's office. When his turn came, he found his colleagues sitting around a table.

Chairman: 'Bill, have you been having an affair with my secretary, Miss Jones?'

Bill: 'Certainly not.

'Are you sure?'

'Absolutely. I've never laid a hand on her.'
'Are you absolutely certain?'
'Of course I am.'
'Very well, Bill, then *you* sack her.'

References

'I am pleased to recommend him, for any other job . . .' or 'I am pleased to provide him with a reference for any other job . . .' or 'He was fired with enthusiasm . . .'

Erratic leadership

The following is a useful analogy, when explaining why the Prime Minister, president, managing director or other adversary is likely to perform some unpredictable and dangerous act.

Mr Brown is like the cross-eyed javelin thrower who does not break any records, but who certainly keeps his audience on its toes!

80 Business, companies and professions

Auditors

An auditor is an accountant who comes onto the field after the battle is over and bayonets the wounded. (*Don Hanson [Arthur Andersen]*)

Auditors – and actuaries

An auditor is like an actuary who has had his personality removed.

Accountancy

If someone asks me: 'What is two and two?', I answer: 'Are you buying or selling?' (*Lord Grade*)

Accountants

Three men apply for a job as an accountant. They are asked one question: 'What is two times two?' The first two fellows got it right. The third one replies: 'What figure did you have mind, sir?' He got the job.

Capitalism and Bankruptcy

Capitalism without bankruptcy is like Christianity without hell. (*Eastern Airlines' Chief Executive*)

Risks

A 'calculated risk' was defined by an airline pilot as 'when the engineers on the ground make the calculations and the pilots take the risk'. [*Adapt for any situation where others make the calculation but the risk is yours. GJ*]

Flotation

An accountant and a client were swimming in the sea when the client was swept away. The accountant swam after him, dragged him towards the shore and when he was nearly in, said: 'Are you OK now? Can you float on your own?'

The client replied: 'Even when I'm dying, he wants to talk business!'

Good company

Lawyer to judge, well known for his puritanical views and as a pillar of the Church: 'I appear for the plaintiffs – a God-fearing, limited libility company.'

Companies
Lord Thurloe once said: "A corporation has no body to be burned and no soul to be damned . . .'

Unanimity
Two directors were doing a crossword. One asked: 'How do you spell "unanimously"?'

The other: 'I am not surprised that you can't spell it. It's only a miracle that you can pronounce the word . . .'

Partners?
The owner of an hotel quietly watched as his barman put 50p in his own pocket out of every £1 he took from a customer. When he saw the barman putting an entire £1 into his wallet, he pounced. 'What are you doing?' he asked. 'I thought we were partners!'

Civil servants
A civil servant – one who has a valid objection to any possible solution.

Success and failure
The head of the Civil Service, Sir Douglas Wass, pointed out to a distinguished and private dinner of top business executives and lawyers that *they* could measure *their* success by winning or losing cases and by their balance sheets (respectively). 'We have no such base to judge ours,' he said. 'The success of a civil servant can only be judged by the absence of obvious failure!'

Police
A teacher in a local school required his class to write an essay on the police. Martin wrote: 'Them police are bastards.'

The teacher told the police of the comment. They invited Martin to the station and gave him the most marvellous day of his life. The next day the teacher set the boys another essay on the police. Martin wrote: 'Them police are *cunning* bastards!'

Spies
A Russian spy went to Wales and was told to see their contact in Abergavenny, who lived at

25 Cwmbran Terrace. The password: 'The space ship is in orbit.'

By mistake, he called at number 5 Cwmbran Terrace. A woman opened the door. 'Yes?' she enquired.

'The space ship is in orbit,' said the Russian.

'Oh,' said the lady, 'you've come to the wrong address. You will be wanting number 25. That's where Dai the Spy lives.'

Public relations

Fact: In places, the fabled River Jordan is nothing more than a trickle.

Comment: 'That is what public relations can do for a river!' (*Henry Kissinger*)

Brains

Two army captains were grousing about the stupidity of their respective batmen. They decided to have a bet on which one was more stupid. Captain X called for his batman and said: 'Take this £5 note and buy me a colour TV set down in the village.' 'Yes, sir. Certainly, sir.' He saluted and went out into the mess room.

Captain Y then rang for his batman and said: 'Go to the orderly room immediately and see whether I am there.' 'Yes, sir. Certainly, sir.' The batman saluted and left.

The two batmen met in the corridor outside and compared notes.

'Fancy asking me to buy a colour TV set on an early closing day,' said the first. The second replied: 'Imagine making me walk half a mile when he could have used the telephone to see if he's in the orderly room!'

Class distinction

When I was serving in the British Army of the Rhine, I found a notice on our HQ board at Christmas. It read: 'Christmas parties will be held as follows: Officers and their ladies, 24 December; non-commissioned officers and their wives, 25 December; and other ranks and their womenfolk, 26 December.'

Press men

Newspapers are fiercely independent of pressure from their advertisers. Or are they?

Some years ago, I campaigned for legislation to ban the fraudulent 'guarantee' or 'warranty', which in reality removed more rights than it gave – especially when provided with a motor vehicle. I was commissioned to write a full-length feature for a London Sunday paper which carried the front page banner: 'THE fearless newspaper'.

My piece was pungent, accurate, documented and devastating. It was not published. Instead, I simply received my fee. I telephoned the Features Editor. He said: 'I'm sorry, but to publish your piece would have cost us a fortune. You effectively attacked every car manufacturer in the business.'

'So what?' I retorted. 'I thought you were "The fearless newspaper"!'

'That's all very well,' he retorted, "but you have to have a newspaper to be fearless in!"

Insurers

Insurance people present plans to keep you poor while you are alive so that you may die rich.

Insurance

The favourite uncle at a wedding dinner announced that he was going to give the bridegroom a life insurance policy. The bride burst into tears. When she was finally calmed, she blurted out: 'I don't like it . . . I don't like it . . . I don't want father to set light to Harry like he did to the warehouse . . .!'

Whose worry?

A man owed $100,000. The night before the sum fell due for payment, he could not sleep. He tossed and he turned and he strode up and down. Eventually, he walked around to his creditor's house and knocked on the window. 'What is it?' asked the man.

'I'm very sorry,' replied the debtor, 'but I shan't be able to pay what I owe you tomorrow morning. I've been so worried about it that I couldn't get to sleep. Anyway, I've decided to wake you so that you can now stay awake worrying, while I get some sleep!'

Whose trade?

Morgan and Dai went on safari. Suddenly, a woolly creature dropped from a tree onto Morgan's back. 'What is it? What is it?' he cried out.

'How should I know?' Dai replied. 'Am I a furrier?'

Enterprise

Cohen owned a small tailor's shop and made a modest living. Then two firms of multiple-tailors opened on either side of him. 'What are you going to do now?' asked a friend.

'Don't worry,' said Cohen, 'Everything will be all right. I'll just change the name of my shop.'

'What good will that do you?'

'Plenty.'

'What will you call your shop?'

'I shall call it . . . *Main Entrance*!'

Jewish business

Three Jewish men met for dinner.

The first one said: 'Oi!'

The second one said: 'Oi yevay!'

The third said: 'If you boys are going to talk business, I'm off . . .'

Antiques

An American and his wife were in Portobello Road. 'It's not bad, Bessie,' he said. 'But they don't make antiques like they used to, do they?'

Wedding present

A father-in-law gave his son-in-law 5,000 shares in his business. 'There you are, lad,' he said. 'Anything else I can do for you?'

The son-in-law replied: 'Yes, Dad. Please would you buy me out?'

Commercial progression

A businessman gets on . . . then he gets honest . . . then he gets honoured . . .

Business talk

Movie Mogul Lou Wasserman once invited Sam Goldwyn to meet Clark Gable. 'But you mustn't talk business with him,' he said. 'Promise me – nothing about business and nothing about money.' Goldwyn agreed.

He duly arrived for the lunch with a briefcase which he promptly opened, emptying onto the table $100,000 in 10 dollar notes. 'There you are,' he announced. 'This is what I am not allowed to talk to you about!'

Golfer – a top surprise

'I know you're not meant to take bets when you play against members,' said John Jones to the club professional, 'but I want to ask you a very special favour. As it's my silver wedding, I'd like to play one round with you for £100.'

'You know I can't do that,' said the professional. 'Anyway, I'd have to give you a very large handicap.'

'No,' said John, 'all I want by way of handicap is three gotchas.'

The professional, who did not want to let on that he did not know what 'gotcha' meant, said: 'OK. But keep it quiet.'

As they were about to tee off at the first hole, the professional felt a hand coming between his legs and grabbing him. 'Gotcha!' John shouted.

Discomfited, the professional prepared to tee off for the second time.

'Gotcha!' yelled John, as he grabbed his opponent.

'That's very nasty,' said the professional. 'But we've 18 holes to go and you've only got one gotcha left!'

'That's right' said John. 'But how will you enjoy playing 18 holes, never knowing when the next gotcha's coming?' (*Bob Monkhouse*) [*Monkhouse used this joke to massive effect at an entertainment industry dinner – his speech won a standing ovation from his colleagues. Used with sensitivity, it may be told to illustrate any other situation in which you are proposing to keep your opponents, competitors, rivals or enemies in Damocletian suspense! GJ*]

81   Finance, sales and insolvency

Follow-up

Fred won a million pounds in a lottery. His wife said to him: 'What shall we do about all the begging letters?

'Just keep sending them!' Fred replied.

How to become a millionaire

A bedraggled beggar wheedled a dollar out of Rockefeller, outside his Manhattan apartment block. After handing over the money, the millionaire enquired: 'Why don't you invest in some clean clothing, young man?'

'I appreciate the suggestion,' the beggar replied. 'But if you don't mind my asking, do I try to teach you *your* business?'

Fellow feeling

A burglar was caught in the garden of a millionaire's mansion, a transistor radio in his pocket.

'What do you want us to do with him?' asked the police.

'Let him go,' answered the millionaire. 'We all started small.'

The gift of language

Sign on shop: '30 languages spoken here.' Customer comes in and tries to make herself understood in French, but nobody can manage. Another customer says to the shopkeeper: 'I thought you spoke 30 languages here?'

Shopkeeper replies: 'That's the customers . . . not us . . .'

Honour

'Next time a man says that his word is as good as his bond, take his bond!' (*Lord Home of the Hirsel – formerly Prime Minister Alec Douglas Home*)

Energy

Britain is a lump of coal in a sea of oil on a bubble of gas. (*Clive Jenkins*)

Oil wealth

It's not clever just to have oil, you know. Sardines have oil and they are really stupid. They even get inside the tin and leave the key on the outside. (*Bob Monkhouse*)

Prophecies

It is very difficult to make a prophecy as to the future . . . and in Israel, it is very difficult to be a prophet at all, because of the competition . . .

Cash management

We have just created a new cash management programme. This means that we pay when we wish to . . .

Debtors

If you owe £50, you are a *shnorrer* (a beggar, in Yiddish). If you owe £5000, you are in business. If you owe £500 billion, then you are Chancellor of the Exchequer (*or Minister of Finance*).

Hyper inflation

The Chancellor of the Exchequer went into a shop and said: 'I don't think inflation is that bad. Look at those handkerchieves – £1 each. And shirts for £10. And trousers for £15.'

His aide whispered quietly in his ear. 'I'm sorry, Minister. We're not in a man's shop. This is a laundry . . .'

Rise – or raise?

The Head of a vast company whose parsimony to his employees was matched by his generosity to the currently governing political party was awarded a knighthood. At Buckingham Palace he knelt before Her Majesty, who tapped him on his right shoulder: 'Rise, Sir Frederick,' she said. Fred remained on his knees.

The Queen tapped him on his left shoulder. 'Rise, Sir Frederick,' she pronounced. Still no movement.

The sovereign lifted her sword and patted the tycoon gently on his head. 'Rise, Sir Frederick,' she said. Still nothing.

A knowledgeable equerry whispered into the royal ear: 'I'd give up, Your Majesty,' he said. 'Sir Fred does not know the meaning of the word "rise".'

233

A capital story	'Where is the capital of Saudi Arabia?'
	'A third in Switzerland; a third in London; and the rest in Germany and the USA.'
	This story is matched by one I was told in Canada: 'What was the first Polish settlement in the Province of Ontario?'
	'30 cents in the dollar!'
Bankruptcy	'Nothing in your deposit box? Nothing in your wife's name? Nothing dug into the ground? – You're not bankrupt, brother, you're skint!'
Ultimate insolvency	Jack went bankrupt so often that he even put his tombstone into his wife's name.
Liquidation	Noah was the bravest man in history. He floated his company when the rest of the world was in liquidation.
Recession	A deep-sea diver feels tug on rope. Voice on intercom says: 'Come up quickly, the ship's sinking!' [*Suitable for comment on invitation to join political party currently in eclipse. GJ*]
Fair exchange	An accountant opened a new office and a client ordered flowers to be sent to him. The next day a splendid arrangement arrived with a card containing the message, 'Rest In Peace'.
	The accountant spoke to his friend and told him what had happened. The friend apologised. 'But,' he said, 'just think of the pleasure that will have been given at the funeral by the card reading "Good luck in your new location!" '

Objectivity	Those who are prominent in political life are objectively described only in their own memoirs. (*Abba Eban*)
Politicians	A politician is a person who approaches every problem with an open mouth. (*Adlai Stevenson*)
Principles	I am a man of principle – but one of my principles is expediency. (*Lloyd George*)
Compromise	Compromise is when you do today that which you swore yesterday that you would not do – and while all politicians compromise, none of them like to be photographed doing so . . .
Balanced concerns	'If I am not for myself, who will be for me? But if I am only for myself, what am I? And if not now, then when?' (*Rabbi Hillel*)
Middle of the road	The only part of the road worth driving on is the middle – each of the extremes is in the gutter. (*General Eisenhower*)
Experience	Experience tells us that politicians do not *always* mean the opposite of what they say.
Eggs and baskets	British aircraft manufacturers once suggested to Winston Churchill that he, the Cabinet and 40 other MPs should go up in the newly invented Comet jet aircraft, so as to give confidence to the public. One of his ministers complained that if anything happened to the aircraft, it would be disastrous. The country would be plunged into over 60 by-elections at the same time.
	Reluctantly, the old man agreed. 'It all goes to show,' he said, 'that it is potentially disastrous to put all your baskets into one egg . . .'
Opposition	To be in Opposition is no disgrace. In fact, it is

an honour. It is the only honour which politicians do not actively seek!

Governmental philosophy

If you do not know where you are going, you will probably end up somewhere else . . .

Publicity

He is the sort of politician who gets an erection evey time he sees a microphone or TV camera. (*Cabinet Minister describing a colleague.*)

Media attraction

A microphone has the same effect on him as a lamp post has on a dog.

Sleep

Members of Parliament and of Congress are people who talk in other people's sleep.

The oldest profession?

Some say that gardening is the oldest profession – because Adam was the first man on earth. But the Bible tells us that before the world was created, all was chaos and confusion. And you all know who created that . . . politicians!

Incipient modesty

Your first two weeks in Parliament, you wonder how you got there. Thereafter, you wonder how the others got there.

Substitute?

An MP died. Within a day, a young hopeful telephoned the national agent. 'I hope it's not too soon,' he said, 'but I'm wondering whether I might not take the place of the deceased . . .'

The national agent replied: 'If the undertaker has no objection, I certainly have none!'

Divisions

Two tourists were standing in the central lobby in the House of Commons when the division bell rang. 'What's that?' one of them asked the other. 'I don't know,' she replied. 'I suppose one of them must have escaped . . .'

Person unknown

A Tory Whip telephoned one of his Members in the middle of the night, to tell him to come in to vote. A woman's voice answered the phone – but he heard a male voice in the background saying: 'Tell him I'm not here . . .'

'I'm afraid Mr . . . is not here' said the voice.

Quick as a flash, the Whip replied: 'In that case, please tell the man who is in bed with you, whomever he may be, that he is required at the House of Commons to vote . . . at once!'

New councillor

Dai Jones is elected a Councillor for the first time. Delighted, he goes to the pub to celebrate.

'Your usual, Dai?' asks the barman.

'*Councillor* Dai, if you please,' Dai retorted.

When he went to collect his coat in the cloakroom, the attendant said: 'Good evening, Dai.'

He replied: '*Councillor* Dai, if you please.'

On the bus, the conductor said: 'Nice to see you, Dai.'

'*Councillor* Dai, if you please,' he replied.

And so it went on with everyone he met. And when he got home, he heard his wife's voice from upstairs: 'Is that you, Dai?'

'*Councillor* Dai, if you please,' he replied.

'Then you'd better hurry up,' his wife called out. 'Dai will be home at any moment!'

Surprise

St Peter provided a distinguished Pope with a bare cell, while giving a Congressman a fine, carpeted and thoroughly heavenly apartment. When challenged by the Pope, St Peter replied: 'We've had plenty of popes up here – but this is our first Congressman!'

Alas

There is nothing so 'ex' as an ex-MP.

Spot the wise man

Reagan, Mitterrand and Thatcher met at a Conference. 'I need your help,' said Reagan. 'I have a problem. I have 18 guards. One of them is a KGB agent. And I cannot find out which one it is!'

'I have a problem that, in its own way, is even worse,' said Mitterrand. 'I have 18 mistresses. One of them is unfaithful to me. And my problem is that I cannot tell which one.'

'My problem is worst of all,' said Mrs Thatcher, 'I have 18 people in my Cabinet. One of them is very clever . . .' [*This happy and – I hasten to to add – apocryphal tale may, of course, be adapted to whichever Cabinet, committee or other national or organised leadership you may desire to defame. GJ*]

Economy

A politician who claimed that it would be possible to get much the same results with half the expenditure illustrated his case with the tale of a Scottish riding school. They supplied each rider with only one spur on the principle that if you can get half the horse to go, there is a good chance that the other half will follow.

83 Parliament, government democracy and elections

Differences of opinion
We specialise in harmonising contrariness. (*Sir Shridath [Sonny] Ramphal, Secretary General of the Commonwealth*)

Family tradition
Franklin D. Roosevelt was asked why he was a Democrat. He replied: 'Because my great grandfather and my grandfather and my father were Democrats before me.'

'What would happen if your great grandfather, your grandfather and your father had been horse thieves?' retorted the questioner.

'In that case,' President Roosevelt replied, 'I would have been a Republican.'

News – and advertising
'News is what somebody somewhere wants to suppress; all the rest is advertising'. (*Lord Northcliffe*)

Mania
Soviet dissident Leonid Plyush told a group of MPs the sad story of his incarceration in Soviet mental institutions. When asked what diagnosis he had received from the Soviet psychiatric experts he replied: 'Reformist mania with messianic tendencies.' His listeners agreed that he would have made an excellent MP.

Princely politics
It is very difficult to avoid making party political statements when you talk about almost anything. Sometimes, I fall into great elephant traps and no one notices. Other times, I trip into a very small trap – and all hell breaks loose . . . (*Prince Charles*)

Open government
Sunlight is the most effective of all disinfectants . . . (*US Supreme Court Justice Brandeis*)

Parliament
Our parliamentary system is not good – but it's the best we've got. (*Winston Churchill*)

239

Parliamentary democracy is the worst form of government – until you look at all the others. (*Winston Churchill*)

Committees

If Moses had been a committee, the Israelites would still be in Egypt.

A Parliamentary committee is a cul-de-sac into which ideas are lured, there to be quietly strangled . . .

Committee inventions

A camel is a horse invented by a committee.

Committee of one

Every committee must be made up of an odd number of people. Three members is too many.

Whipping

An MP complained that the 'whipping' had been so heavy that he could not even get out of the Commons to attend the christening of his son. His friend replied: 'You're lucky. You weren't there when your son was christened. I wasn't there when mine was conceived!'

Elections

A Scottish jury was informed by the judge: 'This is a simple case and no doubt it will not take you long to reach your verdict.'

After the jury had been out for three hours, the judge called them in. 'What's happened?' he enquired.

'We had no difficulty in reaching our verdict,' he was told. 'But the trouble is that we're still trying to elect a foreman . . .'

The right of citizens in a democracy is to make the wrong decision. That right is one which the British people have exercised massively.

Democracy

We cannot complain if a democracy exercises the rotary principle and electors vote the wrong party into power . . . (*Abba Eban*)

Russian elections

In the Soviet Union they have what are called 'Adam elections' – you have the same choice as he had.

Withdraw, withdraw!
MP Willie Hamilton was criticising Harold Wilson for wanting to go into the Common Market . . . then out of the market . . . then into the market again . . . He described such behaviour as: 'The politics of *coitus interruptus*.' The MP in front of him yelled: 'Withdraw . . . withdraw . . .'

The truth
An opponent said: 'How do you know when ex-President Nixon is lying? When he spreads his hands out, he's telling the truth . . . When he wags his finger, he's telling the truth . . . When he shakes his fist, he's telling the truth . . . But when he opens his mouth . . .'

Emigration
A professor decided to emigrate. The Dean called him to his office: 'Why do you want to go?' he enquired. 'You have a very good job . . . an excellent home . . . splendid prospects . . .'
'There are two reasons,' the Professor replied. 'The first is that when I come home in the evenings, I usually find my neighbour outside my door, dead drunk. He keeps swearing at me: "Just wait till we get rid of this Tory government and then we'll slit the throats of all you useless academics!" '
'But the Tory government is in for years yet', replied the Dean.
'Precisely,' said the Professor. 'That's my second reason.'

Tory advance
Conservative statesman: 'I see the *status quo* as the way forward.'

The choice before us
Vicar, blessing all parties before British election: 'We shall have three hymns today. In honour of the Conservatives: Now Thank We all Our God . . . In honour of the Labour Party: Oh God Our Help In Ages Past . . . And in honour of the Social Liberal Democrats: God Does Move In Mysterious Ways . . .'

Why we lost
If you are travelling in a rocky ship and feel

241

seasick, it is quite understandable that you would wish to throw the navigator overboard. (*Denis Healey*)

Advice to successor

When Harold Wilson handed over the premiership to James Callaghan, he is said to have left three envelopes in a drawer. They were to be opened in turn, in times of disaster.

Opening the first envelope, after the first disaster, Callaghan read: 'Blame your predecessor.'

After the second, he read: 'Sack your assistant.'

After the third: 'Prepare three envelopes . . .'

Successors

After Mrs Thatcher took over from Mr Callaghan, she is reported to have said to him privately: 'You certainly left us a lot of problems.' Jim replied: 'I didn't ask you to take them on, did I?'

Deterrent

Lord Birkett liked to tell the classic tale of the woman in the train who watched the man opposite her tearing up a newspaper and every now and again throwing tiny pieces out of the window.

'Why are you doing that, sir?' she enquired.

'To keep the elephants away,' he replied.

'But there are no elephants,' she protested.

'Yes,' he answered. 'It is indeed wonderfully effective.'

Hardly ever

The Captain of Gilbert and Sullivan's *HMS Pinafore* was asked whether he was ever sick at sea. He replied: 'Never.'

'What never? chorused the sailors.

'No, never.'

'What, never?' the sailor insisted.

'Well . . . *hardly ever* . . .' the Captain admitted . [*Similarly: The Government – or the Opposition, or the company, or you – may* hardly ever *be mistaken, out of step, cheating . . . GJ*]

**Political
punishment**

W.S. Gilbert suggested that a judge should 'let the punishment fit the crime'. The following story may be adapted to suit whichever politicians you feel most inclined to insult at the time.

When Winston Churchill died and went to heaven, he was greeted by St Peter who directed him to his room: 'Straight down the corridor, eighth door on the left.' As he walked by, he saw Neville Chamberlain in a cubicle, embracing that great cabaret artist, Mae West.

When Winston arrived at his cubicle, he discovered his old sparring partner, Lady Astor – the first woman MP – lying on the bed. He stormed back to St Peter: 'It's disgraceful,' he thundered. 'After all that I've done for the world. It's bad enough putting me in a room with old Nancy Astor. But how can you do that while putting that dreadful Neville Chamberlain with the delicious Mae West?'

'Now, you mind your own business, Sir Winston,' Peter replied. 'How I punish Mae West is my affair!'

84 Foreigners and diplomats

Foreign Office A tourist recently asked a policeman in Whitehall: 'Which side is the Foreign Office on?' He replied: 'It's supposed to be on our side – but I sometimes wonder . . .'

The chop Sign seen on rear window of car in London: Convicted Saudi shoplifter. No hand signals.

Ex When you are a distinguished ambassador, everyone wants you to make speeches and to be guest of honour. When you are an extinguished ambassador, you have to look both for a platform and for a livelihood . . .

Ambassadors and journalists An ambassador is a man of virtue sent to lie abroad for his country. A newswriter is a man without virtue who lies at home for himself. (*Sir Henry Wootton. The first quote, written in 1604, is well known. He added the second part later when a newswriter teased him about the lack of diplomacy inherent in his first definition.*)

Peaceful solution Our government is prepared to solve any industrial relations problem peacefully if no other solution is available. [*Adapt to suit your circumstances – government, committee, organisation or as the case may be. GJ*]

Silent diplomacy Scientist Mark Azbel told of the need for silence by Jews and others oppressed by their rules: 'A little bird freezes on a cold day and falls to the ground. A passing cow drops a cow pat on it. The bird, revived by the warmth, begins to chirp. A fox appears, hears the chirping, cleans the bird and eats it.

Moral: 'Not everyone who covers you with manure is your enemy and not everyone who cleans you off is your friend.

'More important: If you are deep in the shit, don't make a sound!'

Democracy?

Ivor Richard, former British Ambassador to the UN, was asked by an American friend why the United Nations is so undemocratic.

'Undemocratic?' he replied. 'Why do you say that?'

'Because we keep getting outvoted!'

Christmas gifts – and diplomatic problems

A newly appointed British Ambassador to the USA arrived in Washington DC in mid-December. A newspaper man was chatting with him and asked: 'Ambassador, what would you like for Christmas?'

He replied: 'Well, a small box of American chocolates would do nicely.'

On Christmas Eve, the Embassy was shocked to hear the following broadcast: 'We asked various Ambassadors what they would like best for Christmas. The German Ambassador replied: "A generation of peace for all the world." The French Ambassador replied: "Love and fraternity between nations." The United Kingdom envoy replied: "A small box of American chocolates would do nicely."'

American and English

The American language differs from English in that it seeks the top of expression while English seeks its lowly values. (*Salvador de Madariaga*)

Never has one language done more to divide two nations. (*George Bernard Shaw*)

Solution

Whenever a government thinks that it has solved the Irish question, the Irish change the question.

Idealism

Yes, India is a country with great ideals – but it is peopled entirely by human beings. (*Prime Minister Mrs Indira Gandhi*) [*or the UK – or anywhere else! GJ*]

United Nations?

Former Secretary of State, Dean Acheson:

When the United Nations is divided by 50/50, then the decision does not represent 'world conscience'. Add Yemen, Haiti and Portugal and it becomes world conscience.

Equality?

Re Israel and her Arab foes: 'They are many and we are one, but we represent 50 per cent of the conflict.' (*Yigal Allon*)

Mind your language

Many years ago, a Canadian MP replied to a suggestion that their proceedings ought to be held from time to time in French by saying: 'If the English language was good enough for Matthew, Mark, Luke and John, it is good enough for us!'

Lost opportunities

The Jordanians never miss a chance to lose an opportunity. (*Abba Eban*) [*Adapt to suit circumstances/nation/government/situation. GJ*]

Promotion refused

The Arab General who conquered Egypt some 1,300 years ago expected the Caliph of Arabia to appoint him governor of the country. In fact, the Caliph only offered him the command of the troops in Egypt, while another man became governor.

The General refused this command, with the memorable phrase: 'Why should I hold the cow's horns whilst someone else milks her?' (*Anwar Sadat*)

Pure bred?

A polar bear has his little boy in tow. Son pulls at his tail. 'Dad,' he says, 'do we have any brown bear blood in us?'

'Certainly not, son,' replies the father. 'We're pure polar bear.'

A little later, tail tugged again: 'Dad. Have we any grizzly bear blood in our veins?'

'How many times do I have to tell you, son – we are absolutely pure polar bear'.

A little later: 'Dad, are you sure that we haven't any koala bear blood in our family?'

'Son, I've told you often enough, we are absolutely pure polar bear – with no other sort of blood in us at all. Only polar bear. But why do you ask?'

''Cos I'm flipping freezing!'

EEC virtues

What we need are all the attributes of our colleagues in the Common Market. We should have the sovereignty of Luxembourg, the even temper of the Italians, the flexibility of the Dutch, the initiative of the Belgians, the good nature of the Germans, the reasonableness of the French . . . But we do have in any event the sheer hard work and culinary art of the British . . .

Is there life on Mars?

Yugoslavia is full of delegations. Like Romanians, Yugoslavs remain terrified by the memory of Chamberlain's infamous description of Czechoslovakia: 'That small, distant country, of which we know so little . . .' So they welcome guests and their country is almost overrun by delegations, from East and West.

Three scientists were recently discussing whether or not there is life on Mars. The American said: 'We think, on the whole, that there probably is some form of primitive life on the planet . . .' The Russian said: 'We are far more sceptical. On the whole, we think that there is probably no form of life, however primitive, on the red planet.' The Yugoslav said: '*We* are absolutely *certain* that there is no life on Mars – otherwise we would long ago have had delegations from there.'

Precedence

When the late Aga Khan was due to be guest at a luncheon in the House of Lords, the host wrote to the Garter King of Arms on the question of precedence. After a long wait, he received the following reply: 'The Aga Khan is believed to be a direct descendent of God. English Dukes take precedence . . .'

247

Brainwashing

Chief Rabbi Rosen of Romania tells of his first visit to America. On landing, he was surrounded by press men who asked him some very abrupt and even rude questions. For instance: 'Rabbi, are you not brainwashed in your country?'

He replied: 'Yes, I suppose we are. But then so are you, in a different way. The difference between us and you, though, is that *we* do not believe what *we* read in the newspapers and you do.'

One of the problems of their suspended disbelief is that even when Romanian newspapers or radio are telling the truth while other people's are lying, Romanians are so suspicious that they still prefer to believe other people's lies.

Peace

A peace treaty is more impressive when it has two signatures on it.(*Abba Eban*)

Negotiating with Russians

'They can't accept a big concession. They have got to extort it from you'. (*Henry Kissinger*)

Socialist

Why is the Soviet Union like an aeroplane in flight? Because it's cold; it makes you feel slightly sick; and you cannot get out of it.

Ignorance

About the policies and motives of the Soviet Union, there is no knowledge – only varying degrees of ignorance. (*President Truman*)

Sharing

A Soviet citizen who wished to join the Communist Party was interviewed by an official, who asked: 'If you were given two houses, what would you do?'

He replied: 'Give one to the Party, comrade, and keep one for myself.'

'Now suppose that you are given two cars. What would you do?'

'Give one to the Party and keep one for myself.'

'Now suppose that you were given two shirts.'

'Oh, I'd keep both of them for myself.'

'Why would you give one of your houses and one of your cars to the Party and not one of your shirts?'

'You don't understand. I've already got two shirts.'

Siberian parrot A Russian dissident trained his parrot to say: 'Down with Brezhnev . . . Down with Marx . . . Down with Lenin . . .'

One day, the KGB called on the dissident. In panic, he shoved the parrot into his refrigerator.

The KGB men searched the house and eventually opened the refrigerator. The parrot emerged, shivering.

After an expectant pause, the parrot talked: 'I love Brezhnev . . . I love Marx . . . I love Lenin . . .'

'Little bastard,' snarled his master. 'After 5 minutes in Siberia, you join the Party . . .'

Communist society An East European was asked the following question by his 18-year-old son: 'Do you think that we already have 100 per cent Communism here, or is it going to get worse?'

State secret Some years ago, a Moscow man was arrested for rushing naked through the streets, yelling: 'Krushchev is a fool!'

The judge sentenced him to 25 months' imprisonment. 'You get 6 months for indecent behaviour,' he said, 'and 19 months for betraying State secrets.'

Love of Russia And old man was studying Hebrew on a park bench in Moscow. A KGB man came up to him and said: 'What are you reading?'

'I'm studying Hebrew.'

'What's the use of that to you?'

'It's the language of Israel.'

'Old man – you will never get there . . .'

'Never mind, then. It's the language of Paradise.'

'But what happens if you go to the other place?'

'That will present no problem. I already speak Russian.'

Long distance

When Kosygin died, he entered hell. He begged the devil to be allowed to keep in communication with friends on earth. 'Certainly,' Satan replied. 'But you will need plenty of change for the telephone.'

'What do calls cost from here?'

'To the United States, 50 roubles; to South America, 40 roubles; the United Kingdom, 50 roubles; to India, 55 roubles . . .' and so on, in a long list, ending with: 'and to the USSR, one rouble . . .'

'Why is it so cheap to the USSR?'

'Because,' replied Satan, 'it's only a local call . . .'

Patriotism

Kogan in Kiev applies for a visa for Israel. A few nights later, he hears loud banging on his door. He pulls the blankets over his head. The banging continues. Eventually, he calls out: 'Who is it?'

'The postman.'

'Go away, please.'

The banging restarts. Eventually Kogan opens the door and five KGB men rush in, knocking him to the ground.

'Which is the best country in the world?', one of them asks, sitting on his head.

'The Soviet Union.'

'And where do children get the best education?' demands another, twisting his leg.

'The Soviet Union.'

A third twists his arm behind his back. 'Where is the best food, the best culture, the best of everything?'

'The Soviet Union.'

'In that case,' enquires the man in charge, 'why do you want to leave for Israel?'

'Because in Israel,' said Kogan, 'the postman does not come at 2 o'clock in the morning.'

Moscow morale A man phoned his friend in Moscow: 'How are you, Ivan?' he asked.

'Fantastic . . . marvellous . . . unbelievable . . . fabulous . . .'

'OK,' said his friend. 'I see you've got someone with you. I'll phone back later . . .'

Emigration Brezhnev once asked Kosygin: 'How many Jews are there in the Soviet Union?'

'About 3 million,' Kosygin replied.

'Then tell me: if we opened the doors and allowed as many Jews to leave as wanted to go, how many would emigrate?'

After a moment's thought, Kosygin replied: 'I'd say about 15 million!'

Vive la différence! Malcolm Rifkind, Minister of State at the Foreign Office, tells of his discussion with his Soviet opposite number on a visit to Moscow. He complained about the Soviets' failure to allow Jews to emigrate from their country. The Russian replied: 'The matter of emigration from the Soviet Union is a controversial one. But how would you like me to raise with you the question of immigration into the United Kingdom, which is also a controversial matter?'

Rifkind replied: 'I would be happy to discuss that with you. But there is a difference, you know. People are trying to get *into* my country . . .'

Russian tragedy Moshe Goldstein, a long-serving activist in the Communist Party, applied for a visa to emigrate to Israel. He was called before the Commissar who said to him: 'Goldstein, I don't understand. You have always been a loyal member of the Party. And a proud Soviet citizen. Why do you suddenly want to go to Israel?'

Goldstein replied: 'Comrade Commissar, you do not understand. I am a Jew.'

Commissar: 'So what? Are you not in a position of authority within the Party? Have you not a good living, a nice flat, a fine *dacha*, a car? You are not discriminated against in any way. So why should you want to leave?'

Goldstein: 'But Comrade Commissar, what if things change and unrest grows in the villages and the towns and they start hanging Jews and chess players?'

Commissar: 'I don't understand. Why should they want to start hanging chess players?'

Detente

A Soviet dignitary boasted to an American acquaintance that they had found a new way to make a lion share a cage with a lamb. 'If you don't believe me,' he said, 'then when you come to the USSR we will show you . . .'

True enough, on his next visit the American was taken to Moscow Zoo and there in a cage was a lion lying in one corner and a lamb in another.

'That's wonderful' said the American. 'You must have a very remarkable lion and a very wonderful lamb . . .'

'The lion is a good one,' replied the Russian. 'But we have a new lamb every morning.'

One all

For years I had written to Ambassador Smirnowski, Head of the Russian mission to the UK. My complaints about their treatment of Jews, dissidents, Baptists and other minority groups were all ignored. Then, one day, he came to the Commons for tea, as guest of the Anglo-Soviet Parliamentary Group – of which I was and remain a member in good standing. The Chair introduced us. I said: 'Your Excellency, I am very pleased to meet you. I did not believe that you really existed.'

'Why not?' he asked.

'How could I accept the existence of a person who fails to answer so many letters?'

Ambassador: 'Well, I am very pleased to

meet you too. I did not believe that a man who wrote so many contentious letters could be so pleasant . . .'

Match drawn . . .

Dissidents

My wife and I were invited by the Prime Minister to an official luncheon for Egyptian President Mubarak.

Introducing me to the guest of honour, Mrs Thatcher said: 'Now, Greville Janner is one of my favourite dissidents. In the Soviet Union, of course, they lock up their dissidents. Here we invite them to lunch!'

85   Faith, religion and ethics

Faith

An Italian priest was walking along a cliff top when he slipped and fell – but was caught by a slender sapling, growing out of the cliff. He looked down 300 feet at the sea and up at heaven and cried out: 'Is there anyone up there – help!' And a mighty voice cried out: 'I am here. Fear not. Let go of the tree and I will keep you safe.'

The priest looked down 300 feet at the raging sea and the rocks. Then he cried out: 'Is there anyone else up there – help, help!'

Greater faith

A nun was driving her little Fiat along the road when it ran out of petrol. She left the car and walked 10 miles to the nearest filling station. Regretfully, they said that they had no jerry can and no other container of any sort. 'Surely you have something which I could put the petrol into?' she pleaded. Thoughtfully the attendant said: 'Well, I can only offer you an old chamber pot . . .'

Gratefully, the nun accepted. The pot was filled with petrol; she walked back to the car. And as she was pouring it into the petrol tank, a passing motorist leaned out of the window, saying: 'Well, sister, I wish I had your faith!'

Fowl language

A man was standing on the steps of the cathedral, shooing away the pigeons. 'Bugger off . . . bugger off . . .' he said.

A priest emerged and listened to this performance. 'My man,' he said, 'you really shouldn't talk to pigeons like that. Not on the steps of this House of God. You should say: "Shoo . . . shoo . . . shoo . . ."

'Look, ' he said. 'I'll demonstrate. Shoo . . . shoo . . . shoo . . .' he said to the pigeons. They all flew away.

'There,' said the priest to the visitor. 'I told you all you had to say was: '"Shoo . . . shoo . . . shoo. . ."' and they'd all bugger off, just the same!'

End of the World Prominent physicists predicted that a flood would signal the end of the world in three days.

A television station called on leading religious personalities to advise on how people should act.

The Pope urged his flock to repent their sins; the Buddhist monk instructed his people to seek inner peace by searching for their inner selves; the Rabbi told his followers: 'OK. We've got three days to learn how to swim.'

Spoilsport The advantage of having a Scottish granny is that though she doesn't prevent you from falling into sin, she does prevent you from enjoying it . . .

Optimism An optimist thinks that all is for the best in the best of all possible worlds. But they say in the Vatican that a pessimist is one who thinks that he is right.

Outside support I am afraid that I cannot be called a pillar of your church. But I would like to be described as a buttress – supporting you from the outside! [*Ideal for speeches in other people's churches. GJ*]

Civilisation Mahatma Gandhi was asked: 'What do you think of Western civilisation?'

He replied: 'I think it would be a very good idea.'

Double crossing I once travelled from Amman in Jordan to Damascus in Syria and back again in a day. I was somewhat surprised to find a large sign at the frontier: 'Double crossing only permitted for diplomats and for certain priests.' (*Rt Rev. Robert Runcie, Archbishop of Canterbury*)

True

A man writes to God: 'I am desperately in need of £100. Please, God, help me!' He addresses the letter to heaven – and posts it.

In a special, kindly, post office department, the letter is opened. The clerks decide to have a whip-round. The collect £80 and post it back, 'with love from God'.

The following day a letter arrived at the post office: 'Thank you, dear God, for answering my letter. But I think I ought to tell you that those wretched people in the post office stole £20!'

Whose religion?

Father Brown (Roman Catholic) and the Reverend Green (Anglican) were arguing furiously over a theological matter.

The priest held up his hand: 'Come, let us not quarrel,' he said. 'You and I are both doing God's work – you in your way and I in His!'

Us

We are proud of the inhabitants of our island. There are the Scots who take themselves seriously – as well as anything else they can lay their hands on; the Welsh, who pray on their knees and on each other; the Irish, who will die for what they believe in, even if they do not know what that is; and the English, who proclaim that they are self-made men, thereby absolving the Lord from a heavy burden.

Ethics

A son asks father at dinner: 'What are ethics?'
'Leave me alone to eat,' father replies.
'But I must know. I have to write an essay tonight, which I must hand in tomorrow. Ethics is the title.'
'I see. Well, suppose I am closing the shop at night and I find a £10 note on the floor. I check the till and make sure that we are not £10 light. Then, what do I do? I tell my partner, that's what. And I split it with him. That's ethics.

256

Jewish jokes A Jewish joke is a joke which Jewish people have heard and non-Jewish people would not understand.

Recognition It was Balaam who said: 'How goodly are thy tents O Jacob, thy dwellings places O Israel' – and he was not Jewish. (*Parasha Balak in Exodus*)

Apartheid During the Second World War, the United States fleet paid a courtesy call in Durban. A society lady who was running a big dance one night asked the American authorities to send half a dozen boys along, but to ensure that they included no Jews.

Six big black men duly arrived.

'I'm terribly sorry,' said the hostess, 'but I'm afraid that there must be some mistake.'

'No, ma'am,' replied the leader of the party. 'Major Rabinowitz never makes mistakes!'

Jewish wedding The Jewish bridegroom traditionally treads on glass, breaking it into thousands of pieces. Why? 'To celebrate the last occasion when he will be able to put his foot down . . .'

Persistence A woman was lying on a beach in Miami. She turned to a man lying alongside her and asked: 'Excuse me, are you Jewish?'

He replied: 'No, I'm not.'

A few minutes later, the woman turned again to the man and said: 'Are you sure you're not Jewish?'

He replied: 'I'm certain.'

Five minutes later, the woman again addressed the man: 'Excuse me, are you absolutely certain that you're not Jewish?'

He replied, angrily: 'All right. So I'm Jewish.'

The woman paused: 'Now isn't that funny,' she said. 'You don't look Jewish!'

Half Jews How come that when someone is half Jewish, we so seldom get the top half? (*Chaim Weizmann*)

Anti-anti-Semitic

A Jewish man was sitting in the corner of a compartment, while two other travellers sat chatting. One said to the other 'Where are you going?'

'To Brighton.'

'Oh, that used to be a nice place. But it isn't any more. It's full of Jews.'

'Where are you going, then?' asked his friend.

'To Bournemouth.'

'Bournemouth! You talk of Brighton but you should see what's happening to Bournemouth, with all those Jewish hotels . . .'

The Jew lowered his newspaper and looked at them over the top. 'You know where you two boys should go,' he said. 'You should go to hell. There are no Jews there!'

Many of my best friends . . .

When King Khaled of Saudi Arabia first greeted US Secretary of State, Henry Kissinger, he launched into his renowned attack on the Jews and Israel . . . and how they had taken over the world's banks and financial institutions, its communications and its newspapers, its television and its radio. 'They have even infiltrated into positions of high power in the Foreign Ministries of the world,' declaimed His Majesty.

Then, realising what he had said, the King added: 'But you, sir, we welcome warmly – not as a Jew, but as a great human being . . .'

Secretary Kissinger replied quietly: 'Your Majesty, many of my best friends are human beings . . .'

Repeat business

A tailor made a suit for an Anglican parson. He refused to accept any charge. The parson sent him a lovely Bible.

Two weeks later, the same tailor made a suit for a Roman Catholic priest. Again, he refused to charge. The priest sent him a magnificent prayer book.

The tailor was later visited by a Rabbi and

258

made a suit for him. He made no charge. The Rabbi sent him another Rabbi.

The curse of the Plotnik diamond

Dealer shows woman a magnificent diamond. 'This, madam, is the Plotnik diamond. Is it not beautiful? It is one of the largest in the world and is very valuable. But there is a curse which goes with the Plotnik diamond . . .'

Customer: 'What curse is that?'

Dealer: 'Mr Plotnik!'

Oedipus

A Jewish couple sent their son to a psychiatrist. He returned and his mother enquired what had happened. '*Nu?*' she said.

'He says, I've got an Oedipus complex.'

'Oedipus shmoedipus,' his mother retorted. 'You just go on loving your mommy!'

Blessing

'God bless the Tsar – and keep him far away from us!' (*Fiddler on the Roof*)

Perspective

Ezra Kolet, leader of India's tiny Jewish community – about 7,000 souls out of a population of some 800 million: 'You may take it from me, Ladies and Gentlemen. Numbers are not important!'

Permanent job

Teddy Kollek, Mayor of Jerusalem, kept seeing a man sitting on the roof of his house, looking up at the sky with binoculars. One day, he called out to him: 'What are you doing up there?'

'Looking out for the Messiah' came the reply.

'Why are you doing that?'

'I am being paid for it.'

'How much?'

'Not much. Just a few pence a day . . .'

'That's pretty poor pay . . .'

'I know. But at least the job is permanent!'

86   Sex, love and marriage

Sex – with pleasure

George Bernard Shaw was once asked to give a lecture on sex. He rose to his feet and began: 'It gives me great pleasure . . .'And he sat down.

Love and money

'If I lost all my money, darling, would you still love me?'

'Of course I would, darling. But I'd miss you . . .'

Uncertain future?

A sex questionnaire to college students included: 'Are you a virgin?'

One girl replied: 'Not yet.'

A shepherd's tale

Dai and Morgan went for a dirty weekend in Snowdonia. They found a beautiful shepherdess in a hut and had a lovely time with her.

Three months later, they each received a letter. The shepherdess was in a certain condition.

Dai: 'What shall we do, Morgan?'

Morgan: 'We'd better go and see her, hadn't we?'

Dai: 'I can't get away from work. Tell you what, you go and see her and I'll meet you when you get back and we'll split my day's earnings.'

So off Morgan went, returning that evening. Dai met him at the station.

Morgan: 'I've got some very bad news to tell you. There's been two disasters.'

Dai: 'So what are they, then?'

Morgan: 'The first is – that it's twins.'

Dai: 'Oh God, that's terrible. So what's the second?'

Morgan: 'I regret to inform you that mine has passed away.'

Premarital

Two businessmen talking: 'I never slept with my wife before I was married. Did you?'

'I don't know, John. What was her maiden name?'

Welsh virgins

The day after his wedding, Dai returns home.
'What's happened?' asked his mother.
'I found out that Bridget is a virgin', he said. 'So I left her.'
'Quite right,' said his mother. 'If she's not good enough for the rest of the boys in the village, why should she be good enough for you?'

In love

A well-known peer married at a comparatively advanced age. His wife is an attractive Mediterranean lady. When the noble lord fell ill, his wife replied to a telephone enquiry as follows: 'He is much better, but he is still under heavy seduction.'

A wife in the business

I went into the beer business. My wife said: 'I'll drive the people to drink and you can sell it to them.'

Always right

Wife: 'I have my faults. But being wrong isn't one of them.'

Stupidity

Smith came home and found his wife in bed with another man. 'What the hell do you two think you are doing?' he asked.
The wife turned to the other man. 'There you are,' she replied. 'I told you he was stupid!'

Naked truth

Man comes home and finds his wife lying naked on the bed. 'Why aren't you wearing anything?' he asks.
'I keep telling you,' she replies, 'I haven't anything to wear . . .'
He marches over to the cupboard, throws open the door and then says: 'Hello Persian lamb . . . Hello ocelot . . . Hello mink . . . Oh, hello Sam . . .! Hello Persian lamb . . . Hello coney . . .'

Wrongdoing

Mabel, aged 18, arrived home at four in the morning wearing a mink coat.

'Did I do wrong?' she asked her mother.

Mother replied: 'I don't know whether you did right or wrong dear – but you certainly did well!'

Love My wife liked to talk to me while she was making love. She used to phone me from a motel room . . . Got me so used to it that she would use me to time a boiled egg. It was always soft-boiled . . . (*Bob Monkhouse*)

Three speech A woman sued for divorce, claiming that her husband had only spoken to her three times in the course of their marriage. She applied for custody of the three children.

The fodderless child Our daily diet grows odder and odder.
It's a wise child who knows his fodder.
(*Reproduced by kind permission of Ogden Nash*)

Fertility A turtle lives 'twixt plated decks
Which carefully conceal its sex.
I think it clever is the turtle
In such a fix to be so fertile! (*Ogden Nash*)

Garlic The Italians invented birth control – they call it 'garlic'.

Necessity Gwyneth was on night shift. She arrived home to find her husband, Morgan, in bed with her best friend. She looked down at her sadly and said: 'Bridget – I have to – but you!'

Birth control When people talk to me about the need to keep down the number of children, I remind them that I was the fifth! (*Clarence Darrow*)

Mothers A parent's place is in the wrong . . .

Pen pals For many years, Charlie in London and Bill in New York were pen pals. They had never met.

One day, Charlie received a letter from Bill, saying that he intended to come to London. 'Please cable back if it's convenient,' Bill wrote.

The following exchange of cables ensued:

Charlie: 'Delighted to welcome you. Will meet you at station.'

Bill: 'Thanks – am black.'

Charlie: 'Don't care if black. Come. Will meet you at station.'

Bill: 'Am Catholic.'

Charlie: 'Don't care if black Catholic. Come. Will meet you at station.'

Bill: 'Am hunchback.'

Charlie: 'Don't care if black Catholic hunchback. Come. Will meet you at station.'

Bill: 'Have only one eye in centre of forehead.'

Charlie: 'Don't care if black Catholic, hunchback with only one eye in middle of forehead. Will meet you at station. How do I recognise you?'

Don't wait
Two men were due to fight a duel. One telephoned the other: 'Charlie, don't wait for me . . . If I'm not there within 5 minutes, please start without me!'

Romance
Fall in love with yourself and you are in for a lifetime of romance. (*Oscar Wilde*)

Self-love
He is a self-made man, and he worships his creator. (*Disraeli on John Bright*)

Identification
A man was lying naked on a beach, sunbathing, when he saw three beautiful girls coming towards him. He grabbed at the only clothing within reach – his hat – and put it over his face.

The three girls stopped and looked down at him. The first said: 'Well, it's not my husband.' The second said: 'You're quite right. It is not your husband.' The third one said: 'He's a stranger – he doesn't live in the village . . .'

The bird
A farmer came to town and bought a live chicken. Waiting for his train home, he decided to go to the movies. The woman at the cash desk said: 'I'm sorry, young man, but we don't allow animals in here.'

263

The farmer went round the corner and stuffed the chicken into his trousers. He returned to the cinema, paid for his ticket, and sat down in the stalls. Eventually, two women came and sat beside him.

It was very hot and the chicken became itchy. So he opened up the front of his trousers and the chicken extended its neck.

One woman said to the other: 'Mary, do you see what I see?'

'Certainly I see what you see. If you've seen one, you've seen them all!'

'I'm not sure,' said Mary. 'This is the first one I've seen that eats crisps!'

Evolution

In life, each of us must look after our 'neighbours' – or, as it is sometimes put, we are our brother's keeper. Which reminds me of the monkey in the zoo discussing the principles of evolution and asking: 'Am I my keeper's brother?' [*There is also the tale of the herring, who was separated from his best friend, the whale. He responded to enquiries about his friend's whereabouts with the world's worst pun: 'How should I know? Am I my blubber's kipper?' GJ*]

87 Law and lawyers, crimes and courts

The rule of law

This country is planted thick with laws from coast to coast. If you cut them down – and you're just the man to do it – do you really think you could stand upright in the wind that would blow then? (*Robert Bolt – from* A Man for All Seasons)

Justice

Former Lord Chancellor, the genial Lord Elwyn Jones, often says: 'Welsh juries believe in justice. But they are not too dogmatic about it.'

Which is matched by the story of the Glasgow Baillie who sentenced a criminal to 30 days without the option of a fine. 'And count yourself lucky,' he said. 'If there had been a shred of evidence against you, it would have been 60!'

International law

Famous professor, Hersch Lauterpacht used to say: 'International law is not much good. It creates laws which the wicked do not obey and the righteous do not need.'

Single-handed

A man asked to be recommended to a one-armed lawyer. When asked why, he replied: 'I'm sick of being told: "On the one hand this – and on the other hand that".'

Lawyers

It is untrue that lawyers do nothing. They just get together and decide that nothing can be done.

Alleged motto of the Law Society: The man who is his own lawyer has a fool for a client.

Respected professionals

A foreigner was being shown around Westminster Abbey. His guide pointed to a splendid monument: 'There lies a great and honest man and a most distinguished lawyer,' he said.

'That's interesting,' the foreigner replied. 'I never knew that in England you buried two men in the same grave!'

Oh, hell!

A businessman arrived at the pearly gates and was cross-examined by St Peter. He demanded his basic civil right – to be represented by a lawyer.

'Sorry,' said St Peter. 'We haven't any up here.'

Socialist lawyers

The expression 'socialist lawyer' is a contradition in terms – like 'military intelligence'. (*Michael Foot*)

Bright boy

A car dealer's son was trying to sell his own vehicle – but failing. His father told him to turn back the clock to 6,000 miles. The following week, father asked his son whether he had sold the car. 'Certainly not.'

'Why not then?'

'Well, it's only got 6,000 miles on the clock so I decided to keep it . . .'

Costs

Two partners fell out and sued each other. Their lawyers tried to settle the disputes, but failed. Eventually, the case reached court.

Outside the courtroom, Morgan said to his counsel: 'Look, Dai and I used to be very good friends. We were in happy partnership for years. Perhaps we can have a chat and see if we can settle our differences on our own?'

The lawyer replied: 'Why not? But I must warn you. The amount in dispute between you is now less than the legal costs. So even if you settle your dispute, you've got to decide who is going to pay the costs.'

Morgan went to Dai and the two of them disappeared. Half an hour later they returned, beaming.

'Have you settled the case?'

'We have,' replied the partners in unison.

'Well, who's going to pay the costs then?'

'Oh, that was easy,' said Dai. 'We've solved the problem. He'll not pay his and I'll not pay mine!' (*Judge Bernard Gillis*)

Wrongdoing

When visiting Egypt, one of our guides explained his *modus operandi*. 'If you have to do wrong,' he said, 'you must know the right way to do it.'

Ears

The famous American lawyer, Clarence Darrow, told the story about how easy it is for a lawyer to ask one question too many.

A man was accused of biting off another man's ear. His lawyer cross-examined the witness: 'Did you see my client biting off the victim's ear?'

'No sir.'

Instead of stopping there, he went on in triumph: 'So how can you testify that my client bit off the victim's ear?'

'Because I saw him spit it out!'

Banks – and logic

A bank robber came up for sentence. It was his fifth conviction for the same offence and he had been in and out of prison for years.

'Why do you keep robbing banks?' the judge asked him.

'Because that is where the money is,' he replied.

Conducting a case

If the facts are on your side, hammer on the facts . . . if the law is on your side, hammer on the law . . . if neither is on your side, hammer on the table . . .

Modesty

So I asked myself the question . . . We lawyers frequently ask ourselves questions because in that way we know that we will get prompt and intelligent answers . . . (*Lord Denning*)

Lawyers – and rats

Why do they use lawyers instead of rats as laboratory animals in the USA?

There are four reasons:

First: There are more of them.

Second: Laboratory assistants get less attached to them.

Third: There is less outcry if something terrible happens.

And fourth: There are some things that rats just won't do!

Chancery

The court of a well-known Chancery judge, now retired (and nameless) became known at the Bar as the 'din of inequity'.

Justice?

When I was a puisne judge – sitting on my own, in my own court – I could be sure that justice would be done in that court. But now I sit in the Court of Appeal with two brother judges, the odds against justice being done in my court are two to one!' (*Lord Denning*)

Interviewed on his 81st birthday, Lord Denning was asked whether it was not correct that he bent the law in order to do justice. He replied: 'Certainly not. I just develop it . . .'

Whisky and water

Former Lord Chief Justice, Lord Goddard, was asked what was the difference between whisky and water. He replied: 'If you make the former in private, that is a felony; if you make the latter in public, that is a misdemeanour.' [*The distinction between felonies and misdemeanours has gone, but both acts remain criminal. GJ*]

Dissenting voices

Master of the Rolls, Sir John Donaldson, tells of an occasion when he sat in the Court of Appeal with his great predecessor, Lord Denning. At the end of a case, Denning turned to him and said: 'Well John, I think we must allow this appeal, don't you?'

Donaldson replied: 'No. It must be dismissed.'

Denning turned to the third judge: 'What do you say?' he asked.

'I'm sorry, Tom,' he replied, 'but I agree with John. The appeal must be dismissed.'

'In that case,' said Lord Denning, 'the two of

you will just have to deliver dissenting judgments!'

Equality of opportunity

Courts of this country are like the Waldorf Hotel – open to all! [*High Court judge, explaining the inaccessibility of justice. GJ*]

Perjury

Counsel, cross-examining a man who alleges his arm and shoulder were hurt in an accident: 'Show me how high you can raise your arm, please . . .' The witness raises his arm a few inches, clearly with great effort and difficulty.

'Now show me how high you could raise it, *before* the accident . . .'

The arm goes high into the air. [*This tale is, of course, best told with the appropriate demonstration. GJ*]

Chinese praise

Chinese man in the witness box in a stamp theft case was praised by the judge. He replied: 'Philately will get you everywhere . . .'

The truth

There are three stories in any law suit: the plaintiff's, the defendant's, and the truth.

Ducking the question

Lawyer to witness: 'Did you get the letter?'

Witness (contemplating whether he should answer yes or no – and after a long pause): 'Not necessarily.'

Evidence

Lawyer defending client on charge of causing grievous bodily harm: 'It is our case, my Lord, that there is no evidence that any such affray took place. If it did, we shall prove that my client was not there. If he was there, there is no evidence that he took part in the affray. And in any case, the other man hit him first.'

Unwise counsel

Counsel: 'I hope that you are following me . . .'

Judge: 'Yes – but where are you going?'

Trials

At the 1981 Sheep Dog Trials, how many were found guilty?

Appeal

A businessman had to leave court before the

end of the long, hard-fought trial. He left word for a telegram to be sent to him, to inform him of the result.

At the end of the case, the lawyer sent a telegram as arranged: 'Justice has been done,' it read.

The client immediately sent a reply: 'Appeal at once.'

Forgiving

An old Cockney usher used to take visitors to the Lord Chief Justice's Court when Lord Goddard presided: 'Lord Goddard,' he would say, 'is famous as a forgiving judge. Very forgiving. For giving five years . . . ten years . . . life . . .'

Language problems

Policeman giving evidence of arrest: 'So I cautioned the man and asked him if he could explain his presence, in the early hours of the morning, carrying what appeared to be a house-breaking implement. He made a lengthy reply in a language which I subsequently discovered to be Greek. I told him that I was not satisfied with his explanation and I duly arrested him.'

Cross-examination

The policeman gives evidence of having observed disgusting behaviour by a courting couple in a car. They deny it, maintaining that had he been in a position to observe, they would have heard him coming.

Counsel: 'Was it not a gravel path? What size shoes do you take? Was it not in the silence of the night? I put it to you that had you been near to that car, they would have heard the tramp of your feet . . .'

Constable: 'No sir.'

Counsel: 'You say that they would not have heard the tramp of your feet? Why do you say that?'

Constable: 'I was riding my bicycle.' [*This sort of horror explains why young lawyers are enjoined: 'Never ask a question in cross-*

examination unless you know the answer.'
Theoretically, splendid advice . . . GJ]

No charge
PC: 'You are under arrest, sir. I am taking you to the police station where you will have to stay the night.'
'And what's the charge, officer?'
'No charge sir. All part of the service.'

Balls
A prisoner went round the cells, selling tickets for the Warder's Ball. One of his mates complained: 'I don't want to buy a ticket for any screw's dance!' The seller replied: 'It's not a dance. It's a raffle!'

Bribery
Lord Goddard once remarked: 'Bribery is like a sausage – difficult to describe, but very easy to smell!'

Commission
A well-known company found difficulty in putting its 'commission' (*slush, payola, or what-have-you*) through its books. But as it had a hunting lodge in Scotland, it listed the items as 'hunting expenses'.
A visiting customer from Nigeria was provided with a suite at Claridges and a girl in it. Unfortunately, he contracted a certain illness for which he had to be treated at the London Clinic. The cost of that treatment went into the books as: 'Repairs to gun . . .'

Corruption
Be specially careful not to bribe tax or factory inspectors or other public officials. 'Do not feed the hand that bites you . . .'

Gifts
Sir Joshua Hassan, Chief Minister of Gibraltar, making a presentation of small Wedgwood box to British Foreign Secretary: 'This comes well within the parameters of what a Minister is permitted to accept!' [*In other words – it did not cost much, but what a charming way to put it! GJ*]

Written evidence
A man appeared in a lawyer's office: 'I have

come to you because God has told me you are the best lawyer in the country.'

The lawyer replied: 'If that happens again, please get it in writing.'

Rubbish

To get rid of rubbish nowadays, all you have to do is to wrap it in silver paper, put it on the back seat of your car, and some silly sod will steal it. (*Bob Monkhouse*)

Tact

A company official was in the witness box, giving his opinion. 'Do you consider yourself an expert?' asked the cross-examining lawyer.

'Well, no,' said the man modestly. 'But I am something of a judge.'

'What is the difference between an expert and a judge?' asked the lawyer.

'An expert sometimes makes mistakes,' replied the official. 'A judge – never!'

Judge's functions

Lord Asquith was discussing the functions of the various branches of the judiciary. He said: 'It is the function of the judge in the Queen's Bench Division to be quick, courteous and wrong. But it must not be supposed that it is the function of the Court of Appeal to be slow, crapulous and wrong – for that would be to usurp the function of the House of Lords.'

Conviction

A famous hanging judge, Mr Justice Avory, was discussing with Mr Justice Travers Humphreys the unhappy way in which the courts were being conducted by their junior colleagues.

Avory: 'Any of these young members of the Queen's Bench Division can secure the conviction of a guilty man. But it takes an old hand like you or me to make sure that the innocent do not escape!'

Leading counsel

Litigant arrives at court to find that whilst he is represented by junior counsel only, his opponent has both a junior and a leader. He tugs the gown of his advocate: 'How are you going to

manage?' he says. 'The other side have a QC
and a junior . . .'

'I'm as good as any two of them,' replies the
junior.

A few minutes later, the client again tugs the
barrister's gown. 'I'm worried,' he says. 'I've
noticed that when the QC is talking, the
barrister behind him is thinking. But when you
are talking, no one is thinking!'

Speed   An American criminal complained that in New
York you are liable to get mugged between
the time that you rob the bank and the time that
you reach the getaway car.

Terrorism   The Mafia Godfather arrived at the Pearly
Gates.

St Peter: 'I'm not sure that we will have you
in here. 'I'll have to ask The Boss.'

'I haven't come to be invited in,' said the Godfather. 'I have come to give you three minutes to
get out.'

Food for thought   Political life has many drawbacks, one of which is *not* malnutrition.

Shortage   What is 200 yards long and eats cabbage? A queue outside a food shop in Warsaw.

Patience – and head waiters   Inscription on head waiter's tombstone: God finally caught his eye.

We serve all . . .   A man came into Grubbs with an alligator on a leash. He said: 'Do you serve lawyers here?'

Mr Grubb replied: 'Of course we do.'

'In that case,' said the man, 'I'll have two salt-beef sandwiches for me and a lawyer for my alligator . . .' [*For lawyers, use doctors, Methodists, Mongolians – or whatever other audience you are addressing. GJ*]

A fare charge?   In some countries, cab fares are charged per head. In one of these, a couple with three children stopped a cab and asked what it would cost to be taken to the next town. '5 dollars for each of you grown ups,' the driver smiled. 'I'll not charge for the children.'

'In that case, said the father, 'please take the children. My wife and I will take the bus.'

Never satisfied   The host asked his house-guest: 'Will you have coffee after dinner?'

'No thank you. Just brandy.'

'Will you have cocoa before you retire?'

'No thank you. Just tea.'

'Will you have tea for breakfast?'

'No thank you – coffee.'

'Would you like boiled eggs or scrambled eggs?'

'One of each please.'

After breakfast, the host asked his guest: 'How were your eggs?'

Food, drink and travel

'Not good.'
'Why?'
'You boiled the wrong one!'

Staff training

Two waiters pass behind diner's chair. One says to the other: 'Look – she's eaten it!'

Fifty-fifty

A well known hotel in London's West End became a favourite haunt of Arab guests. So it started serving a new delicacy: camel and chicken stew.

A dissatisfied diner called after the head waiter. 'This is meant to be camel and chicken stew,' he said. 'But I can't taste any chicken.'

'Oh, I can assure you, sir,' the waiter replied, 'it's fifty-fifty – one camel, one chicken!'

Prescriptions

A down-and-out tries to beg a pound from a passer-by.

'What is it then? Drugs?'
'Don't indulge.'
'So I suppose you smoke yourself silly?'
'As a matter of fact, I never smoke at all.'
'Then there is only one answer. Gambling...'
'Certainly not. That's a mug's game . . .'

'Then never mind the quid. You come into the car with me and let me take you home to meet my wife. I would like her to see what happens to a man who doesn't drink, take drugs, smoke or gamble!'

Conferences

Some politicians and many business people suffer from a disease called conference syncopation – making irregular movements from bar to bar . . .'

Glass houses

Two guests at a cocktail party. One says to the other: 'Look, old man I shouldn't drive if I were you. Your face is getting all blurry.'

Drink and drive?

A Scottish hotel applied for a drinks licence. This was refused because 'the roads in the vicinity of the hotel are unsuitable for drunken driving.'

'Blood thicker than whisky . . .' A Scottish friend of mine always carried a hip flask of whisky. One day he fell and felt damp around his hip. 'My God,' he said, 'I hope it's only blood!'

Ugh! After a party, Fred was found wandering on the rooftops. The drinks were on the house.

Mirage 'Drink makes you look really beautiful, Brenda.'
'But I haven't been drinking, Charlie.'
'I know. But I have!'

No room at the inn? Smith is refused a room at a famous hotel. 'I'm sorry, sir, we are full up,' says the head receptionist.

'If Prince Philip were to come here,' said Smith, 'you'd find a room for him, wouldn't you?'

'I suppose we would,' said the receptionist.

'Well, I've got news for you,' Smith retorted. 'He isn't coming. So I'll have his room.'

Early bird Cyril decided to beat the latest Underground strike by hitch-hiking to work – he got up at 5.30 so as to beat the traffic.

89 Time

Procrastination

A visitor to Ireland asked a professor: 'What is the Gaelic for *mañana*?'

The professor replied: 'I regret that we do not have any word in the Irish language that conveys quite that same sense of urgency!'

Brevity

We no longer know how to be brief. For instance: the Lord's Prayer consists of 56 words; the Ten Commandments 297 words; the United States Declaration of Independence 300 words; and the EEC Convention on the Importation of Caramel – 26,911 words.

I am sorry that I have had to write such a long letter. I did not have the time to write a short one. (*Horace Walpole*)

God gave man two ears and one mouth so that he may listen twice as much as he speaks! (*King Faisal*)

Time limits

No man can enjoy the sunset for more than 15 minutes. (*Goethe*)

Former Israeli Prime Minister Levi Eshkol once chaired a meeting. A speaker who was likely to be boring asked him: 'How long shall I speak? There's so much to say. I don't know where to begin . . .'

Eshkol replied: 'Then I suggest that you start at the end . . .'

Apologies

Counsel apologises for the length of his speech.

Judge: 'Don't worry – you have shortened the winter for us . . .'

Apologies for lateness

Better the President late than the late President. [*Favourite apology of the late Lord Fisher of Camden, my predecessor as President of the Board of Deputies of British Jews. GJ*]

277

Time and tide	They believe in casting the bread on the waters – but only when the tide is coming in. (*James Callaghan*)
Take your time	An El Al plane was landing in New York. The pilot announced: 'Ladies and Gentlemen, we hope that you enjoyed this flight on El Al and that we shall have the pleasure of your company on future flights.' Then, forgetting that his loudspeaker was still switched on, he added: 'Now all I need is a nice cup of coffee and a woman!'
	A pert air hostess rushed up the gangway towards the cockpit. An old Mama put her hand gently on he passing arm: 'Don't hurry, darling,' she said. 'Give him time to have his coffee!'
Confidence	Cricketer Learie Constantine told how he was once walking down the steps of a pavilion on his way to bat when he heard the following telephone conversation: 'You want to speak to Learie Constantine? Oh, I'm sorry, he's just going in to bat. Would you like to hold on?'
In conclusion	'Has he finished?'
	'Yes, he finished a long time ago, but he is still going on.'

90   Health and hospitals

Communication

The operator at a London hospital received a call asking for the sister in charge of a particular ward. When the sister was put through, the caller enquired: 'How is Mrs Goldberg?'

'Doing very well,' sister replied.

'Is her stomach condition improving, then?'

'Yes. The doctor is very pleased with it.'

'Is her blood pressure better?'

'Yes, much better.'

'And how about Mrs Goldberg's chest. Is the infection clearing well?'

'Very well. But tell me, who is enquiring?'

'This is Mrs Goldberg. Nobody tells *me* nothing, *dollink*!'

Ambition

The Minister of Health visited a hospital and was introduced to three international rugby players, lying in adjacent beds. He asked the first man: 'What's the matter with you?'

'I have piles, sir,' replied the man.

'And what are they doing for you?'

'They give me a brush and some ointment and I apply it to myself.'

'And what's your ambition now?'

'To get back to the rugger field to play for England, sir, as soon as possible.'

'Well done, my boy. I wish you luck.' And he turned to the second man.

'What's the matter with you, then?'

'I'm afraid that I've got venereal disease.'

'Oh dear. And what treatment are they giving you?'

'They give me a brush and some ointment and I apply it to myself.'

'And what's your ambition?'

279

'To get back to the rugger field to play for England again, as soon as possible,' he said.

'Well done, my boy,' nodded the Minister and turned to the third bed.

'And what's your trouble?'

'I have laryngitis,' the man whispered.

'What are they doing for you?'

'They give me a brush and some ointment and I apply it to myself.'

'And what is your ambition?'

'To get the brush before the two other fellows . . .'

Majority for good health

In 1982, my car suffered a blow-out on the M1 and we were all saved by the presence of a crash barrier – and the driver and myself wearing seat belts. At Question Time the following week, I paid tribute to that crash barrier – and asked the Minister of Transport to ensure that any road works which meant that traffic had to flow in both directions on the same side of the road should be kept as rare and as brief as posible.

She started her reply by saying 'how glad the whole House would be to hear of the Honourable Member's fortunate escape – and at his presence in good health here today.'

This evoked cheers from my side and laughter and cries of 'resign' from that of the Minister. Which reminded me of the classic story of . . . The lone Conservative Councillor in a Welsh Labour stronghold who fell ill. He was visited in hospital by the mayor, who said:

'My dear Dai, I am here not only in my personal capacity, but especially as mayor of our town, deputed to bring to you a resolution which I will now read: "We the City Council of Ebbw Vale do wish Councillor Dai Jones a most speedy recovery to robust good health." I am pleased to tell you, Dai, that this resolution was passed – by 13 votes to 12, with 6 abstentions!'

Rare? Patients in a psychiatric hospital were under-going group therapy. One asked: 'Why are we all here?' Another immediately replied: 'Because we're not all there . . .'

Mad? A psychotic builds castles in the air; psychopaths live in them; psychiatrists collect the rent.

Listen! Man visits a psychiatrist's office and says: 'My trouble is no one listens to me.' The psychiatrist says: 'Next . . .'

Lost voice A singer who had lost his voice knocked on the door of his doctor's surgery. A nurse appeared. The man whispered: 'Is Dr Jones in?' The nurse whispered in reply: 'No – come in quickly.'

The doctor arrived after about 15 minutes, wrote out a prescription and recommended 'plenty of ice cream.'

The singer duly lodged the prescription with the chemist and went off to the ice cream parlour. He whispered: 'What flavours of ice cream do you have?'

The ice cream man replied, whispering: 'Strawberry and vanilla.'

Singer: 'Do you have laryngitis too?'

The ice cream man whispered: 'No – just strawberry and vanilla.'

Limits on DIY John needed a pacemaker but could not get one swiftly under the National Health Service. So he went privately to a distinguished consultant. 'I can do the job for you with pleasure,' said the surgeon. 'But I'm afraid it will cost you £5,000. These gadgets are very expensive.'

'I have a friend who is brilliant with electronics and gadgets,' said John. 'If I provide my own pacemaker with his help, will you do the implant for me?'

The surgeon agreed. John produced the pacemaker and the surgeon planted it in his chest and wired him up.

Three months later, John returned for a check-up. 'Any problems?' The surgeon asked.

John replied: 'Only one. Whenever I get an erection, the garage door opens!'

Just right   Sign over pharmacy: 'We dispense with accuracy.'

Fair   Dentist to patient: 'Now, we're not going to hurt each other, are we?'

Medical prophecy   An American doctor gave his patient six months to live – and sent him a bill for $500. By the end of the six months, the bill was still not paid. The doctor then gave his patient another six months . . .

Nurses   Occupational nurses are a race apart. I once asked one 'What do you do when you have a patient brought in with a bleeding leg?' She replied: 'You bind up the bleeding wound; you elevate the bleeding leg; and you call in the bleeding doctor.'

Accidents at work   There is no such things as an Act of God when you are dealing with accidents in industry. The fact is that God has a down on inefficient managers . . . (*Bill Simpson, then Chairman of the Health and Safety Commission*)

Emergencies   An employee was lying on the operating table in the factory's sick bay, clenching his teeth, while a doctor sewed up a large wound on his scalp. A pair of pliers had fallen from a scaffold and split open his head. I asked him: 'Haven't you got a hard hat?'

'Yes' he said.

'Where is it, then?'

He replied: 'It's in my locker.'

'Why do you keep it in your locker?'

'It's there for emergencies,' he answered.

Deafness   Doctor to personnel manager at very noisy steel works. 'I don't know why you don't just hire deaf people in the first place and then you wouldn't have to worry . . .'

Too late

When I asked a steel worker why he was not wearing his ear muffs, he replied: 'I'm already deaf!'

Compensation

Apprentice: 'What is a cubic foot?'

Foreman: 'I don't know – but I will make sure that you get full compensation.' [*Or could be a reply by a shop steward. GJ*]

Fall from grace

Fred fell 80 feet from a scaffold. By good fortune, he managed to clutch hold of a rope about 20 ft from the ground. After a few moments, he let go and fell on his head.

His friend picked him up and said: 'Fred – why did you let go of that rope?'

He replied: 'I was afraid it was going to break.'

Self-recognition

An employee had his ear cut off at work. He was told to go to the local hospital and have it stitched back on. When he arrived, he had left the ear behind.

'Where is the ear?' they asked. 'Why didn't you bring it with you?'

'I couldn't tell whether it was mine,' he replied. 'It had no pencil behind it!'

Useless remedy

A man suffering from constipation went to his doctor who provided him with a suppository, telling him to leave it in his back passage overnight and that if it did not do the trick, to come back in a couple of days.

Two days later, the patient returned. 'It was useless,' he said.

'Did you do as I recommended?' asked the doctor.

'Well,' said the patient, 'we haven't got a back passage in our house. So I put it on top of the refrigerator. For all the good it did me, I might just as well have shoved it up my rear end!'

Open certificate Morgan was an overworked businessman. He suffered a severe heart attack and his doctor told him that he had to keep 'very quiet' until further notice – no stress, no excitement, no exertion.

'But what about bed with Gwyneth?' he asked. 'Bed is for sleeping purposes only,' said the doctor.

Some months later, when Morgan was feeling much better, he said to Gwyneth: 'Well, it's Friday night and I am quite recovered now.'

'I'm not taking any chances,' said Gwyneth. 'You'll have to get a doctor's certificate before I am prepared to resume our previous arrangements.'

So Morgan went back to the doctor, who examined him and proclaimed himself fully satisfied. 'You may return to work on a part-time basis,' he said. 'You are doing very well.'

'Then how about bed, with Gwyneth?'

'That should be all right. Everything in moderation, of course.'

'Gwyneth won't allow even moderation without a certificate from you.'

'Then I shall provide one,' said the doctor, and sat down at this desk, took out his pen and began to write.

Morgan came quietly up behind him. 'If it would not be a nuisance,' he said, 'would you be kind enough to head your certificate: "To whom it may concern"?'

91   Age, death – and the end

Age

The young look forward, the old look back, and the middle-aged look around.

You are young if it is as easy to go upstairs as it is to go down; you are middle-aged if it is easier to go down than up; and you are old if it is just as difficult to go in either direction.

Two elderly men were visiting a brothel on the top floor of a 20-storey block. The lift broke down and they started to climb. One said to the other: 'Wouldn't it be awful if we got to the top and found that the girls weren't there.'

After 10 floors, the other replied: 'Wouldn't it be awful if we got to the top and the girls *were* there!'

Boss to secretary: 'I don't look 50, do I?'
Secretary: 'No – but you used to.'

Distinction

To appear really distinguished, you need grey hair, a wide girth and piles. The grey hair gives you an appearance of wisdom; the girth an appearance of prosperity; and the piles a look of anxiety that can easily be mistaken for true concern.

Alternatives

A distinguished US Senator was asked how he felt on his 80th birthday. 'Very well, thank you,' he replied, 'considering the alternative . . .'

Very nearly

A friend asked an 80-year-old man who had just married a young girl: 'How are you managing?'

'Marvellous,' he replied. 'We do it nearly every night. Nearly on Monday . . . nearly on Tuesday . . . nearly on . . .!'

Don't delay	A streaker ran across Westminster Bridge and passed three elderly ladies. Two of them immediately had a stroke. The third one did not reach out her hand in time.
Pensioner's marriage	Two pensioners married. On their honeymoon night, the husband reached for his wife's hand – and held it tenderly. On the next night, he did the same. On the third night, he reached out for her hand but it was not there. 'What's the matter, Mary?' he asked. 'I am sorry, dear,' she replied. 'I am too tired tonight . . .'
What for?	Two old men were sitting on a bench in a boulevard. One said: 'Do you remember how we used to run up and down here when we were young, chasing girls?' The other replied: 'I remember running up and down – but I've forgotten what it was for.'
Reason to mourn	A man was sobbing his heart out at a millionaire's funeral. No one knew who he was. 'Are you a relative of the deceased?' someone asked him. 'No.' 'So why are you crying?' 'That's why!' he replied.
Wrinkles	Two old ladies in an old people's home decide to go streaking. A retired sailor is sitting with his wife watching them. She says: 'Look at those two. What are they wearing?' 'I don't know – but whatever it is, it needs pressing!' [*This may be adapted for a named hotel, club or other institution. GJ*]
Happy ending	Goldstein, aged 75, married a 30-year-old. He boasted to a friend how they had done it six times every night during their honeymoon. Friend: You can die from this! Goldstein: So she dies, she dies!

Age, death – and the end

Enjoy!

Sound, sound the clarion, fill the fife,
Throughout the sensual world proclaim
One crowded hour of glorious life
Is worth an age without a name. (*Thomas Mordaunt [1730–1809]*) [*Both these last two quotations are especially useful in eulogies – the second one, for those who died young. GJ*]

Time – and life – and death

Days are scrolls; write on them that which you want to be remembered. (*Spanish-Jewish Sage, Bachya*)

Tact

Jones the Bread, Morgan the Tailor and Evan the Bookie went to the races. Unfortunately, a horse leapt over the rails and smashed into poor Jones, knocking him down and killing him. Morgan and Evan considered the problem: 'Who should tell Mrs Jones?'

Morgan said: 'I'm only a tailor. I have no tact. Evan, you tell her. You're a bookie, so you know how to explain losses . . .'

So Evan went to the village and knocked on the door of the Jones's terraced home. A lady came to the door.

'Excuse me, madam,' said Evan. 'I'm sorry to disturb you. But are you Widow Jones?'

'There's no Widow Jones here,' she replied.

'Do you want to make a bet?' asked Evan.

Will

An old man was dying. His children and his grandchildren were gathered round his bed, waiting patiently. Every few minutes, the old gentleman pointed down to the floor with two fingers of his right hand. Eventually, the eldest son said: 'He is trying to tell us that's where he's put the money . . .'

So they started pulling up the floorboards all over the house – but they found nothing.

That evening, the father rallied and started to chat. Eventually, the son said to him: 'Tell me, father, what were you pointing two fingers at the floor for?'

287

'Oh that,' replied the father. 'I was just too weak to point them upwards.'

Wills

A man climbed to the top floor of a block of apartments, to the home of a well known call-girl. As she opened the door, he had a heart attack and dropped down dead. His executors asked their lawyers this question: 'Are we bound to carry out the testator's last wish?'

Eternal distrust

During the Congress of Vienna, Metternich was informed that the Russian ambassador had died. 'I wonder what was his motive!' he exclaimed.

Right dead

Here lies the body of William Jay
Who died defending his right of way
He was right – dead right – as he walked along
But he's just as dead as if he'd been wrong.
(*Epitaph on pedestrian's Tombstone*)

Floral tribute

Everyone is condemned to the sadness of attending funerals – I treasure one true anecdote which has added a moment of consolation to many a cremation service.

An elegant lady cousin had to attend both a funeral and a wedding on the same summer's afternoon. So she donned a smart, navy blue suit, but put her attractive new floral hat into a paper bag. As it was covered with gay and realistic artificial flowers, it was hardly suitable headgear for a cremation.

In the entrance of the crematorium, a solemn black-clad man – obviously a cloakroom attendant – held out his hand for her parcel and she gave it to him. Then she sat quietly at the back.

Moments later, the coffin was wheeled noise-lessly into the funeral hall. It was cowned with a magnificent floral tribute – her hat!

My cousin sat transfixed during the service, which reached its silent climax as the doors at the far end of the hall slid apart and the coffin rolled gently away, still bedecked with her hat.

The service over, she joined the mourners around the back where all the wreaths had been laid against the chapel wall, accompanied by a simple sign: 'In memory of the Departed'. She stood silently – wondering whether she dared remove her floral tribute from the rest. Watching the sad faces of the family of the deceased, she decided that her hat must be sacrificed. She went to the wedding hatless. When she returned that evening, her hat was gone.

Brotherly love   During the lingering final illness of my wife's beloved uncle, Emeritus Chief Rabbi Sir Israel Brodie, I often sat by his bedside while he told me marvellous and generally whimsical tales from the Talmud. My favourite explains the nature of brotherly love: I have used it often and always with impact at functions of and for charities, fraternal organisations and the like . . .'

A father died and left his fields in equal parts to his two sons, one of whom was a bachelor and the other married with many children.

One moonless night, after the harvest had been brought in and stacked, the bachelor brother crept into his field and carried half a dozen sheaves from his pile, took them across the boundary line and quietly placed them on his brother's heap. The next morning, he was amazed to find that the two piles were still the same size.

The following night, the brother repeated the process. Still the piles were no different.

The next night, the bachelor tried again. This time, as he was carrying the bundles across his field, he met his married brother, coming in the other direction and himself laden with sheaves. 'What are you doing?' he asked. 'Please let me give you some of my wheat. I do not need it, I am single and have no family to keep. You have a wife and children – many mouths to feed.'

'Not so, brother,' came the response. 'You must save for your old age. You will have no wife or children to look after you. You must keep the corn for yourself.'

So the two brothers stood together and looked up to heaven and called on the *Holy-One-Blessed-Be-He*. 'Tell us,' they called out, 'which one of us is correct?'

A voice descended from above. 'You are both right,' it said. 'And so great is your love that upon these fields will I build my Temple.' And tradition has it that He did.

Death

Cicero: Life is a great play. The final act is a tragedy.

De Gaulle: Life is a magnificent voyage, ending in a shipwreck.

Hell

Stalin died and went below. Shortly thereafter, St Peter answered a knock on the door. He found the devil outside, seeking political asylum.

Life after . . .

'The House of Lords? Life after death, my boy . . .' *(Ex-Cabinet Minister – now a Peer)*

Index

Index